KATHARINE HEPBURN

A Hollywood Yankee

GARY CAREY

A DELL BOOK

Published by
Dell Publishing Co., Inc.
1 Dag Hammarskjold Plaza
New York, New York 10017

This book is a revised and updated version of *Katharine Hepburn*,
originally published in 1975 by Pocket Books.

Film stills from the Museum of Modern Art Stills Archive, courtesy
of RKO, MGM, United Artists, Columbia Pictures, and Avco-
Embassy.

Dell ® TM 681510, Dell Publishing Co., Inc.

ISBN: 0-440-14412-4

Reprinted by arrangement with St. Martin's Press, Inc.

Printed in the United States of America

First Dell printing—December 1984

Contents

Katharine Hepburn

1

Connecticut Yankees

"Two of an actress' greatest assets are love and pain," Katharine Hepburn once said. "A great actress, even a good actress, must have plenty of both in her life."

She knows what she's speaking about—there has been both love and pain in Katharine Hepburn's life. Today it is generally assumed that she was born into a fabulously wealthy family, rose in a flash to the top of her profession, stayed there for three decades that were filled with awards, triumphs, and unflagging public devotion, and finally emerged in the late 1960s as one of the screen's great, indestructible stars. It wasn't that easy. There were many setbacks during Hepburn's early stage career, and, on her arrival in Hollywood, her looks were considered odd, her behavior eccentric, and her appeal too special for mass consumption. Few of her films were financial blockbusters, and quite a number were fiascos—not just mediocre pictures that could be shrugged off lightly, but outright clinkers that had audiences screaming for her blood.

Kate was tough. Whenever she took a tumble, she jumped back into the saddle and trotted off as though nothing had happened. She always went her own direction, even if it took her down a road crowded with obstacles and unnecessary hardships. She had no time for pretense or stupidity, no stomach for pandering to the press and public, as was expected of stars in the 1930s. When challenged, she could become haughty or even downright rude, and soon she had enough enemies to fill all the pages of a little black book.

Sometimes Hepburn was her own worst enemy. When she arrived in Hollywood, she gave some sophomorically supercilious interviews, and reporters retaliated by roughing her up whenever they got the chance. Occasionally they stooped to fabricating incidents that had never occurred: one story that received wide circulation had Kate squatting leisurely in the middle of Hollywood Boulevard to read her fan mail. Newsmen cynically dismissed Hepburn's eccentric behavior as a ripoff of the Garbo "I-want-to-be-alone" act, and a large portion of the public also assumed that her staunch show of individualism was just another publicity gimmick to cash in on the Garbo-Dietrich craze.

Perhaps in the early days it was dressed up with a bit of showmanship, but Hepburn's individuality is the real McCoy. She comes by it naturally—for more than two generations, all members of her family have shared that spirit of feisty independence that is her chief characteristic as a woman and an actress. "Probably it all goes back to Grandfather," Kate says. "He used one cake of soap for everything—for washing, shaving, brushing his teeth. He even used a washcloth instead of a toothbrush."

Washcloths were honored commodities for the Hepburns; in their household, cleanliness ran neck-in-neck with godliness, so much so that some of the neighbors decided soap had won out over the Lord. The Hepburns had money and impeccable social credentials, but they didn't

2

live like other members of the New England aristocracy. Outwardly, they seemed respectable enough—they had a big house; five servants, a summer cottage; they were Protestant teetotalers who served nothing stronger than sherry at their dinner parties. But the upright citizens of Hartford, Connecticut, couldn't enter the Hepburn drawing room without blushing. Kate's father, a doctor, was fascinated with a disease that couldn't be discussed by nice people, and Mrs. Hepburn dressed up in an ornamental Chinese robe for afternoon tea. Worse yet, she was a suffragette and an advocate of birth control. People looked the other way as she walked down the street with pamphlets in one hand and a "Votes For Women" placard in the other.

No one who had known Mrs. Hepburn as a young girl had dreamed she would grow up to be a woman suffragist. The oldest of three girls, Katharine ("Kit") Martha Houghton had been born in Corning, New York, to parents who originally came from Boston. The family had a fine social pedigree—Kit's cousin, Alanson Bigelow Houghton, was ambassador to the Court of St. James's—and generally the daughters of the family were educated for nothing higher than marriage and an occasional bit of charity work. This tradition was upset when Kit was orphaned at the age of thirteen; before dying, her mother had made her promise she would go to college and find a career that would make her financially independent. Her guardians disapproved of higher education for women, but Kit badgered them until she was allowed to enter Bryn Mawr in the fall of 1894.

Not a very diligent student, she crammed for good grades at exam time and spent the rest of the year running a small "salon" in her dormitory room. Her classmates described her as a handsome, carefree, extravagant girl who was totally oblivious of outside events. Once she saw a newspaper carrying the headline, MAINE IS SUNK, and asked a companion, ''How could Maine sink? Was there an earthquake?''

After graduating from Bryn Mawr, Kit received an M.A. in art history from Radcliffe. Then she toured Europe, and on her return took a teaching job in Baltimore to be near her sister Edith, a student at Johns Hopkins University. Edith enjoyed fencing, and once when she was playing an exhibition match with a Johns Hopkins medical student, Kit stopped by to watch. Edith's opponent was named Tom Hepburn, and Kit Houghton thought he was ''the most beautiful creature'' she had ever seen. They were introduced, started courting, and, in 1904, Tom's last year in medical school, they were married.

A Virginian by birth, Thomas Norval Hepburn was the son of an Episcopalian minister. Husky, hearty, and handsome, he had been a crack athlete as a Randolph-Macon undergraduate, and physical fitness was to be a lifelong obsession: he believed a flaccid body produced a flaccid mind. Tom Hepburn was strong, upright, and outspoken, the possessor of a gruff sense of humor that was directed against ''the Dumb, the Complacent, and the Conservative''—a caste system he and his family worked out to categorize the different types of American untouchables. All through his years at Johns Hopkins he had been a top student, and when it came time for his internship, he received several offers. He didn't want to live in a big city, so he chose Hartford, Connecticut, where there was a fine hospital that would allow him to pursue his special interest in urology.

Young Dr. Hepburn didn't have a nickel, and while his wife had a small inheritance, they couldn't afford a luxurious home. On arrival in Hartford, the couple rented half of a two-family house directly across from the hospital, and it was there that their first child, a boy named Tom, was born. Three years later came Katharine, who, like all the Hepburn children, was given Houghton as a middle name. She was born on November 8, 1907 or 1909—Kate says 1909, but most theatrical reference books list the earlier date.

"I don't believe in marriage," Hepburn has said on many occasions. "One of the few happy marriages, possibly the *only* happy marriage I've known, was my parents'. They never argued about things—my mother never wanted 'things' the way most people do—they only argued about ideas."

For a while Mrs. Hepburn was happy playing wife and mother, but one day as she was out strolling, dragging Tom by the hand and wheeling her daughter in a carriage, she suddenly thought—this is Kate's description of her mother's politicalization—"Now this is great, and these two little things are fine, but is this the end of my contribution to the world?"

She went home and discussed her discontent with her husband, who was sympathetic. He had read Ibsen and Shaw, who had alerted him to the frustrations of the modern woman. As an antidote for his wife's boredom, Dr. Hepburn suggested she attend a lecture given by a famous suffragette who was passing through Hartford; she wasn't interested, but he made all the arrangements and went along with her.

Mrs. Hepburn was very excited by what she heard at the lecture. Soon she was deeply immersed in feminist literature and political philosophy, and the more she read, the more radical her views became. She was, her daughter later said, "far left" while Dr. Hepburn was merely "a liberal"; when they argued about politics, Mrs. Hepburn could become violent, even to the point of throwing things at her husband. In later life, when she had mellowed somewhat, she was still known to open conversation with a new acquaintance by asking, "How do you stand politically?" If the answer sounded conservative, she would murmur, "How dull, how awfully dull!"

Shortly after her indoctrination, Mrs. Hepburn began parading around Hartford with a bag of feminist literature under her arm. She received a cool welcome from passersby. "My mother was considered a dangerous and wicked woman," Kate recalls. "When I was a small child, we'd meet a neighbor on the street. My mother would say 'Good morning,' and the neighbor would look through us as if nobody was there. My mother didn't mind. She kept saying 'Good morning,' and pretty soon the neighbor, faced with such good manners, felt compelled to return the greeting."

Although she was a tireless worker for the cause of the vote for women, Mrs. Hepburn was never so preoccupied that she slighted her family. Following Kate's birth, she decided there were enough babies around the Hepburn household, but after a short sabbatical, she had four children in rapid succession. There were two boys—Robert and Richard—and two girls—Margaret (Peggy) and Marion. Dr. Hepburn had prospered in his career, and he'd invested his money shrewdly. By the time Kate was three, he was able to buy a large brick house on Hawthorne Street, and then a few years later, an even bigger home on Bloomfield Avenue in fashionable West Hartford.

The Bloomfield Avenue house was spacious and well shaded, with verandas, rolling lawns, and lots of room for children and visitors. Mrs. Hepburn's tea parties were the talk of the neighborhood—dressed *à la chinoise,* she was known to entertain such celebrated feminists as the militant Emmeline Pankhurst, Charlotte Perkins Gilman, and the notorious Emma Goldman, who had been jailed for promulgating anarchy among the working class.

Another frequent visitor to the Hepburn home was novelist Sinclair Lewis, a resident of Hartford during the early 1920s. Mrs. Hepburn had met Lewis at a gathering and invited him to dinner. Then she had second thoughts. She told her husband that the author was known to drink and wondered if they shouldn't serve cocktails before dinner. Dr. Hepburn went to the phone, called Lewis, and said, "I'm Dr. Hepburn and I'm to be your host on Saturday night. I suggest that if you must get drunk, you get drunk before you come here, because we do not serve liquor in our home." Mrs. Hepburn was mortified, but Lewis came to dinner stone cold sober and lasted out the evening with only a glass of sherry for spiritual comfort.

At the Hepburn parties, children were both seen and heard. "My parents taught me not to be afraid of expressing my opinion," Kate once said. "We were encouraged to argue with our parents, but not idiotically."

There were no forbidden topics of conversation in the Hepburn drawing room: social hygiene, sexual relations, Shaw, Fabianism, socialism, Marx, anarchy—all were discussed openly in front of the children. "From the time she could sit up and listen, baby Katharine heard talk which in those days was little short of revolutionary in the purely social sense," wrote author Nina Wilcox Putnam, an occasional guest at the Hepburn home. "The child heard many a convention denounced as rubbish, and had the praises of self-development and self-expression sung to her constantly."

At first, Mrs. Putnam was impressed by "the new mode of child-rearing," but after observing Kate's development, she began to have doubts. "I can assure you that when

Katharine was about seven, I saw her take food from the plates of distinguished guests—at will and unreproved. . . . I remember her interrupting the conversation of her elders—unreproved. I remember her snatching ladies' hats and putting them on her own head—unreproved.'' The child was, according to Mrs. Putnam, ''totally undisciplined by her clever mother.''

Kate tells a different tale. She says she was periodically spanked until she was nine years old; then she learned to take her thrashings without tears and her parents turned to other forms of punishment. The Hepburn household was run along Spartan lines. The child who complained of aches and pains was told to ''take an aspirin and lie down for half an hour.'' Each day began with a plunge into a cold shower, a piece of masochism that affected Kate's character development. Those icy baths gave her the impression ''that the bitterer the medicine, the better it was for you,'' and were responsible for what she calls her ''perversity.''

Dr. Hepburn's favorite maxim was ''Exercise is the surest road to health.'' He encouraged his children—both girls and boys—to run, wrestle, climb trees, skate, sled, swim, and play tennis. This physical-fitness program turned Kate into a roughneck, a tempestuous little tomboy who dressed in trousers and cropped her hair into a short Dutch bob. One summer she shaved her head, explaining that her bangs gave an unfair advantage to wrestling partners of the opposite sex.

Kate's boyish appearance and behavior caused lifted eyebrows among the Hartford matrons. One of Mrs. Hepburn's guests watched the girl whoop and race around the yard after brother Tom, and cooed sarcastically to her hostess, ''Ah, Kate's so fragile!'' Overhearing the remark, the child howled, ran across the lawn and dashed headlong into a tree. It was her way of proving that she was just as strong and vigorous as Tom.

Tom was a handsome, healthy, highly intelligent boy, and Kate adored him. Because of the gap in the ages of the Hepburn offspring, Kate and Tom were particularly close, growing up together in "an idyllic, wonderful childhood" that came to a tragic end in 1920. That year Kate and Tom spent Easter vacation in New York and saw a stage version of *A Connecticut Yankee in King Arthur's Court*—in it, the hero escaped hanging by steeling his neck muscles so that the rope couldn't cut off his windpipe. Both children were very impressed by this trick. A day or so later, they attended a party where Tom was ribbed about his good looks and his enormous appetite for birthday cake.

Back in Hartford, Kate came down for Easter breakfast and was surprised to find her brother not sitting in his usual place. She ran through the house looking for him, and finally found him hanging from a rope tied around a rafter of the attic, his feet just brushing the floor. Kate ran for help, but fifteen-year-old Tom was already dead. An official investigation turned up no proof of suicidal intent, and the Hepburns preferred to think that their son had died in a foolish attempt to duplicate the rope trick in *A Connecticut Yankee*.

After Tom's death, Kate became moody and despondent. Up till then she had been doing well in school, but her grades began to fall off and her teachers worried about her lack of interest and poor deportment. Kate's spell of depression lasted until early summer, when she discovered the world of make-believe, and then, almost magically, her spirits began to lift. She hadn't previously shown any particular interest in the theater or even in the "let's pretend" games most children play. Of course, like most children her age, she loved the movies, especially the cow-

9

boy films starring W. S. Hart and the society dramas with
Leatrice Joy, one of Cecil B. De Mille's flamboyantly
dressed flappers. She could cry on cue—when Dr. Hepburn
said no, she turned on the tears, and usually got what she
wanted; and she was noted for her spirited classroom ren-
ditions of such poems as "The Wreck of the Hesperus."
Otherwise, the Hepburns had no idea they were raising a
budding Eleanora Duse—and if they had, they would have
been horrified at the idea. To them, the theater was only
one step up from the gutter or the circus. It was one thing
to write plays like Shaw and Ibsen, but to put one's personal charms on public display was little short of pros-
titution.

They were pleased, however, when Kate showed an enthusiasm for amateur theatrics during the summer of 1920.
She rounded up a stock company of neighborhood children
and staged a backyard pageant called *Bluebeard*. It was a
huge success, and with the help of her friend, Alice Barbour, she wrote and directed a second production, *Beauty
and the Beast*. "It called for a large cast," Hepburn remembers. "We knew the children's mothers would have to
come. We were doing it for the Navajo Indians, of whose
troubles we had heard a missionary tell."

Alice Barbour played Beauty, and Kate, dressed "in a
gray flannel beast's head with long ears, and a Little Lord
Fauntleroy suit," took on the role of the Beast. "Valuing
ourselves highly, we asked seventy-five cents a ticket, but
New England thrift almost did us in," Hepburn recalls.
Several mothers decided seventy-five cents was too much
for a kiddy show, and they ordered their children to go on
strike. Learning the profits would go to a good cause, they
reconsidered and the show went on; the Navajos eventually
received seventy-five dollars from the Hepburn stock company.

In the fall, Dr. Hepburn sat down and reconsidered his eldest daughter's education. He had never much approved of the American public-education system, and, considering Kate's recent problems, he decided she would be better off with private tutors. She was delighted, since her lessons could be scheduled around her major interests—skating, tennis, and golf.

As a teenager Kate said she wanted to be a doctor, but instead of studying chemistry and physics, she was making a name for herself as an ace athlete. At age fourteen, she won a bronze medal for figure skating and a year or so later reached the semifinals of the Connecticut Young Women's Golf Championship.

Even at this young age she had flair and individuality. On the green she had two caddies—one carried her bags, the other held aloft a parasol that shielded her freckled skin from the sun. Kate—or Kathy and "Redtop," as her family called her interchangeably—had grown into a handsome young woman. She was a bit plump and would remain so until she entered her early twenties, but her long reddish hair, her smoky gray eyes, and her aristocratic bearing made her a striking figure as she strode across the golf course. Her looks didn't appeal to everyone—not by a long shot. She wasn't a long-stemmed American beauty like the Gibson girls or a vanilla ice cream valentine like Mary Pickford; she was decidedly modern, with the angular, coltish appeal of those emaciated young ladies who were just beginning to flitter into the pages of *Vanity Fair* and *Smart Set*.

As a young girl, Kate impressed people as being brash and very self-assured, but one family friend believed that she was "shy—not in the ordinary sense, but with a profound basic shyness that was hidden under an arrogant front." After she was taken out of school, Kate relied on

11

her family for friendship, growing progressively less easy with people her own age. To make her parents happy, she joined the Hartford Junior Assembly and accepted invitations to parties and dances, but usually she sat on the sidelines, bored and confused as the other girls chattered excitedly about makeup and dresses and other adolescent preoccupations that were outside her range of interest.

One of her first teen-aged buddies, Kate recalls, "was a bad lot" who encouraged her to break into deserted Hartford homes. Later on, when she started dating, Dr. Hepburn dismissed most of her beaus as "boring," and nearly died of shock on learning that she was keeping company with a Catholic. In advanced circles, Catholics were regarded as the enemy—they were against birth control, votes for women, and practically everything else that was progressive and promised a better future for mankind. Dr. Hepburn greeted the Catholic boy with such "chill politeness" that, from then on, Kate decided to meet him outside her home. Sometimes she accompanied him to Sunday Mass, but she never went further than the church steps. While he attended service, she sat outside and was mortified when her father rode by and waved hello. Kate kept up her church-side vigils for a few weeks and then allowed the friendship to peter out.

Kate was never much of a student—she flunked Latin the first time around and never had the foggiest notion of what physics and chemistry were all about. It became clear that becoming a doctor was out of the question, and for a time it seemed as if she'd never pass college entrance exams at all. Her parents, however, were determined that she should receive a B.A. in some field of study, and after a crash course with her tutors, she was admitted to Bryn Mawr, her mother's alma mater, in the fall of 1924. She elected world history as her major field of interest.

There's always been a snobbish aura about Bryn Mawr—it's the epitome of Main Line Philadelphia posh, and soon it would be renowned for rearing young ladies who spoke like the young Katharine Hepburn: broad "a," swallowed "r," a vocal tilt at the end of sentences. But for all its spacious lawns and ivy-covered dorms, it has never been a playground for rich debutantes. Its academic standards are stiff, and Kate was almost dismissed before the end of her sophomore year.

2

Conscious Beauty

On the day she first entered the Bryn Mawr dining hall, Hepburn was wearing a bright blue skirt that buttoned down the front and a matching blue-and-white ski sweater that accented the highlights of her auburn hair. The ensemble was smashing, and Kate was sure it would draw gasps of admiration. As she passed over the threshold, she posed dramatically, and a hush fell over the room. "Ah," exclaimed one of the senior students, "conscious beauty!" There was a ripple of laughter, and Kate ran back to her room. It was seven months before she returned to the dining hall. In the meantime, she spent most of her pocket money on meals bought in a neighborhood tearoom.

Kate's dining-hall ensemble was one of the more conventional items in her Bryn Mawr wardrobe. It had a skirt, and usually she preferred pants, tailored blouses, and bandannas that she tied around her head. In cold weather she wore a bright green coat, well-tailored but missing most of its buttons and fastened with a safety pin. She used no powder or paint, just scrubbed her face with a strong medicinal soap that turned her complexion a tingly pink.

Kate was fond of baths—sometimes she took four or five a day, and her hair was washed nightly. By morning, it was unmanageable, a tangled jungle that couldn't be tamed by comb or brush.

Her behavior was as eccentric as her appearance. She jumped in the campus fountain and then rolled in the grass to dry herself. During a blizzard, she went out on a roof, stripped off her clothes, and stood in the freezing wind until she was blanketed with snow. She defied the 11 P.M. curfew, coming and going as she pleased by climbing up and down the ivy outside her dorm window.

One day a friend gave her a pack of perfumed cigarettes. Kate sat down in the lobby and puffed nonchalantly until a monitor tapped her on the shoulder and told her smoking was strictly forbidden at Bryn Mawr. There was talk of expulsion, but she pleaded innocence and received a lesser punishment—restriction to campus for several weeks.

Kate's exhibitionistic pranks were possibly a defense mechanism, a way of using up her nervous energy and concealing her inadequacy in dealing with people her own age. But they didn't succeed in making her popular with either her classmates or her teachers. She was a poor student, she cut classes regularly, and she looked bored and restless when she did attend lectures. She was envious of other girls' scholastic application. "I'd go to the library to study," she recalls, "and I'd sit next to my best friend. I could hear the wheels whirring in her head. I was insanely jealous, and so, naturally, I loved her."

Kate got by during her freshman year, but, as a sophomore, she suffered an attack of appendicitis, and after it her grades dropped way below the Bryn Mawr standard. The dean sent Dr. Hepburn a letter suggesting that his daughter drop out of school. "If I had a patient who was sick," Dr. Hepburn answered, "I wouldn't release him

15

from the hospital.'' The dean saw his point and allowed Kate to stay on at Bryn Mawr.

In her junior year, Kate tried out for the college dramatic society—and discovered that all participants in extracurricular activities had to maintain a B average. Suddenly there was a marked improvement in her grades. Performing in a stilted, awkward manner, she appeared as a young man in *The Truth About the Blayds* and as a Spanish novice in *The Cradle Song*. She caused little excitement. By this time, she had decided she was going to be an actress, though she hadn't dared to tell her parents and friends. The one time she did speak of her ambitions, a confidant looked at her and said, ''You! An actress? You're too skinny and funny-looking!''

Undeterred, Kate wangled a letter of introduction to Edwin H. Knopf, the manager of a top-flight stock company in Baltimore. During Easter vacation, 1928 (the spring of her senior year), she visited the producer's office and handed her note to a secretary, who looked her up and down—she was wearing a floppy angora sweater, a beret, and flamboyant slippers—and decided she was a freak. Shaking her head, the secretary passed the letter to Knopf, who read it and said, ''All right, send her in and I'll get rid of her.'' He soon learned that it wasn't that easy to get rid of Katharine Hepburn.

''I tried to explain that the theater was a dreadful place, that she'd be miserably unhappy there,'' Knopf later recalled. ''She didn't agree; she said she'd been born to be an actress. I suggested that she return to her family, till after the summer at least.'' Kate dismissed all his arguments with a cool front of invincible determination. As a last resort, he said his plans for the season were already made and there was no place for an untrained actress. Kate walked to the door, turned around, and smiled. ''Thanks,

Mr. Knopf,'' she said graciously. "I'll be back as soon as school is finished.''

A few weeks later, at the Bryn Mawr Day festivities, Kate played Pandora in an Elizabethan pageant, *The Woman in the Moone*, and made a big hit when she appeared in a flowing white gown with a laurel wreath crowning her disheveled auburn hair. She looked lovely, though she winced a little as she skipped about the gravel path that led to the stage. The director had asked her to wear sandals, but Kate was a stickler for realism. "Pandora went barefoot,'' she explained, "and so shall I.''

Dr. and Mrs. Hepburn attended the pageant and were impressed by their daughter's performance. On their drive back to Hartford, Kate decided it was time to tell her parents that she was going to be an actress. Her mother said nothing—secretly she was pleased that Kate had chosen a career, any career, rather than marriage—but Dr. Hepburn was outraged. There was a stormy argument that ended with Kate bursting into tears. "All right!'' her father snapped. "I'll give you fifty dollars to get started, but that's it!''

A few days later, Hepburn crept into Knopf's theater and took a seat at the back of the darkened auditorium while the producer conducted a rehearsal. She sat there for five hours, never daring to move—not even to go to the bathroom—for fear someone would notice her and ask her to leave. At the end of the day, Knopf walked past her and said, "Report for rehearsals on Monday.'' He never looked at her, he didn't wait for an answer, but Kate was content—she had a job in the theater.

On Monday morning, Knopf told her she could play a lady-in-waiting in his next production, *The Czarina*, a comedy about Catherine the Great. Kate looked happy. There were no lines, the producer warned, but she would have plenty of curtsies. Kate nodded. And when she got on stage—"My God!" Knopf remembered. "Did she curtsy!"

While waiting for her cues, Kate stood in the wings, trying to absorb the tricks and techniques of Knopf's stars. Mary Boland, a leading Broadway comedienne of the period, was spooked by her hovering presence. "Eddie," she whispered to Knopf, "I can't stand it! That Hepburn girl's only on stage five minutes, and the rest of the time she sits over there staring at me. I feel her every minute."

Knopf's stage manager, Kenneth MacKenna, was more sympathetic toward Kate's rapturous delight in being part of the theater. He was taken with her unusual personality, but realized she was green and knew nothing about stage deportment. Her body was stiff, she didn't know what to do with her hands, her voice was liable to jump from contralto to castrato without a moment's notice. Taking her aside, MacKenna advised her to find someone who could give her lessons in voice and movement. A week later, after playing a small part in *The Cradle Snatchers*, Kate left the Knopf stock company and headed for New York in search of an acting coach.

"I distinctly remember the day she came to me," said Frances Robinson-Duff. "It was raining. She had run up the stairs. She burst in the door, unannounced, and flung herself on the settee. Rain ran from her red hair and down her nose. She sat in a dripping huddle and stared. 'I want to be an actress!' she exclaimed. 'I want to learn everything!'"

At the time she met Kate, Frances Robinson-Duff was a white-haired dowager of ample girth and impressive hauteur. She held tenaciously to the old, aristocratic traditions of the theater—there was nothing scruffy or bohemian about the Robinson-Duff academy. Her classroom was a Louis Seize studio on the top floor of an East 62nd

18

Street townhouse. Against its back wall was a platform; on the platform stood a gilt and velvet throne chair; on that chair sat Miss Robinson-Duff, as regal and ramrod straight as the Queen Mother of England. In front of her was a music stand holding innumerable charts of the human body and its modes of emotional articulation. Acting, the teacher claimed, was a matter of breathing and pantomime. A certain position of the arm—fist closed and brought up against the breast—signified defiance; vary the gesture slightly—fingers resting lightly across the bosom—and that was placidity.

One lesson required that the student hold a lighted candle before his mouth. He then pronounced a series of vowels, and if they were said properly, the flame would quaver without going out. "I never got the hang of it," Kate says. "As soon as I opened my mouth, that damn flame went out."

Today the Robinson-Duff method sounds antiquated and faintly absurd, but in the 1920s Ina Claire, Helen Hayes, and many of the great Broadway stars studied with her— she was considered America's best acting teacher. She was also expensive—ten dollars a lesson—more than Hepburn could afford. Swallowing her pride, she called her father and told him her dilemma. "Well . . ." he answered, "I've won some money gambling at bridge. I don't approve of gambling and I don't approve of your career, so I guess you should have the money."

Miss Robinson-Duff and Michael Mordkin, Kate's dance teacher, had their work cut out for them. At this time, Hepburn had a repertoire of two gestures—arms vertical and stiff, and arms bent with clasped fists—and a voice that twanged and quivered uncontrollably. She also had a peculiar way of walking. These were the days when vamps slunk, debutantes slouched, and leading ladies glided gracefully on and off the stage. Not Kate—she loped or strode like a marathon hiker. That walk has never changed much, and the voice, even in the actress' prime years, was never a very flexible instrument. Miss Robinson-Duff and other coaches and directors refined, but never eliminated, Kate's now famous mannerisms. If they had, she might have become a better or worse actress, but she wouldn't have become the Katharine Hepburn of today.

While still studying, Kate started making the rounds of the agents' and producers' offices. Like most actors, Kate hated this routine. "By the time I had made one or two stops, my face would be moist with perspiration, my hair disarranged, and my clothes in disarray," she recalls. "But I was too bashful to ask anyone where the ladies' room was and would spend minutes roaming around the building trying to find it myself."

After only a few weeks in New York, Kate won a part in a play Edwin Knopf was bringing to Broadway. Called *The Big Pond*, it was the story of Barbara Billings, a rich American debutante who falls in love with a French courier named Pierre de Mirande. Originally Kate was cast in a bit role, but once rehearsals started Knopf became dissatisfied with the actress playing Barbara and elevated Hepburn to the leading part.

Miss Robinson-Duff and Knopf drilled and coached and rehearsed their protégée until all three were exhausted. Kate was stubborn—she had ideas of her own and fought Knopf every inch of the way. On the opening night of the tryout engagement in Great Neck, she was "in actual terror." To calm her nerves she went for a long walk and almost missed the curtain. When she arrived at the theater, Knopf was tearing his hair—he thought she had skipped town.

Just before she made her entrance, Kate's underpants

20

began to scratch; nervously, she stepped out of them, handed them to a nonplussed stage manager, and then went out to face the audience. For a while, everything was smooth sailing: Kate was still jittery but she didn't blow her lines, and the first-nighters seemed to like her.

Then, just as she was beginning to feel comfortable in the role, disaster struck. Early in the first act, Barbara imitates her boyfriend's French accent, and Hepburn's mimicry got the first big laugh of the evening. It threw her for a loop. She missed her next cue and then began reciting her lines so rapidly that no one could understand her. When she came off stage, limp and close to tears, a Knopf representative gave her the bad news: she was fired.

The next morning, Kate kept a scheduled appointment with Frances Robinson-Duff. "Well," she said, "I'm not crying." The teacher was not impressed. "That's just the trouble with you, Kate," she said. "You're not crying! A real performer would take the loss of a leading part a lot more seriously. If you're to succeed in the theater, you'll shed a lot of tears—mark my words!"

Others have also implied that the young Hepburn was not really dedicated to learning the craft of acting: her father said she was just "showing off," and around Broadway, she was considered "a rich, stagestruck debutante who dabbled at acting." And Kate now admits that when she started out she didn't have any burning desire to be an actress; she just wanted to be famous. Still, she showed amazing fortitude. In the next few years she was to face many setbacks and overcome them all with great resiliency, buoyed perhaps by her conviction that "the bitterer the medicine, the better it was for you."

Kate's big problem in this period was her lack of technique. She was a good "flash read"—at auditions, she could tear through a part at first glance, hitting all the

21

right emotions, laughing and crying with conviction, acting circles around the other candidates. As a result, she received larger parts than she could handle. Sometimes she managed to get through the rehearsal period, but then, as soon as she faced an audience, her face turned red, she went up in her lines, her voice rose several octaves, and by the end of the evening she was out of a job.

Somehow she always managed to get another—even her one-night fiasco in *The Big Pond* brought her offers from two leading Broadway producers. John Golden saw a photograph of Hepburn as Barbara Billings, liked her face, and cast her in a lurid speakeasy melodrama called *Night Hostess*. When the show opened in Milwaukee, Kate was improbably cast as a lady of easy virtue, and before the week was out, Golden had, predictably, fired her as being too wholesome for a B-girl.

On returning to New York, Hepburn received a call from Arthur Hopkins, a modest, soft-spoken little man who was Broadway's leading producer of quality drama. He had seen her in *The Big Pond* and decided she had the makings of a first-rate actress. He didn't have much to offer her, just a small part in one of his lesser productions, but Kate jumped at the chance.

Hopkins had given Broadway *What Price Glory?*, John Barrymore's *Hamlet, Anna Christie,* and the first Philip Barry comedies, but he also made plenty of mistakes, and producing *These Days* was one of them. Most of the cast knew they were trapped in a quick flop—only Kate failed to note the atmosphere of doom that hovered over the production. Playwright Katharine Clugston used most of her ingenuity on naming her characters—Virginia MacRae, Pansy Larue Mott, Guadalope Gorham, Dorothea Utterback, Cleo Almeda Young, Signhild Valdemir Van-Alstyne, and Veronica Sims (Hepburn). The plot is slim:

Virginia MacRae, the unhappy daughter of an alcoholic billionaire, runs away from school and, after two turgid acts, ends up as the unhappy wife of a Parisian ne'er-do-well.

On opening night—November 12, 1928—Kate got on and off the stage without any mishaps. "I thought I had done a good job," she recalls, "but then I sensed that the same coldness was in the air that I had noticed when the curtain came down on *The Big Pond*."

"Anything wrong?" she asked a stagehand.

"Yes," he snarled. "The closing notice is up." Hepburn was very surprised. "I didn't realize then that shows folded up. I thought they sort of opened and then went on indefinitely."

These Days closed after eight performances, but before the end of the run, Arthur Hopkins had another job for Hepburn. In two weeks he was opening a new Philip Barry comedy, *Holiday*, and though the show was already cast, he hired Kate as understudy for the star, Hope Williams, a socialite-actress who was a popular light comedienne of the 1920s.

The play was a great success—it is the most winning of all Barry's plays—and the leading role was perfect for Kate. It was also perfect for Miss Williams, a blonde with shingled hair whose arch mannerisms and boyish appeal may have influenced Hepburn's development as an actress.

Hope Williams didn't take her career very seriously—she looked on Broadway acting as just a more elaborate game of East Hampton charades—and though she was blooming with good health, she told Kate that she would call in sick at the drop of a hint. Hepburn wasn't interested. Two weeks after the opening, she turned in her notice, and on December 12, 1928, at a wedding ceremony in her parents' home, she became Mrs. Ludlow Ogden Smith.

3

"The Warrior's Husband"

A date with Kate was lots of conversation and no kisses. On and on she went about Shakespeare and Shaw, the plight of the poor, the moon, the flora and fauna, the sick and the downtrodden until her beaus were too tired to make a pass. Robert McKnight, a Prix de Rome sculptor, had met Kate when he was at Yale and she was at Bryn Mawr. Hepburn loved picnics, and he decided an *al fresco* luncheon was the proper time for a proposal of marriage. She went on and on about the *divine* landscape until McKnight, who couldn't get a word in edgewise, decided to forget the whole thing.

At about the same time, she met Ludlow Ogden Smith—or "Luddy," as Hepburn called him. The elder son of a Philadelphia social-register family, he was French-educated, handsome, sophisticated, tall, and impeccably tailored. Kate liked him and so did her parents, and they went on seeing each other even after she had rejected marriage in favor of a Broadway career. She saw other men as well, but when she became disenchanted with the progress of her career, she turned to Luddy and marriage.

From the start, there were indications that Kate wasn't ideally cast in her new role. First of all, she didn't like her name. Mrs. Smith had a plebeian ring, and as for Kate Smith, that was impossible. Dropping Smith and reversing the order of her husband's given names, she came up with Mrs. Ogden Ludlow, a title that inspired respect and befitted her station in life.

After a Bermuda honeymoon, the couple returned to Philadelphia, but Kate didn't like the city. Luddy pulled up stakes, found a job as a New York stockbroker, and soon Mr. and Mrs. Ludlow were living in a two-room, fourth-floor walkup on East 39th Street in Manhattan. The tiny apartment was furnished with a few tables and chairs, a phonograph, and lots of classical records. While Luddy was at the office, Kate sat home listening to Bach, Beethoven, and Brahms—and nearly died of boredom. Four weeks later, she called Arthur Hopkins and asked to be rehired as Hope Williams' understudy.

This signalled the end of the marriage, which had lasted less than two months. Kate has taken much of the blame for its failure. "I behaved very badly," she admits. "I was not fit to be married, because I thought only about myself. An actor, whose temperament tends to be egocentric, has to be very careful about getting married, because he's likely to make somebody else very unhappy."

The separation was amiable, and actual divorce was postponed for several years. Kate and Luddy maintained a close, platonic relationship throughout the early 1930s, and continued to see each other until Smith's recent death. To the Hepburns, Luddy was always "family"—as late as 1940 there was a room reserved for him in their summer cottage.

Kate stayed with *Holiday* until it closed in the spring of 1929. Then she went off on a European holiday with

Luddy, and on her return, she received a frantic call from Arthur Hopkins' office. *Holiday* was tuning up for a national tour at the Riviera Theatre on upper Broadway; Hope Williams was sick, there was no understudy—could Hepburn pinch hit for one evening? Kate went on that night and turned in a polished performance. "She was beautiful," said one cast member. "She amazed us all."

A few weeks later, Hepburn was selected for a small role in S. N. Behrman's *Meteor,* a Theatre Guild presentation starring Alfred Lunt and Lynn Fontanne. Higher company than that a young actress couldn't aspire to, but Kate gave it up for a leading role in *Death Takes a Holiday.* A Shubert production, this macabre, sub-Pirandellian fantasy takes place in an Italian *palazzo* overflowing with world-weary aristocrats. Moving among them is Death, alias Prince Sirki of Vitalba Alexandri, who has taken a vacation to discover why mortals fear the hereafter. Kate played Grazia, a doe-like creature who swoons at first sight of Sirki and eventually returns with him to his Kingdom of Darkness.

Moony roles often brought out the worst in Hepburn, and throughout rehearsals of *Death Takes a Holiday,* she battled continually with director Lawrence Marston. There was talk of firing her, but Philip Merivale (who played Sirki) sprang to her defense and managed to keep her in the show until its Philadelphia tryout. The local critics were divided in their reactions. "One lot said I was a lovely young creature," Hepburn recalls. "Another lot said I was gawky, hoydenish, gaunt, like something escaped from a tomb."

Producer Lee Shubert sided with the second group. He decided Kate had to go, but he gave her an easy, face-saving out. One day, his assistant appeared in Hepburn's Philadelphia dressing room and handed her an envelope. "Mr.

Shubert would like you to read this, and, if it's all right, sign it."

"What is it?" Kate asked.

"Mr. Shubert is giving you a chance to resign from the cast," he mumbled.

"I won't resign!" Hepburn shouted. "If he wants me out, he'll have to fire me!"

On the day she was given her notice, Kate called her father, who drove from Hartford to Philadelphia in time for the last act. When the curtain came down, he hurried backstage and told his daughter, "They were right to fire you. Who's going to believe that my daughter, a big healthy girl like you, could fall in love with Death?"

Kate laughed, cleaned out her dressing room, and went back to Hartford with her father. Her roots were in Connecticut, and she went there whenever she was troubled, unhappy or lonely—as she recently said, she never really grew up, never really left home. The members of her family were her best friends, and they were always there when she needed them. Though she loved both her parents equally, she particularly admired her father's ability "to make a game interesting, and life interesting, and an evening interesting." Boredom was unknown around the Hepburn household. From early morning rising to 10 P.M. curfew, there was always something happening—enormous breakfasts, picnics, afternoon teas, hikes, sports, and talk, talk, talk. Kate adored it all—like her father, she had the capacity for finding or making every moment of her life interesting—and she always came away from Hartford refreshed and bursting with energy.

After a few weeks with her parents, Kate had recovered from her *Death Takes a Holiday* setback and was ready to start making the rounds for a new job. It was late in the season, and the best thing that came her way was an offer

27

to understudy the ingenue lead in the Theatre Guild's revival of *A Month in the Country*. It was a comedown, but she accepted it without any false show of pride. The play was directed by Rouben Mamoulian; he took a liking to Kate and later promoted her to an important supporting role. The promotion came after the play had been running for a month, so she received no reviews—which was just as well, since her name was listed in the playbill as Katherine Hapburn.

When the play closed, Frances Robinson-Duff suggested that Kate and another prize pupil, Laura Harding, take summer-stock jobs at the Berkshire Playhouse in Stockbridge, Massachusetts. The heiress to the American Express fortune, Laura was a boyish, plump blonde with charm, wit, and enough vitality to keep up with Kate on even her most frenetic days. The two girls became fast friends—that summer, Hepburn cried "Laura! Laura!" when the script instructed her to summon her best friend.

These interpolations did not endear Kate to the Berkshire company. She was, say members of the troupe, difficult and egocentric, insisting that she alone was suited to the leading role in each play. The director disagreed—her appearances were limited to supporting parts in three productions: *The Torchbearers, A Romantic Young Lady*, and *The Admirable Crichton*.

On her return to New York in the fall of 1930, Kate tried out for the ingenue lead in *Art and Mrs. Bottle*, an English comedy about a fallen society lady and her bohemian daughter. Mrs. Bottle, the leading role, was played by Jane Cowl, a lady who had been one of the great stars of the American theater for much longer than she cared to remember. Twenty years earlier, she had been New York's favorite Juliet (a part she had played for over nine hundred performances), and from Shakespeare she had gone on to successes in a string of popular melodramas, some of which *(Lilac Time, Smilin' Through)* she had written herself. In 1930 she was still handsome, witty, and intelligent, but she was also a little selfish about sharing the spotlight with a younger actress.

Hundreds of girls auditioned, but Miss Cowl liked none of them until Hepburn appeared. "Can you act, my dear?" the star asked.

"I think so," said Kate. "At least I'd like to try. . . ."

Jane Cowl smiled and nodded her approval, but playwright Benn Levy was appalled. "She's revolting!" he shrieked. "She's got Vaseline on her face; her skin glistens; she's got no allure! Impossible! Out with her!"

Hepburn says Jane Cowl came to her rescue. After Levy's outburst, the actress took Kate aside and said, "My dear, on the stage you must use makeup. Otherwise you'll look dull, commonplace. Mr. Levy does not want you in this show. I'll fight for you . . . but I don't know how successful this effort will be."

Kate was hired; then Levy prevailed and Kate was fired; then she was rehired; then she was fired again. Several replacements came and went until everyone agreed that Hepburn was the best of the lot. The part was hers, and everything went smoothly until the first dress rehearsal.

Miss Cowl stumbled over half-learned lines, looked distraught, buried her head in her hands, invoked the gods, and moaned a few strangled sobs. Then, according to producer Joseph Verner Reed, she sat bolt upright and announced, "There's someone here who wishes me evil—someone who doesn't like me. . . . I've been fighting an unseen foe. . . . Let him speak! Who is it that wishes to destroy me?"

Pointing at Kate, she cried, "It's you, my girl . . . all through Boston, Baltimore, and even now, you have been wishing me evil!'' As politely as possible, Hepburn explained that she had never played Boston or Baltimore or any other city with Miss Cowl. The actress looked suspicious, but when the cast supported Kate, she smiled, patted Kate's cheek, and purred, ''We must love each other. Let us go on! Where were we?''

On opening night—November 18, 1930—Jane Cowl pushed Kate out for her first solo bow, and the audience gave her a mild ovation. The next day, the play, Cowl, and Hepburn's height (five foot seven) made her unfashionably tall; Howard shared this opinion—he thought she was much too gangling and affected to play a romantic heroine. her ''agreeable to look at, assured, and altogether a proficient actress.''

Art and Mrs. Bottle, which played in repertoire with Miss Cowl's production of *Twelfth Night,* had only a short run; it closed in January 1931. The Depression had severe repercussions along Broadway—the number of productions fell from around two hundred and fifty in the late 1920s to less than half that number at the beginning of the 1930s. Audiences became more selective in their theatergoing; plays had to receive really strong reviews to run an entire season. As a result, there were many unemployed actors. Some went into radio, others tried Hollywood, and a few, like Kate, hung on in hope of Broadway success.

After being out of work for several weeks, Hepburn accepted a summer-stock job at the Ivoryton, Connecticut Playhouse. This was a pleasant assignment—Ivoryton was only a short distance from the Hepburns' cottage at Fenwick, a resort town where many prominent Hartford families had summer homes. In her free time, Kate swam and sailed on Long Island Sound, fished and dug clams, and spent many peaceful hours on her parents' private beach. During the summer, Kate appeared in *Just Married, The*

Cat and the Canary, and *The Man Who Came Back,* and made a hit in all three. She found a sympathetic director in Julian Anthalt, who recognized her talents and helped her refine her stage technique. Years later, Hepburn was to say Anthalt was the single most important influence on her early development as an actress.

At the end of the season, Kate was engaged to play an important role in Philip Barry's new comedy, *The Animal Kingdom.* This looked like the break she'd been waiting for, but Leslie Howard, the star of the show, took an instant dislike to her. According to the tastes of the time, Hepburn's height (five foot seven) made her unfashionably tall; Howard shared this opinion—he thought she was much too gangling and affected to play a romantic heroine. Kate tried to please—she bent her knees and slouched, she toned down her mannerisms—but Howard was not impressed. At one of the first rehearsals, she asked, "Mr. Howard, what would you like me to do next?" He hesitated for a moment and then answered, "My dear, I really don't give a damn."

Though Kate recognized the threat behind Howard's words, she was still surprised when, a few days later, she was sacked. Enraged, she called Philip Barry and insisted she was being treated unfairly. "You can't do this to me!" she shouted. "I'm perfect for the part!" The playwright liked Kate, but was irritated by her temper tantrum. "Listen!" he cut in, "I'm glad they fired you. You just weren't good enough."

Today Kate admits that Barry was right. "I didn't know how to support the other actors," she says. "It's expected of you—you have to make the star look good. I didn't know how to do that. I was out for myself."

Kate was desolate after losing the role in *The Animal Kingdom.* For several weeks, she felt blue and cried a lot—

a friend remembers seeing her weep in an elevator—but her spirits revived when producer Harry Moses offered her a part in Julian Thompson's *The Warrior's Husband*. Harry Moses wasn't one of Broadway's great producers—two years earlier, in fact, he had been Chicago's leading hosiery manufacturer—and *The Warrior's Husband* wasn't one of Broadway's great comedies. A bawdy burlesque of the Greek legends of Hercules, Theseus, and Hippolyta and her tribe of female warriors, it was no more than a string of cheap gags about mincing men and militant women. There were, however, several flashy roles in the play, including Antiope, an Amazon tomboy who loses her virility—and virtue—on learning the Greek art of "osculation."

Moses gave this part to Hepburn, and, on opening night, she made one of the most spectacular entrances in Broadway history. Clad in a short tunic, bronze helmet, breastplate, and armored leggings, she sprinted down a ramp, sprang onto a platform, and hurled a dead stag, which was draped over her shoulder, at Hippolyta's feet. Later on, she hoisted an actor over her head, wrestled him, and swaggered around the stage with the prowess of a champion athlete. She was dazzling, and, at the final curtain, the audience rose and hailed Kate as Broadway's brightest new star.

The next morning, the critics dismissed the play and concentrated on the performances. Romney Brent, as Sapiens, the pansy husband of a butch Amazon matron, got most of the praise, but Hepburn was also favorably mentioned. "Excellent," said Brooks Atkinson of *The New York Times;* "a tougher and more dynamic version of Maude Adams' Peter Pan," wrote the man from the *Herald Tribune*. Best of all was Robert Garland's rave notice in the *World-Telegram:* "Miss Katharine Hepburn comes into her own as Antiope. Ever since she supported Miss Jane Cowl in *Art and Mrs. Bottle,* I've been waiting for Miss Hepburn to fall heir to a role worthy of her talent and beauty. Antiope is that role. . . . It's been many a night since so glowing a performance has brightened the Broadway scene.''

The Warrior's Husband ran for only eighty-three performances, but while it lasted, Kate was the talk of New York. Publicly she scoffed at her success, saying, ''Nobody ever noticed me until I was in a leg show''; privately, she was, of course, very pleased. She even consented to talk to reporters, a breed of humanity she soon came to loathe. One of her first interviews centered on the reversal of sexual roles in *The Warrior's Husband.* ''Men know damned well they're the bosses,'' Hepburn told a *World-Telegram* journalist. ''And it's all right with me. I haven't had time to think about whether I'm a feminist or not—but I guess I'm not.''

Kate's triumph as Antiope soon attracted the attention of the film studios. Fox bought the rights to the play, and asked Hepburn to make a screen test; she did, but lost the role to one of the studio's contract players, Elissa Landi. Kate didn't really care; like many theater people, she considered film an inferior and rather tawdry medium. She turned down a Paramount contract that paid well but would have kept her off the stage for years.

One night, Lillie Messenger, a talent scout for RKO-Radio Pictures, saw *The Warrior's Husband* and wired David O. Selznick, the studio's production chief, that Hepburn had potential as a screen actress. Selznick was then preparing a screen version of Clemence Dane's *A Bill of Divorcement,* an international stage success that had made Katharine Cornell a Broadway star a decade earlier. Nearly every actress in Hollywood and New York had tested for the role of Sydney Fairchild. Irene Dunne, Anita Louise, and Jill Esmond (the first Mrs. Laurence Olivier) were leading contenders, but no one had been signed when Selznick received Miss Messenger's telegram. He wired back, asking that Hepburn be tested in New York.

All the applicants for the role of Sydney Fairchild had been requested to film a scene from the play, but Kate reasoned that the RKO executives must be weary of watching *Bill of Divorcement* over and over again, so she chose a scene from *Holiday*. Miss Messenger supervised the test, with Alan Campbell (an actor who later married Dorothy Parker) playing opposite Kate. Hepburn persuaded the handsome and debonair Campbell to keep his back to the camera. "I'd seen too many girls make screen tests with juveniles, only to have the juveniles hired, while the girls were forgotten," she later confessed.

The test was shipped to the West Coast, where an assemblage of RKO brass greeted it with boredom and derision. At first, director George Cukor found Hepburn clumsy and too odd for the screen, but then he was caught by a small detail of her performance. "At the end," he recalled, "she placed a glass on the floor, and something about the gesture was very, very, *very* moving. She was like no one I had ever seen."

Many years later when Hepburn filmed *Holiday*, she showed her original screen test at a cast party. "They laughed themselves sick," Hepburn recalls. "But I didn't think I looked so awfully funny in it. There was something awfully heartbreaking about the girl I was in those days. I was trying so hard—too hard. I was so eager—too eager."

Most of the RKO executives thought Hepburn "looked like a cross between a horse and a monkey" (her words), but Cukor and Selznick decided she was the right actress for *Bill of Divorcement*. Salary negotiations began between RKO and Kate's new agent, Leland Hayward, a tough operator who pulled off some of the shrewdest deals in show-business history. RKO offered $500 a week. Kate wasn't impressed. "How much do you want?" Hayward asked. "Fifteen hundred," she answered. The agent stared at her—for *The Warrior's Husband*, she had earned $100 a week, and later, when audiences started to fall off, that was cut to $79.50. Hayward told RKO Kate's price; the studio countered with $750, then $1,000, and finally $1,250. Kate wavered, but after consulting her father, she refused to compromise. "Daddy," she told Dr. Hepburn, "I'm going to show them I mean business."

Eventually, RKO met her terms. Kate signed a contract that guaranteed $1,500 a week for four weeks (the shooting time of *Bill of Divorcement*) with options for five years; round-trip transportation to the West Coast; and a delayed starting date so that she could fulfill a previous engagement with a stock company in Ossining, New York.

Kate was shocked when RKO met her terms. "They must be insane out there!" she told Laura Harding on the phone. "You'd better come to the Coast with me." Laura happily accepted the invitation.

Hepburn played *The Bride the Sun Shines On* in Ossining, returned to Manhattan, and went shopping for a Hollywood wardrobe. As a traveling costume, she selected a three-piece pearly gray ensemble (cutaway jacket, bias-cut skirt, cowl-necked blouse) with a matching hat that looked like a collapsed soufflé. The outfit had been designed by Elizabeth Hawes, one of New York's leading couturiers, and Kate felt terribly chic whenever she put it on. Apparently no one told her it made her look like a female Miles Standish, so she wore it on July 1, 1932, when she and

Laura boarded the Stratoliner and started their journey to California.

The cross-country trip was a great adventure—train travel was fun in those days, with lots of stopovers, good food, first-class service, and time for reading, rest, and relaxation. The girls lived it up until they reached New Mexico, where Kate got a cinder in her eye.

4

Katharine of Arrogance

The only unpleasant part of the trip was the heat—it was a hot summer, and it got hotter as the train dipped into the southwest corner of the country. The rising temperature sent Laura and Kate scurrying for the observation platform, where there was a breeze—and dust and hot cinders from the tracks. One of the embers flew into Kate's left eye, and it couldn't be dislodged; checking herself in a mirror, Kate looked on in pain and horror as first one eye and then the other—"out of sympathy," she says—turned bright pink.

When she stepped off the train at Pasadena's Union Station, she was a symphony in pink and rumpled gray. Leland Hayward and his West Coast partner, Myron Selznick, had come to welcome her, and as she climbed into a chauffeured Rolls-Royce, she heard Selznick mutter, "My God! Are we sticking David fifteen hundred a week for that?" (Myron was David Selznick's older brother.) In physical and emotional agony, Kate sat in the back seat, staring straight ahead and barely speaking as the car drove from Pasadena to the gates of the RKO studio.

Though its corporate history can be traced back to the 1880s, RKO was a fairly new studio, dating from 1929, when the Radio Corporation of America bought a nearly defunct film company and merged it with the Keith-Albee-Orpheum theater chain. At the time Kate arrived on the lot, the top RKO stars were Irene Dunne, Ann Harding, Constance Bennett and leading men Richard Dix, John Boles, and Ricardo Cortez—who today are all but forgotten except by trivia experts. RKO was one of Hollywood's "Big Five" studios, but it ranked after MGM, Paramount, Warners, and Fox in prestige, glamour, and quality. Things had started to improve, however, in 1931, when David O. Selznick was appointed head of production; with the help of director George Cukor and executive assistant Pandro S. Berman, he had raised the level of the RKO product several notches.

On arriving at the studio, Kate was introduced to Selznick and Cukor, who were both appalled at her appearance. The director looked her up and down and said, "What is that thing you have on your head?"

"It's a hat," she answered. "It's very smart. Don't you like it?"

Cukor didn't like it, but he kept quiet. So did Kate; she was doing her best to look aloof and disdainful. To make conversation, the director showed her sketches of her *Bill of Divorcement* costumes. Peering at them imperiously, Kate shook her head and said she'd prefer to have her clothes designed by Chanel or Schiaparelli.

"Considering the way you look, I can hardly take your judgment seriously," Cukor retorted. Kate looked stunned for a moment. She turned on her heel, headed for the door, and was almost out of the office when she stopped and walked back with her hand extended. "I shook it," Cukor recalled, "and we've been friends ever since."

When Kate first met him, Cukor was thirty-three and portly, with dark hair and bespectacled, intense eyes. After a short but solid career on Broadway, he had arrived in Hollywood in 1929 as an authority on spoken dialogue, and worked first at Paramount, then at RKO. He quickly established himself as a master adaptor of stage and literary material—he considered himself an "interpretive" rather than a "creative" director—and as a Svengali who could bring out the best in any actor. Because of his fruitful relationships with Hepburn, Crawford, Garbo, Garland, and Judy Holliday, he was frequently called "a woman's director," but the label is too limiting; James Stewart, James Mason, Ronald Colman, Cary Grant, and Spencer Tracy also flourished under the Cukor touch. "George was happiest," reports a friend, "when he was making actors comfortable"—and it made no difference whether the actor was male or female.

"He makes you trust yourself," Hepburn once said. "He maintains your illusion of yourself out of the ebullience of his energy and the immense generosity of his spirit."

Cukor was a witty and enthusiastic conversationalist with a habit of repeating all superlatives and descriptive adjectives at least three times. (Producer Charles Brackett remembers that Cukor used to look at a piece of dialogue and "tell us it was phony, phony, phony, *phony*. When he got to the fourth phony, we knew he was serious!") He had a waspish sense of humor, and when thwarted in his perfectionist drives or displeased with an actor's performance, he could be very blunt. Shelley Winters played her first important screen role as a frumpish waitress in Cukor's *A Double Life:* she decided to add a little glamour to the part, but when she walked on the set, the director yelled, "Damn it, girl! Take off those eyelashes and that girdle!

You have a perfectly good intelligence—why insult your mind that way?'' Miss Winters was eternally grateful to Cukor. ''All during the film,'' she says, ''I followed him around like he was my daddy.''

Back in 1932, after establishing friendly relations with Kate, he sent her to makeup and found a specialist to look after her eyes. The director realized Kate needed sprucing up—her freckles would have to be covered by makeup, her sharp contours required special lighting, her frizzy hair needed a massive restyling—but he didn't want her overhauled into a glamorous nonentity. At all costs, he wanted her individuality to come through on the screen, and he watched over the experts to make sure they didn't plane away the sharp edges of her looks and personality and turn her into another faceless, characterless, assembly-line RKO starlet.

After their first day at the studio, Kate and Laura checked in at a Beverly Hills hotel and stayed there until they rented a tiny four-room cottage in an unfashionable Los Angeles neighborhood. According to Hollywood legend, Greta Garbo once visited Kate's hideaway and told a friend, ''My God! How dreary it was! But, of course, I love dreary places!''

Hepburn didn't find it dreary. The house was located in a woodsy, middle-class neighborhood near the Los Angeles reservoir; it was peaceful, the scenery was lovely, there was lots of wildlife, and it was blissfully private; no one but Kate seemed to realize that the reservoir was the perfect place for an afternoon hike.

As soon as she had settled in the cottage, Kate started studying the *Bill of Divorcement* script. Originally written in 1921, the play was now awfully musty in its dialogue (''I'm withering without you like cut grass in the sun'') and its overripe dramatic machinations. Playwright Clemence Dane had borrowed the outline of her plot from Ibsen's *Ghosts:* beautiful and gifted Sydney Fairchild fears she may be tainted by her father's insanity and gives up her chance for love, marriage, and children to care for him. The play is hollow and contrived, but Sydney is a showy role for an actress with an elusive and esoteric appeal—she must be offbeat enough to suggest the possibility of future insanity without ever actually playing madness or anything close to it.

As part of her pre-production study, Kate visited the studio daily, watched the RKO stars on the set, and took an interest in all phases of film-making. Nothing escaped her attention. She walked around the lot looking, listening, learning, and asking endless questions of the "little people" who kept the studio running. Eventually she acquired expert knowledge in every field of film production, and bossed the technicians whenever she felt they were falling down on the job. "Jesus, she thinks she could replace us all," one specialist complained to a producer of a later Hepburn movie. "Yes," the producer answered thoughtfully, "and if she put her mind to it, she probably could."

To drive back and forth from the studio, Kate rented a Hispano-Suiza, a huge touring car that one RKO producer described as "a cross between a soda fountain and the Super Chief." Some say she was trying to impress the film colony, others claim she was ribbing the Hollywood life style—either way, she failed to make her point. The Hispano-Suiza was a familiar and unexciting sight around the studios—Garbo rode in one in *Grand Hotel,* and many film heroines had gone from rags to riches after a tryst in the back seat of one. To Hollywood, the car was about as glamorous as a Model T Ford. Kate soon heard about her mistake; she was mortified, but, to save face, she and Laura kept driving around in the oversized hearse as though they were duchesses on a sightseeing tour of the Hollywood aborigines.

On her first day at RKO, Kate had met her *Bill of Divorcement* co-star, John Barrymore. At the time, she was still pink-eyed and dressed in her Puritan traveling suit. Barrymore smiled, took her aside, and said, "You know, my dear, sometimes I drink a little myself. And when I do I always use these eyedrops. They remove the inflammation at once." He pulled a vial of medicine from his breast pocket and tried to hand it to Kate.

"But, Mr. Barrymore," she protested, "I have a cinder in my eye." Barrymore gave her a knowing wink. "That's what they all say, my dear."

Bluestocking Hepburn and lecherous Barrymore—the combination has myth-making possibilities, and there are many stories about their encounters on the *Bill of Divorcement* set. One starts with Barrymore deciding to seduce Kate, a courtesy he extended to many leading ladies. Some people say he removed his clothes before Kate arrived in his dressing room; others claimed he waited till she was in the room and then bared his dishonorable intentions. When Hepburn realized what was happening, she gasped and headed for the door. "There must be some mistake!" she shouted over her shoulder.

Another anecdote has Barrymore and his leading lady conducting open warfare before the entire crew. After one scene had been shot several times, Hepburn turned to Barrymore and shouted, "I'll never play another scene with you!" Barrymore retorted, "My dear, you never have."

In *Good Night, Sweet Prince,* Barrymore biographer Gene Fowler dismisses these stories as malicious fantasies, and Kate agrees. "Barrymore never criticized me," she recalls. "He just shoved me before the cameras. He taught me all that could be poured into one greenhorn in that short a time.''

Perhaps Barrymore helped, but Cukor did most of the work. One of the first directors of the sound era to recognize the difference between acting for the theater and for film, he instructed, corrected, and badgered Kate—sometimes in front of cast and crew—as she struggled to adapt herself to the craft of playing before the camera. It was a slow process. At first, Kate tended to do too much—her gestures were hurried, her movements too quick—but with Cukor's help, she began to learn that in film acting, less is more.

A Bill of Divorcement was shot in four weeks, and the speed shows: it's a peculiarly graceless film, with abrupt transitions and long passages of awkward direction and acting. Barrymore and Billie Burke (as Mrs. Fairchild) are floridly theatrical, and at times Hepburn's performance also has an aura of the theater about it. She comes on too strong, she's too tense—but she makes her personality felt, and, compared to her veteran co-stars, she looks strikingly modern. Many years later, director Rouben Mamoulian was to comment that only three or four actresses in Hollywood history ever had a truly individual and expressive manner of walking. He mentioned Garbo, Cyd Charisse, and Hepburn, who in her very first film, demonstrated what Mamoulian was talking about. Hepburn's walk—really a cross between a stride and a lope—is both stylish and gauche, a description that could be extended to cover her overall performance as well as her off-screen personality.

Shortly after the film was completed, Kate and Laura returned to New York, and Hepburn took off on a European vacation with Luddy. They sailed steerage class because, Kate later explained, she saw no reason why she should "get seasick on a first-class ticket."

She was still in Europe when *Bill of Divorcement* opened at a ten-dollar charity premiere in New York's Mayfair Theatre. The film, wrote the critic for *Stage* magazine, "was ushered in with a discreet blowing of trumpets . . . but once all the ballyhoo had subsided, it turned out that practically the only cause for excitement was a startlingly clear and vibrant performance by Katharine Hepburn. . . ." Other critics were kinder to *Bill of Divorcement*, but all the reviews centered on Kate.

Overnight there was a Hepburn craze, as Nancy Hamilton, who had been Kate's understudy in *The Warrior's Husband*, reported in *Stage* magazine.

Really, the kindest thing Katharine Hepburn could have done for me, short of getting sick last spring (which she did *not* do), was to get famous this fall, which she rather definitely has done. . . . For weeks I have been going around to the various producers in town, having velvet carpets unrolled before me, colored boys waving fans behind me, and champagne waiting to be poured in my slippers. Oh, not immediately upon stepping into an office, you understand . . . but as soon as they would point wearily to the door, I would announce with lovely simplicity that I had been Katharine Hepburn's understudy last year. The change that would come over the whole personnel of an office at this announcement was nothing short of outstanding. Doors would fly open, heads appear through the floor, dictaphones spring out of the air, and heralds with trumpets ushered me into the inner sanctum. . . .

The RKO publicity department was totally unprepared for Kate's success. When she had arrived in Hollywood, Hepburn had refused all interviews, and allowed only a few ''cheesecake'' photographs that showed her doubled up as she executed a jackknife from a high diving board. Lacking biographical details, the publicists made up a life story that described her as heiress to the fifteen-million-dollar fortune of A. Barton Hepburn, the president of Chase Manhattan Bank. At first Kate was amused, then irritated—she had come to resent her image as a wealthy and eccentric dilettante—but she did nothing immediately to alter this impression. RKO told her to come home; she did, and on arrival on the S.S. *Paris*, she gave one of her few mass interviews. It was also one of her worst. Asked if she were married to her traveling companion (Luddy), Hepburn answered, ''I don't remember.'' Did she have any children? ''Yes—two white and three colored.''

Discarding Luddy and picking up Laura, Kate rushed off to Hollywood, where there were more silly questions—and equally silly answers. Finally, Kate refused all interviews, especially those for fan magazines. RKO was shocked. All the studios viewed *Photoplay*, *Modern Screen*, and the other movie monthlies as valuable outlets for publicity, and cooperated with them as long as their reporters steered clear of any real scandal. (The banner headlines often sounded juicy, but the articles that accompanied them were pretty tame.)

In the 1930s the fan magazines were very powerful. They boasted a collective readership of four million people, 90 percent of them women, most in the lower-income bracket. And there was no way of knowing how many people read the fan magazines on the sly—society ladies might pick them up in the beauty parlor, literate and well-heeled gentlemen might find them in the doctor's office—and this secret readership was probably huge. An unflattering article in one of these magazines could offset the box office, so most stars learned to accept the foolish chatter and inane interviews as a part of their jobs. Not Kate. There were to be no inside scoops on her private life. She looked on all members of the press—whether from *Vogue*, *The New York Times*, or *Silver Screen*—as natural enemies.

For the next thirty-five years, Kate waged a vigorous battle to protect her privacy. She concocted elaborate schemes to avoid the press and her fans—some of which backfired and brought her more attention than cooperating by handing out a few autographs or submitting to an occasional interview would have. In a 1965 article (''The Right of Privacy'') written for the *Virginia Law Weekly*, Hepburn says that on arrival in Hollywood, she divided the world into two spheres. One was private territory—''her home, a friend's home, a private club''; the other belonged to the enemy—''railroad stations, airports, restaurants, bars, theaters.'' She avoided public places and expected the public to stay off her private terrain. It sounds like a sensible arrangement, but, as she admitted in her article, it runs counter to the demands of modern society.

There were, of course, times when Kate had to cross over into public territory : she went to the theater, she was an inveterate museum visitor, she enjoyed browsing through antique and second-hand shops. (She has rarely been seen in a restaurant because, she explains, eating in public gives her indigestion.) On these occasions, Kate often had unpleasant encounters with autograph hounds, some of them ending in an exchange of bitter insults. Hepburn once said she took exception to this foolish, but quite harmless form of flattery because she didn't want to be ''spoiled.'' Early in her career, she realized that the star who begins to enjoy the attention of fawning interviewers and fans can be devastated when it comes to an end.

On their return to Hollywood, Kate and Laura rented a

new and slightly larger house with a swimming pool. Later they joined the Bel-Air Country Club so that Hepburn could play golf on Saturdays, but this was their only concession to Hollywood extravagance. Kate lived on a frugal allowance that was doled out weekly by her father. Shortly after her arrival in California, she called Dr. Hepburn to tell him of her adventures and he asked, ''Where's the money?''

''Well, Daddy,'' she answered, ''there isn't any money. I spent it all.'' From then on, she sent her salary to Hartford for her father to bank or invest as he saw fit. Within a few years, he had made her a very rich woman.

Because of her *Bill of Divorcement* success, Kate was a much sought-after guest, but she rarely went to parties or premieres, and never dated Hollywood's eligible bachelors. Other than Laura, Leland Hayward, and ''Murph'' (Eve March), her stand-in, Kate saw no one except the people she met at George Cukor's famous Sunday lunches. A gourmet, an art collector, a bibliophile, a connoisseur of gifted people, Cukor ran the closest thing to a salon ever seen in Hollywood. His elegant lunches and dinners were attended by a glittering array of film and literary celebrities—everyone from Aldous Huxley and Somerset Maugham to Joan Crawford and all three of the Barrymores.

It was at one of these parties that Hepburn met Greta Garbo, her favorite actress. On the day the shy and reclusive star came for lunch, Hepburn arrived at Cukor's house early and went for a swim in his pool. As she was paddling around, Cukor ran out to announce Garbo's arrival; Kate jumped out of the pool, grabbed a towel and ran smack into the Swedish actress—who smiled enigmatically. Greatly flustered, Hepburn stammered out a greeting and then became tongue-tied. Later she and Garbo became good friends.

Through Cukor, Kate also met Mary Pickford and was invited for dinner at Pickfair, the baronial estate Pickford and Douglas Fairbanks had built back in the days when they were America's favorite sweethearts. Kate didn't want to go, but Cukor pleaded with her, and after several more invitations she agreed.

The next morning, she called on Cukor and said, "I hope you're satisfied. I had dinner at Pickfair last night." The director made a quick appraisal of her clothes—slacks and a baggy sweater—and replied, "I assume you ate in the kitchen. Certainly they didn't let you in through the front door."

Kate's clothes gathered a lot of unfavorable comment from the Hollywood elite. For public appearances she had a few dresses, many of them designed by Elizabeth Hawes, most of them making her look like a frump—though one is not sure whether the fault lies with the dresses, with Kate, or with the fashions of the period. In private, she nearly always wore pants; some were so worn and poorly tailored that they might have belonged to a California truck farmer.

This wasn't the proper image for a star, so RKO asked her to throw her pants in the trash bin. When she refused to comply, the studio threatened to steal them. "And one day, they did it," Hepburn recalls. "They stole my trousers. And I said, 'If you don't give them back, I'll walk practically naked through the studio lot.'" The trousers weren't returned. "So I did it. Of course I did it. I walked through the lot in my underpants."

Around the RKO lot Kate was called "Katharine of Arrogance": she was polite to the gaffers and go-fers and petty technicians; she cooperated with the directors and producers she respected; but for the high-salaried, self-important nonentities that cluttered Hollywood, she had nothing but disdain. And she expressed it in bizarre ways.

Invited to a cocktail party, she sent Laura in to excuse her on grounds of illness while she stood outside in full view of the assembled guests. Asked to dinner by a prominent producer, Kate refused, saying that eating in public gave her a nervous stomach. But at the last minute, she decided it might be fun to see what was going on; so she and Laura drove to the producer's house and peeped through the dining-room windows. Then, the two girls crept around to the kitchen, bribed the servants, put on maids' uniforms, and served dessert. As Kate was handing around the cherries jubilee, one of the guests looked up, stared thoughtfully, and said, "My dear, did anyone ever say you look exactly like that new actress, Katharine Hepburn?" Recognizing Kate, the hostess asked her to sit down, but Hepburn refused. "We just dropped by to serve dessert," she explained. "We often do that."

The following day, this escapade was the talk of Hollywood. Kate's friends found it very funny, but the rest of the film colony was definitely not amused.

Hepburn's second RKO film was to have been *Three Came Unarmed,* the story of a missionary family living in Borneo, but this was shelved when a suitable script couldn't be fashioned from E. Arnot Robertson's novel. Instead, the studio assigned her to *Christopher Strong*, the story of a lady pilot and her unhappy affair with a British politician. Kate was fascinated by the idea of playing an aviatrix, and read up on Amelia Earhart and her British counterpart, Amy Johnson—the models for her *Christopher Strong* heroine. She also looked forward to working with Dorothy Arzner, but the making of the film turned out to be an unpleasant experience. The script was pedestrian; Miss Arzner's direction was limp and uninspired; and, worst of all, Hepburn was seriously ill with influenza for part of the production.

Overall the film is mediocre, but it has its memorable moments, including a spectacular entrance for Hepburn. Dressed as a moth for a masquerade party, she floats in wearing a floor-length lamé sheath and a heart-shaped helmet sprouting two antennae from its crown. It's an incredible costume, so bizarre that it can only be described as surreal camp.

On a more serious level, there are several muted and highly effective love scenes in *Christopher Strong,* and an unusually intense bedroom sequence that critic Pauline Kael has rightly called "the intelligent woman's primal postcoital scene." The ending, however, is a cop-out: pregnant and unable to marry the man she loves, the heroine takes off in her plane and kills herself by removing her oxygen mask at an altitude of thirty thousand feet.

Hepburn is almost embarrassingly bad in these final moments, and throughout the picture she's self-conscious, relentlessly high-strung, raspy in her vocal delivery, glowering and overstylized in appearance. There's not a trace of warmth or humor in the entire performance. In some strange, not very pleasing way, she's unforgettable, but she's also very hard to take.

On its release in March 1933, *Christopher Strong* was panned by most critics, and Kate received very mixed reviews. "She leaves some of us who cheered her along during her marvelous performance in *A Bill of Divorcement* aghast at the amateur quality of her histrionics," lamented William Boehnel of the New York *World-Telegram.* "For the first half of the time, she shrieks her lines in an unduly affected voice; for the rest of the film, her diction . . . jars the nerves.'' Several critics compared her to Garbo, which, considering her lacquered appearance, is probably what RKO intended; but at least one reviewer realized the resemblance was contrived and unflattering. "All Miss Hepburn needs is a little more familiarity with the microphone,'' noted Thornton Delehanty in the New York *Post*, "and a firm determination not to let her producers turn her into a second Garbo, a second Joan Crawford, or a second anything."

Christopher Strong was a box-office flop. Audiences hated it, and they hated Hepburn too. Men, in particular, disliked her. The male viewpoint on Kate was best summed up by critic Brendan Gill, who wrote that the early Hepburn heroines gave the impression that "they would make love only after marriage and then only with a certain fastidious reluctance, nostrils flaring." The appraisal is only half accurate: many Hepburn heroines make love before marriage, but their nostrils do occasionally flare when a man approaches. Kate's romantic scenes were always carefully stylized, with lots of mooning and swooning and artful backlighting. At this time, sexual passion lay outside Hepburn's repertoire of screen emotions, but for her fans that hardly mattered. Here, for the first time in American film history, was a woman of breeding and intelligence, spirit and strength, who had more on her mind than bed, babies, and the beauty parlor.

It is, however, possible to admire Hepburn and still see why a large portion of the 1930s movie public positively loathed her. This kind of double vision is rare: if you hate Joan Crawford, it's hard to imagine how anyone can like her; if you love Greta Garbo, it's inconceivable that anyone could consider her less than exalted. But with Hepburn, you know what the opposition is talking about. Yes, she's aggressive, mannered, artificial, and that Bryn Mawr diction can be as nerve-wracking as fingernails on a black-board. But that isn't the entire picture—there's also warmth, vibrancy, individuality, and one of the great, original faces of film history. In her late 1930s films, the contradictory sides of Hepburn's personality don't always mesh, but they are the more fascinating for their harsh, discordant notes. They are, in fact, much more interesting than many of the creamy, bland, overpraised films of her later career.

5

Top of the Heap

While working on *Christopher Strong*, Kate received two scripts from Jed Harris, a prominent Broadway producer who wanted to lure her back to the stage. One play was *The Green Bay Tree*, a love-triangle drama with latent homosexual overtones; the other, *The Lake*, was a love-triangle drama with Oedipal overtones. Kate rejected *The Green Bay Tree*—the leading female role was weak—but liked *The Lake*. RKO agreed to give her time off after she finished three more films. These commitments were worked off in a rush—all three were completed before the end of December 1933.

Kate was already set for a new film—an adaptation of an unproduced play by Zoë Akins, the author of *Christopher Strong*. *Morning Glory*, her new script, was nearly as slapdash, but the leading role was perfect for Hepburn. She played Eva Lovelace (née Ada Love), a Vermont girl who comes to New York as an aspiring actress. Half crazed with ambition, she is a fey creature who talks too much, starves for her art, and regards the theater as a religious vocation. ''There will always be a Shaw play in my repertoire as long as I remain in the theater," Eva says. "And of course, I shall die in the theater. My star will never set."

Zoë Akins said Eva Lovelace was based on her close friend Tallulah Bankhead, whom she had known back in the days when teen-aged Tallulah was the most talked about nonactress on the 1917 Broadway scene. At the time of *Morning Glory*, Bankhead was pursuing a disastrous Hollywood career that had started with *Tarnished Lady*, a George Cukor film. The actress and director had become fast friends, and through him, Bankhead met Kate. At first meeting, the two actresses disliked each other—"A prude," said Bankhead; "Rude," thought Hepburn—but eventually they became great friends, and Tallulah once paid Kate an often-quoted compliment.

"Whenever I see Kate perform," she said, "at first I wonder why she talks that way. And then when I come out of the theater, I wonder why everyone doesn't talk like Kate."

For all her familiarity with Tallulah, Hepburn's Eva Lovelace bears no resemblance to the fabled and easily caricatured Bankhead. Hepburn later said she used Ruth Gordon as a model for some scenes, but that reference doesn't ring true, either. For the most part, Eva Lovelace suggests the young Katharine Hepburn of the *Holiday* screen test— the girl who is too eager and tries too hard to please.

Morning Glory follows the pattern of the typical backstage picture. On her arrival in New York, Eva is ignored by all the theatrical managers until she attends a Broadway party and, tiddly on champagne, gives an amateurish, heartfelt rendition of Hamlet's soliloquy and Juliet's balcony scene. Producer Louis Eaton (Adolphe Menjou) takes her under his wing and (it is implied) into his bed, dresses her in furs and sequined sheaths, and gets her an understudy job in a new play by Joseph Sheridan (Douglas

Fairbanks, Jr.). When the leading lady walks out, Eva goes on and wows the audience. "Now you belong to no man," Eaton tells her. "You belong to Broadway!"

Another friend warns Eva, "How many keep their heads? You've come to the fore. *You* have the chance to be a morning glory—a flower that fades before the sun is very high." Determination shining through her tears, Eva answers, "I'm not afraid of being a morning glory. I'm not afraid ... I'm not afraid!"

At the end, Kate is as tremulous as a plate of Jell-O, and at the beginning, her affectations are in full flower. In many scenes, she is so febrile and overwrought that she seems to be suffering from brain fever like the lovesick heroine of a Russian novel. Less austere and forbidding than in *Christopher Strong*, she is still very bizarre—her reading of the balcony scene in Eva's quavering, untutored voice is extraordinary, but one doesn't know what to make of it. Is this acting or the quirky display of a girl drunk on her own ego? Later in the film when Eva is on the road to fame, Hepburn tones down the intensity and exhibits the mellower side of her personality, and it is only then that the audience is able to relax and enjoy her performance.

"It's a peculiar thing," said George Cukor, "but the movie audience is usually hostile to Kate at the beginning of a picture. You can almost feel the hostility. But then at the middle they're usually sympathetic, and, by the end, they're rooting for her."

Morning Glory is the first of many Hepburn films in which the actress begins by playing directly against the grain of audience sympathy and then slowly wins over the spectator by revealing that purity of feeling and sensitivity that Hepburn alone can command. Sometimes, as in *Morning Glory*, the balance tips dangerously in the wrong direction; sometimes, she goes to the other extreme and falls over into sentimentality. Still, this method of character building was a daring and provocative way of reconciling the contradictions in her personality. Eva Lovelace and all the other eccentric, outwardly brash and inwardly vulnerable Hepburn heroines of the 1930s were self-portraits—or so Kate has implied. At the beginning of her career, she recalls, "Everyone thought I was bold and fearless and even arrogant . . . but inwardly I was always quaking. . . . I've never cared about how afraid I may have been inside—I've always done what I thought I should." This was a lesson Hepburn had learned from her parents. "They taught me not to give in to fear, showed me how to conquer it."

Much of the credit for Hepburn's *Morning Glory* performance must go to director Lowell Sherman. Modestly talented as both an actor and director, Sherman made only a few films before his untimely death in 1934; *Morning Glory* and Mae West's *She Done Him Wrong* stand out as his most substantial credits. All his films are technically very crude—*Morning Glory* looks as if it was shot in three days and edited in two—but this deficiency was offset by his flair for bringing out the best in his leading ladies. (The men in his movies are all pawns or props—in *Morning Glory*, Douglas Fairbanks, Jr. has about as much personality as a dummy in a tailor-shop window.)

Though he really wasn't her kind of man—like his brother-in-law, John Barrymore, he was an alcoholic—Kate found Sherman much more sympathetic than the stiff and domineering Dorothy Arzner. Working with lightning speed, the director rehearsed and shot the film in three weeks, never once deviating from script continuity. This was a great boon to Kate—accustomed to the orderly character development of the stage, she had found it difficult to adjust to the out-of-sequence shooting of her previous films.

When *Morning Glory* came out in August 1933, it received mixed reviews—everyone loved Kate, but many critics rapped the film for its gassy dialogue and fairy-tale triviality. Several months later, Hepburn won her first Oscar for *Morning Glory*, an event that placed her far ahead of her chief RKO rivals, Ann Harding and Irene Dunne. From then on, the studio looked on Kate as their prize prestige star, though few of her films made much money. The pattern was set with *Morning Glory*, which did only moderately well at the box office.

Kate wasn't impressed by her Oscar. Unable to attend the ceremony, she wrote a telegram saying she didn't believe in acting contests, and therefore felt it her duty to refuse the bronze statuette. Leland Hayward read the wire, tore it up, and sent a thank-you note instead. "He was right," Hepburn says today. "I was being childish." She has never, however, picked up any of her four Oscars. "I'm not proud that I didn't," she says, "I just never got around to it."

Jumping ahead for a moment to 1969, there was a blustery, bone-chilling winter day in that year when Katharine Hepburn visited the Museum of Modern Art for a private film screening. Everyone else was bundled up in overcoats and scarves and woolly sweaters, but not Kate. With a book bag slung over her shoulder and wearing only a light jacket to protect her from the near-zero weather, she marched in and exclaimed, "My, isn't it an invigorating day!"

As she strode down the corridors to the screening room, she paused to stare at a still of Clark Gable. ("My Gawd!

Look at Clark! Doesn't he look *awful!*''), delivered a bloodcurdling temperance lecture on smoking, and inquired about future film programs at the museum. Told of a future George Cukor retrospective, she asked, ''Are you going to show my *Little Women*. . . ?'' Her voice trailed off, and for a brief moment, her eyes grew misty with nostalgia.

Made in 1933, *Little Women* is a nearly perfect film, and Hepburn's performance as the gallant Jo March goes beyond perfection—it's sublime. One can fault or praise a particular gesture or movement, but otherwise acting at this level can't be analyzed except to say that it is pure and moving and durable: Kate's Jo lives on in the mind, and one can go back to the film years later and find her as fresh and wonderful as one remembered.

Little Women had been one of David Selznick's pet projects for many years. Shortly after his arrival at RKO he promoted it as a potential Helen Mack vehicle; that fell through, but the project stayed in the back of his mind. He wanted George Cukor as director, but at first Cukor wasn't enthusiastic. He had never read Louisa May Alcott's novel, which he equated with the Elsie Dinsmore school of ''sweetness and light.'' Egged on by Selznick, he read the book and found that it was ''not at all saccharine or sentimental, but filled with strength and seriousness.''

As he read the book, Cukor could see only Katharine Hepburn as Jo. ''There's no reason to make *Little Women* unless you have the right Jo,'' he said. ''Hepburn was born to play the role. She was raised in New England, and she instinctively understood the background and moral values of the story.''

By the time *Little Women* went into production, David O. Selznick had left RKO to become an executive producer, but the film bears the stamp of his fastidious attention to detail: it is carefully researched—all the Victorian decor and bric-a-brac look authentic; the script is remarkably faithful; the casting of the little women, their beaus, and their relatives is nearly perfect.

Hepburn was an inspiration to everyone, said Cukor. "She cast a spell of magic and a kind of power over the picture. You could go with whatever she did." It's a nice memory, but it's not the whole truth: there was a lot of tension between Hepburn and Cukor on this film. One incident involved Kate's wardrobe. Walter Plunkett, RKO's dress designer, had made beautiful costumes out of authentic period material—they were one-of-a-kind, and Kate was warned that they couldn't be replaced if she spoiled them. One shot required her to run up a flight of stairs carrying a dish of ice cream; throwing herself into the gaiety of the scene, Kate forgot the warning and spilled ice cream on her skirt. Outraged, Cukor slapped her across the face in front of the entire cast and crew—an insult that few Hollywood stars would have accepted as meekly as Kate did. She shrugged it off and headed for her dressing room to be refitted for a new costume.

While on location at the Warner Bros. lot—many of the outdoor *Little Women* scenes were filmed there—Kate introduced picnic lunches and tea breaks as part of the daily routine. At first Cukor dismissed these collations as a Hartford affectation, but eventually he came to share Kate's view that they were a gracious way of easing on-set tension. From then on, Hepburn provided picnics for most of her 1930s films.

There were other problems during the making of *Little Women:* the script was revised even after shooting had started; a technicians' strike interrupted production; and Joan Bennett, playing one of Kate's sisters, was pregnant and ballooning in size as each day went by. Cukor kept shooting higher and higher until all that was seen of Miss Bennett was her head and shoulders. The blocking was restaged daily, with Kate and her other screen sisters (Frances Dee, Jean Parker) taking over Bennett's more athletic movements. It was skillfully done, and no one ever realized that one of the little women was about to become a little mother.

When *Little Women* opened at Radio City Music Hall in November 1933, it was welcomed as the best RKO production to date. For Hepburn, there was unstinting praise. "Her playing is superb," wrote *Time* magazine. "An actress of so much vitality that she can wear balloon skirts and address her mother as 'Marmee' without suggesting quaintness, she makes Jo March one of the most memorable heroines of the year. . . ." Released at a time when audiences were fed up with gangster pictures, backstage musicals, and Mae West innuendo, *Little Women* was a huge hit. The big box-office receipts capped Kate's Hollywood success; in her own words, she was now "top of the heap."

Her triumph was short-lived; within a year some people were writing her off as a "flash in the pan." The downward curve of her career began with her next film, *Spitfire*, the story of an Ozark faith healer named Trigger Hicks. "The picture has absolutely nothing to recommend it," said its director, John Cromwell. "The part of Trigger Hicks is about as unsuited to Katharine's talents as anything that can be imagined."

Asked if he thought Hepburn knew she was unsuited to the role, Cromwell replied, "I don't think so. . . . She was much too self-confident for that. She had all the self-confidence in the world . . . so much so that I doubt that even for a moment did she ever think there was anything she couldn't do."

Others say Kate went into *Spitfire* with great reluctance, accepting the assignment so that she could fulfill her RKO commitment and return to the stage. The shooting schedule was limited to four weeks, with the studio agreeing to pay Hepburn $10,000 for any extra work. There are reports of continual on-set friction between Hepburn and Cromwell, but the director minimized their mutual hostility. "I realized that she was instinctively a very good actress," he recalled, "but she had never taken the trouble to learn more about the business. . . . We got along very well, with the exception of one incident."

At the time of *Spitfire*, Cromwell was still new to Hollywood, and he felt uncomfortable extemporizing business and camera setups on the set. Kate always memorized her lines before filming began, but she left details of her characterization to the last minute, expecting that she and the director would work these out together. "I had some movement planned," recalled Cromwell, "and Kate objected to it. She wanted it changed, but I decided it would embarrass the continuity, and, as gently as I could, I refused. She was quite upset and for a while there was a thing between us. I knew that I was much too conservative for her, but I doubt that she ever understood that I was too unsure of myself to throw out my plan for what seemed to be a whim."

At 6 P.M. on the last day of Kate's contract, Cromwell dismissed the company, although two scenes, including the ending, remained to be filmed. Leland Hayward reminded RKO that Kate was now on overtime, but the front office insisted that her contract did not expire until midnight, and therefore she still owed the studio six hours' work.

The next morning Hepburn reported to the *Spitfire* set. Shooting proceeded, but nothing pleased Cromwell, and precisely six hours later, in mid-scene, Kate stopped working. The studio called Hayward and tried to effect a compromise. Kate refused. There was only an hour's filming left, but she insisted on the $10,000 whether she worked five minutes or eight hours.

She got her full fee, finished the film, and flew east to begin rehearsals of *The Lake*.

6

Kate Sinks
in "The Lake"

In Edna Ferber and George Kaufman's *Stage Door*, Broadway actress Terry Randall wonders whether she should go to Hollywood. "For what?" a friend asks. "So that a few years from now they can throw you out on the ash heap? The theater may be slow and heartbreaking, but if you build solidly, you've got something. . . . Look at Katharine Cornell, and Lynn Fontanne, and Alfred Lunt. . . . They've got something that nothing in the world can take away from them. And what's John Barrymore got? A yacht!"

For theater people in the 1930s, Hollywood meant yachts and flash success; the stage was struggle and dedication and glory everlasting. Hepburn shared this attitude—her Hollywood success had been too easily won, too financially rewarding to suit her Puritan sensibility. Returning to the theater was a form of penance. "The idea terrified me," she admits. "It frightened me so much that I thought I must go back and conquer my fear."

Kate's return was so heavily publicized that *The Lake* racked up a $40,000 advance sale—a record for the Depression era. The play had been an enormous success in London, and now it was the most eagerly awaited production of the 1934 Broadway season. Too much anticipation can hurt even a first-rate play, and *The Lake* wasn't first-rate by any stretch of the imagination. Soap opera of the English drawing-room variety, it is the story of highborn Stella Surrege, a mother-dominated young lady who has made a mess of her life: she's in love with a married man and engaged to marry a man she doesn't love. On her wedding day, she and her husband drive off for their honeymoon, their car skids into a lake, and he drowns. This accident gives Stella a new outlook on life, and she sets out in search of a better tomorrow.

Stella is a young lady given to self-pity and languid attitudes, and the play is prone to the same sort of posturing. It's a very flossy drama, but with the right actress as Stella, it might add up to a passable evening in the theater. Hepburn, however, wasn't the right actress.

Kate had hoped to spend a month working with producer-director Jed Harris before starting rehearsals, but *Spitfire* took up the time allotted for this preliminary tuneup, and she arrived in New York only three weeks before the show's Washington tryout. From the start, she was uneasy and tense. Surrounded by a distinguished supporting cast (Colin Clive, Blanche Bates, Frances Starr), she sensed her inadequacies at once, and became irritable and defensive as rehearsals progressed. One day her nerves cracked, and, pointing at the actors standing in the wings, she screamed, ''Get these people away from me! I can't work with them staring at me!''

Jed Harris shouted back, ''If you're to become an actress, you've got to learn the stage tradition of courtesy. Everyone standing around you, obeying orders, is a better trouper than you!''

Jed Harris knew less about stage courtesy than Hepburn. Slim, short, saturninely handsome, with hooded eyes and an all-day five-o'clock shadow, he became a legendary man-about-Broadway before he was thirty. In theater circles, he was hailed as a genius—his hits included *Broadway, Coquette,* and *The Royal Family*—and despised as a monster who brutalized actors. He isn't really cruel, one associate said, "He just enjoys being a sadistic sonofabitch." Some stars accepted his abuse without protest; others fought back. Enraged by his barrage of insults, the elegant and very grand Ina Claire once floored Harris with an unexpected right hook and then kicked him in the stomach with the heel of her custom-made pump.

Harris made a practice of abusing the actors who worked for him, calling them any name that came to mind, gloating over their limitations, and undermining their confidence. Kate got the full Harris treatment. When she arrived late for rehearsal, he talked about the red-carpet pampering expected by film stars; he made demeaning comparisons between her and other members of the *Lake* company; he drove her hard. "If she turned her head to the left, he didn't like it," said one cast member. "If she turned it to the right, he liked it still less."

According to some reports, Kate wanted to buy her way out of the show, but Harris refused. Good reviews or bad, *The Lake* could run for some time on the strength of its advance sale and the box-office appeal of Hepburn's name.

On December 17, 1933, Hepburn arrived in Washington, D.C. for a one-week tryout of *The Lake.* When her train pulled into the station, there was a crowd of shouting fans waiting to welcome her, and, rather than face them, she ducked out a side exit, raced across the tracks and muddy fields, and circled around to a waiting limousine.

On opening night, the National Theatre was filled with

Bryn Mawr alumnae, Washington socialites, and a few prominent politicians. At the end, there was a prolonged ovation for Hepburn, and as she came off stage, Harris said, "Perfection! I can do no more!" Kate brushed him aside—she knew she had been terrible. She also knew that it would take a miracle for her performance to be in working order by the time of the Broadway premiere.

The audience that gathered at New York's Martin Beck Theatre on the night of December 26, 1933, included Laura Harding, Dr. and Mrs. Hepburn, Leland Hayward, Kay Francis, Nancy Carroll, George S. Kaufman, and Dorothy Parker. Kate came on staccato and overwrought, and seemed unable to vary or modulate her performance. At intermission, Dorothy Parker turned to a companion and made her famous quip: "Katharine Hepburn runs the gamut from A to B." This remark quickly became the most quoted nonreview in theater history, and it has left a false impression of the critical reaction to Kate's performance in *The Lake*. The reviews were bad, but they weren't malicious.

Practically all the reviewers echoed the opinion of George Jean Nathan, the acerbic critic of *Vanity Fair:* "Miss Hepburn has many of the qualities that may one day make her an actress of position. . . . She has the looks; the fine body; the sharp intelligence; the determination; and a readily detectable integrity. But that day . . . is still far from being at hand."

Judging from contemporary reports, Hepburn's performance in *The Lake* was all style and no emotion. When in doubt, she posed dramatically, threw back her head, raised a hand to her throat in an artful, strikingly simple gesture. Her voice carried a special kind of theatrical magic—it was a rasp and a sob and a violin all at once—but she couldn't manage it, and after fifteen minutes, magic turned into monotony.

The poor notices came as no surprise to Hepburn—she was in a state of shell shock long before the opening. But she wasn't so numb that she didn't want to work on her performance. On the second night, a woman walked into her dressing room and said, "You're in a lot of trouble." Kate groaned. "Well," the plump lady said, "I'm Susan Steele, and I teach voice. I think I can help you." Kate nodded, and for the rest of the run, Miss Steele watched the show every evening, and then, the next day, she discussed the performance with Kate, and together they worked out a new and better interpretation.

A few weeks later, Kate was giving a good performance. But *The Lake* had been a painful experience, and when she learned that Harris was planning to tour the show after its New York run, she again asked to buy her way out of her contract. This time Harris agreed: Kate wrote out a check for $15,000, and after fifty-five performances, the play closed on February 10, 1934.

For the next few months, Hepburn stayed in New York, living in a rented four-story townhouse in Manhattan's Turtle Bay district. Kate had discovered the house in 1931—the rent was then $100 a month—and she became so attached to it that she bought it outright in 1937. Since then, East 49th Street in New York City has been her only permanent address. She has never bought a home in California, because, she says, "I never intended to stay." Instead, she has moved from one rented house to the next, sometimes shifting quarters as often as twice a year.

Hepburn's Manhattan home has a garden in the back and a fireplace on each floor; the walls are painted white, the stairways are narrow, and the furniture is Colonial antique. With Laura Harding as advisor, Kate decorated the place herself. She loves good furniture, and, during the Depression years, she was able to pick it up at a reasonable price. There's nothing of the interior decorator about the atmosphere—everything is simple and warm and comfortable. "I can't imagine anyone wanting to live there," said one visitor with more formal taste, "but, of course, it suits Kate—a little bit of New England transplanted to New York."

During the run of *The Lake*, Kate acquired a chauffeur-caretaker, Charles Newhill, who was to be in her service for over forty years. When she was out of town, he looked after the house; when she was in residence, he drove her to Hartford or Fenwick nearly every weekend. When the hot weather arrived, the trips to Connecticut became more frequent—Kate hated the muggy New York heat and believed all forms of air cooling were unhealthy. But whatever the season, she was always eager to see her family.

The younger Hepburns had grown into young adulthood during the last few years. Kate's sisters had been tutored at home and later had both attended Bennington; Peggy had shown an aptitude for science while Marion had literary leanings. Richard, a recent Harvard graduate, wrote short stories and plays, few of which were ever published or produced. (His historical drama, *The Sudden End of Anne Cinquefoil,* was produced off-Broadway in 1961.) Robert, the younger Hepburn son, had a brief fling at the theater as a chorus girl in a Harvard Hasty Pudding revue, but later followed in his father's footsteps as a doctor. The busiest member of the clan was Mrs. Hepburn, who was in constant demand as a speaker on women's rights and birth control. There was, of course, something of a contradiction in a mother of five children being an advocate of birth control, but Mrs. Hepburn explained that she had

had the money, servants, and fortitude to cope with a big family.

After *The Lake*, Kate spent a lot of time with her family. The play had been a devastating experience that was to haunt her for many years. For some time to come she was terrified of stage audiences, irrationally believing they were sitting out there waiting for her to fall on her face. Even after a few weeks in Hartford, the bad reviews still rankled. But when she received word that she had won a Cannes Film Festival award for *Little Women*, she was feeling fit enough to pick it up in person. Afterward, she planned to spend a few weeks lolling about the Riviera and touring France.

Laura Harding was busy, so Kate asked Susan Steele to accompany her. This time she booked first-class passage, but on the day of the sailing she entered the S.S. *Paris* through steerage to escape the press. The ruse failed—the next day, all the papers carried pictures of Kate and the oversized Miss Steele scurrying up the gangplank.

After only four days in France, Kate returned on the *Paris,* arriving in New York on April 4. The press was out in force to welcome her. To questions of why she had cut short her vacation, Kate answered, "I was homesick"; her next film, she announced, would be *Joan of Arc* with a Thornton Wilder screenplay; her favorite actress was Garbo. Then, designating Susan Steele as her spokeswoman, she left the ship. The reporters kept asking, was Hepburn planning to remarry? And Miss Steele kept repeating, "No, she has no plans of getting married."

Ludlow Smith (who had been dropped from the Philadelphia social register after his marriage) and his mother were also questioned about this rumor, and they also denied it. But Kate surprised them—she may not have been thinking of remarriage, but she had decided she definitely wanted to divorce Luddy. After a few days in New York she went to Miami, and there, with Laura as her companion, she boarded the *Morro Castle* and sailed for Mexico.

At Mérida in the Yucatán, she registered at the Hotel Itza under the name Katharine Smith, and, on May 8, filed for divorce in a Mexican court. The final decree waived the usual thirty-day restriction on remarriage, which implied that either Kate or Luddy was planning to remarry in haste. Kate seemed the more likely candidate. For the past few months, there had been rumors that she was in love with Leland Hayward, who had recently obtained a divorce from his wife.

Hayward's professional relationship with Kate had taken a romantic turn at about the same time of *Morning Glory*. No one knows how serious their alliance really was (Hepburn has never discussed it), but many people feel that, next to Spencer Tracy, he was the most important man in her life. She found him fascinating—as did nearly everyone. Tall, slender, and handsome, Hayward was a complex, moody man, ruthless in business dealings, sophisticated and fastidious about his pleasures, totally unpredictable in behavior. "Leland shuffled between New York and Hollywood like a man in a fever, sometimes flying his own plane and getting lost for days," recalled his friend and client Ben Hecht. "He was continually vanishing, becoming involved in mysterious enterprises, flying into hysterics, and losing total track of who his clients were and what they were doing."

A voracious reader and passionate brain-picker, he could converse intelligently on practically any subject, no matter how esoteric; his range of interests was wide, and besides being the greatest agent of his day, he was also a crack pilot, camera fanatic, art connoisseur, card shark, man's man, and lady killer. Hayward was fickle in his affections.

All during his romance with Hepburn he had a harem of girl friends; actress Margaret Sullavan gave Kate her stiffest competition.

On the day her divorce was granted, Hepburn told reporters—through Laura—that she had no plans of remarrying. Back in New York, Luddy made no comment. A few days later, he confided to an interviewer that he had always hoped Kate would come back to him, but he bore her no ill will. At the time he had no thoughts of marrying again, and he stayed single until 1942, when he married Elizabeth Albers, a Boston socialite.

Leaving Mexico, Kate and Laura flew to Florida and took the train to New York. First at her townhouse and later in Fenwick, Hepburn read scripts sent her by RKO—Thornton Wilder's first draft of *Joan of Arc*, a screen condensation of *The Forsyte Saga*, a biography of George Sand, a historical drama called *The Tudor Wench*. She had considered appearing in a stage adaptation of *Pride and Prejudice* for Arthur Hopkins, but had decided instead to try out a new American play, *Dark Victory*, at the Ivoryton, Connecticut Playhouse.

Dark Victory was something of a joke: practically every producer in New York had optioned it at one time or another; every major Broadway actress had read it and expressed interest; the authors had rewritten it at least ten times, and still it remained unproduced. The story of horsy, hard-riding, hard-drinking Judith Traherne, a society girl with a brain tumor and only six months to live, the play was a variation on *Camille*, with periodic blackouts substituted for the telltale consumptive cough.

Just before rehearsals began, the Ivoryton engagement was cancelled because of an illness in the family of Stanley Ridges, a minor Hollywood star engaged to play Kate's leading man. Practically any actor could have played the part, and when Hepburn rejected *Holiday* as a replacement for *Dark Victory*, theater people decided she was reluctant to appear on stage so soon after the debacle of *The Lake*.

In the fall of 1934, *Dark Victory* came to Broadway with Tallulah Bankhead as Judith Traherne. Tallulah hated the play, but she adored its silent backer, millionaire John "Jock" Whitney; unfortunately for her, both the romance and *Dark Victory* were fast flops. Whitney was luckier— the film companies were intrigued by the play; RKO considered it for Hepburn while MGM saw it as a Garbo vehicle. Eventually Warner Bros. bought the screen rights, and in 1939, Bette Davis added Judith Traherne to her list of memorable, hyperthyroid heroines.

The my-days-are-numbered plot of *Dark Victory* is trash, but it's fun trash with strong dramatic situations and meaty characterizations. It was exactly the kind of property Hepburn needed at this point in her career, but instead RKO assigned her to a series of fusty, bloodless dramas that bored the public and turned Kate into "box-office poison."

7

Gee Whiz, A Hit!

When Hepburn returned to Hollywood in the summer of 1934, there were conflicting reports about the property chosen for her next film. *Joan of Arc* was still a possibility—Hepburn made technicolor tests for the role—but when Thornton Wilder's final script proved unsatisfactory, the film was dropped. Afterward, the studio and Hepburn couldn't make up their minds: one day, she was to appear with John Barrymore in a modern drama, *Break of Hearts;* a few days later, it was announced that since she was best suited to costume roles, she would return to the screen in James M. Barrie's *The Little Minister*.

Hepburn's experience with period parts was limited to *Little Women,* and RKO was obviously hoping to duplicate that earlier success when *The Little Minister* was chosen as Kate's next film. At first Kate wasn't enthusiastic about the project, but when she learned RKO was planning to film it with Margaret Sullavan, she changed her mind. "I really didn't want to play it until I heard another actress was desperate for the role," Hepburn later said. "Then, of course, it became the most important thing in the world for me that I should get it. Several of my parts in those days I fought for just to take them from someone who needed them.''

Like *Little Women, The Little Minister* is all sweetness and light, but there the similarity ends. The Barrie tale oozes treacly sentimentality and its heroine, Lady Babbie, is insufferably quaint. She's a highborn Scotch lassie who dresses up as a gypsy wench and fraternizes with the starving weavers ''of Auld Licht Kirk in the Thurms of 1840.'' While mixing with these folk, she meets Gavin Dishart, a conservative minister who cares naught for the beauty of any woman save his mother. ''You've spoiled me,'' he tells his mama, ''for ever caring for another woman.'' But after one look at Lady Babbie, he changes his mind.

''Charm,'' says one Barrie heroine, ''is a sort of a bloom on a woman. If you have it, you don't need to have anything else; and if you don't have it, it doesn't much matter what else you have.'' Lady Babbie and the other Barrie heroines have loads of charm and not much else—and charm isn't enough to make them attractive to modern audiences. But in their day they were considered winsome creatures, and actresses like Maude Adams (who introduced Lady Babbie to New York stage audiences) built legendary reputations on the strength of their Barrie interpretations.

At the start of her career, Hepburn was frequently compared to the legendary Miss Adams. After his first meeting with Kate, Lionel Barrymore asked his sister Ethel, ''Who does that girl remind you of?'' Then he asked brother John the same question. Without a moment's hesitation, Ethel and John both answered, ''Maude Adams.'' This was a compliment of the highest order, for Maude Adams was (in the words of a contemporary critic) ''an adored and elusive personality'' to whom acting was both ''a careful science'' and ''a complete enchantment.'' She was one of Kate's idols.

Physically there was only a slight resemblance between the two actresses, but in *The Little Minister* everything possible was done to stress the few similarities that existed. Hepburn's costuming, hairdo, and manner of playing were all in the Adams style, and some critics were very impressed by the likeness. ''The substitution is entirely satisfactory,'' wrote *Time* magazine. On the other hand, the New York *Post* felt that Kate was not Lady Babbie, not Maude Adams, but ''just Miss Hepburn, arch, vivid, varying little, adored by a vast public.''

The *Post* was wrong: Kate's ''vast public'' did not adore *The Little Minister*. Too precious and snobby to have appeal to the Depression audience, it was, despite generally favorable reviews, a box-office flop.

For her next two films, RKO took Hepburn out of petticoats and put her into modern dress. *Break of Hearts* was the story of Constance Dane, a young composer, and her hopeless love for alcoholic Franz Roberti, a rich and eminent conductor. Originally John Barrymore had been scheduled to play Roberti, but by the time of production he was engaged elsewhere, and the role was given to Francis Lederer, a Czech actor who had just scored a major Broadway triumph in *Autumn Crocus*. Hepburn took an instant dislike to Lederer—he was rude, couldn't remember his lines, and insisted on being photographed only in profile— and after a week of shooting, she had him replaced by Charles Boyer.

Kate liked her new leading man. They worked well together, but they could make no headway against the torpor of Philip Moeller's direction. A theater man acclaimed for his productions of *Strange Interlude* and *Mourning Becomes Electra,* Moeller dawdled over *Break of Hearts,* a simple tearjerker, as though he were trying to turn it into another six-hour O'Neill marathon. The picture was slaughtered by the critics, with *Time* warning that "unless Miss Hepburn's employers see fit to restore her to roles in keeping with her mannerisms, these will presently annoy cinemaddicts into forgetting that she is really an actress of great promise and considerable style."

Pandro S. Berman, who was soon to become head of RKO production, agrees that the studio was largely responsible for Hepburn's decline in popularity during the 1930s. "We turned out so many Hepburn pictures every season— right or wrong, ready or not. We hadn't found Kate's right formula. I don't mean that she's limited or has to be typed, but that a certain character line suits her best. And that line happened to correspond to Kate's own character."

Today Kate knows that the strength of her personality limits her as an actress. "I'm a personality as well as an actress," she once said. "Show me an actress who isn't a personality, and you'll show me a woman who isn't a star." Back in the 1930s, however, she seemed to believe—as director John Cromwell pointed out—that she could play anything.

During the filming of *Break of Hearts*, Hepburn suggested Lola Pratt, the baby-talking heroine of Booth Tarkington's *Seventeen*, as her next role. No one was enthusiastic about the idea, and with good reason. Miss Pratt is a birdbrained, baby vamp who carries a pink parasol and a fluffy dog named Floppit, says "ess" for "yes," and awakens teen-aged boys to the joys and frustrations of first love. The role lay far outside Kate's range as an actress and went against all that was best in her personality: she can't play stupid or coarse women; she can't be coy without becoming affected and arch; and it's hard to imagine even the very young Hepburn causing a mass epidemic of teen-age passion.

Instead of Lola Pratt, Pandro Berman suggested Hepburn play Alice Adams, another Tarkington heroine. This role was perfect for her. Alice is a working-class Midwestern girl with airs above her station in life, but underneath her affectations, she is an intelligent, sensitive, lonely, and lovely girl. By nature she is an aristocrat, while her neighbors and friends are snobs or yokels. For a time, Alice is courted by a wealthy out-of-town visitor, and though he truly cares for her, he can't reconcile their differences. As the book ends, Alice abandons her dreams of social success and enrolls in a secretarial school.

The film version of *Alice Adams* closes on a more positive note. Alice invites her suitor (played by Fred MacMurray) home to dinner. Her mother plans an elegant menu—caviar sandwiches, hot soup, creamed sweetbreads, Brussels sprouts, and vanilla ice cream. On the day of the party, a heat wave hits town—the first in a long series of calamities: the food is too heavy, the ice cream melts in the kitchen, Mr. Adams' collar button pops into his soup, the black maid is surly, Alice's brother arrives in the middle of dinner and confesses that he has stolen money from his employer's safe. Through it all, Alice chatters brightly—too brightly—until the end of the party, when the façade vanishes. Looking at MacMurray, she says, "You know, I feel as though I'm only going to see you for five minutes more in my whole life."

For the next few evenings, Alice waits in vain for her boyfriend. Then, just as she's given up all hope, the doorbell rings, she goes to the door, and there he is. "Gee whiz!" she exclaims. The happy ending was scorned by critics, but if Fred MacMurray is a happy ending, then

God didn't make little green apples. He's the only sour note in this charming film, one of the small masterpieces of 1930s' American cinema.

The picture looks as though it was made with love and total harmony on all sides, but that was not the case. At first, there was contention over the choice of director. Hepburn wanted William Wyler, one of Hollywood's top directors, but RKO pushed the relatively unknown George Stevens, whose previous efforts included nothing more distinguished than *The Cohens and Kellys in Trouble* and a Gene Stratton Porter story, *Laddie*. At Pandro Berman's request, Kate agreed to meet the gruff, slow-speaking Stevens, and she liked him. Some friends say she was secretly attracted to him, and later they became close friends, but during the making of *Alice Adams,* they squabbled frequently.

Before starting work, Stevens was told by a previous Hepburn director, "Yell, 'No!' at her seven times. If you try to be tactful she thinks she must be right." Stevens, however, was not the type to be intimidated: he felt he knew more about the Adamses and their Midwestern milieu than did his New England-born star.

The first collision between actress and director occurred as they began shooting a scene in which Alice breaks down and cries after the disastrous dinner party. On screen, Kate's eyes had often brimmed with tears, but she had never really let herself go and sobbed with grief: such an emotional display was repellent to her Puritan temperament. She told the director she would throw herself on a bed and cry into a pillow. Stevens insisted she walk to a window, look out, and then, in full close-up, begin bawling. A lengthy debate ensued until Stevens snapped, "Miss Hepburn, you'll cry at the window or I'll return to my custard pies!" (He had started his career as a director of slapstick shorts.) Kate was jubilant. "A quitter!" she said. "You don't get your way, so you quit. You're yellow!"

Stevens suggested a compromise: Hepburn was to walk to the window and stand there for a few minutes. He'd photograph her from behind, and dub the sound of crying on the sound track. Kate agreed, crossed to the window, and burst into tears.

Later in the picture, Kate was required to cry on the last word of a speech delivered by her father. Tears flow easily for many actors, but it's not a simple task to turn them on at a word's notice. Stevens told Kate that if she couldn't manage it, they'd supply glycerine. On the first take, Alice's father mentioned the magic word "home," and a tear rolled from Kate's eye. Something was wrong with the lighting, then the sound, and the scene had to be photographed again and again and again. Each time, Kate supplied tears at the appropriate moment. Everyone was impressed by the lubricity of Kate's tear ducts, but she explained that she was so moved by Fred Stone (Mr. Adams) that she could have cried "fifty times."

Stevens struggled to soften Kate's mannerisms and to get her to play with greater simplicity. "I never knew an actress of whom I was surer as to potentiality," he once said, "but I never knew an actress of whom I could be less sure that the promise would come through. She not only had no technique, she didn't seem to want any. . . ." The director went on to say that it wasn't arrogance as much as fear of being dishonest that kept Kate from perfecting her technique. She felt that her performances would ring false if she planned them too much or relied on mechanical tricks.

Stevens' perseverance paid off. Kate's performance is warm, beautifully shaded, and filled with funny and poignant little touches. Like all her 1930s heroines, Hepburn's

Alice has her overwrought moments, but this time the posturing belongs as much to the character as to the actress. She achieves the supremely difficult feat of mocking Alice's affectations without mocking the girl behind them. Even when Alice is at her silliest, Hepburn makes her touching, and in the love scenes, she is luminous: soft, vibrant, and without a flared nostril in sight.

When the picture opened in August 1935, it received mainly favorable reviews, and it became a modest box-office success. Hepburn won her second Oscar nomination, but lost the award to Bette Davis for *Dangerous*.

During the filming of *Alice Adams*, Laura Harding decided to leave California and settle permanently in the East. Kate was upset, but she realized Laura had her own life to lead, and there were no hard feelings over the separation. The two women remained close friends, seeing each other whenever Kate was in New York or when Laura paid one of her infrequent visits to the Coast.

Meanwhile Hepburn continued to see Leland Hayward, and there were persistent rumors that they would soon marry. It was a very private romance, with the couple leading the press a merry chase as they popped in and out of airplanes, sometimes risking life and limb to escape detection. Once Kate bet Hayward she could board and leave a plane without being noticed. No one saw her get on, but, on landing, she was spotted by a group of photographers. Panicking, she sprinted across the airstrip, lost her bearings, and came within inches of colliding with a whirling propeller.

If Kate's private life was somewhat unsettled at this time, so was her career. Despite her moving and delicate performance in *Alice Adams*, Kate's hold on the public was shaky—many people still found her too odd and rarefied to be likeable. In retrospect, it is clear that she should have followed *Alice Adams* with another simple and direct little comedy; instead, she chose *Sylvia Scarlett,* one of the most bizarre films ever to come out of a Hollywood studio.

The film was George Cukor's idea. He had read an English novel, Compton MacKenzie's *The Early Life and Adventures of Sylvia Scarlett,* and decided it would make a wonderful movie. Kate agreed. Pando Berman wasn't so sure, but Kate and Cukor convinced him that the confused, overlong novel could be honed into an RKO masterpiece.

Once production was underway, actress and director both started to have misgivings. "We did the picture, although George secretly thought to himself, 'Something is a bit wrong with this,' and I was thinking to myself, 'Something is a bit wrong with this,' but we went on," Hepburn recalls. "The picture was supposed to be magical and hilarious comedy. I played the part of a boy through seven-eighths of it. . . ."

Sylvia Scarlett (Hepburn) is the daughter of an English embezzler (Edmund Gwenn). With the London bobbies hot on the trail, she and her dad hightail it to France, with Sylvia dressed in boy's clothes and calling herself Sylvester. On the way, they join forces with Jimmy Monkley (Cary Grant), a Cockney con man, and work their way back to England as petty thieves and traveling Punch-and-Judy players. During their travels, Sylvia—still in drag—falls in love with artist Michael Fane (Brian Aherne). At this point, the film skids into a twilight zone of sexuality and never regains its balance. Sylvester becomes Sylvia, but Michael Fane isn't overwhelmed by the transformation. "Boy!" he exclaims without much enthusiasm, "you're a girl!" Much of the film seems designed to titillate a small homosexual coterie: "There's something queer about you," one character says to Sylvia/Sylvester, and in one scene, a girl kisses the trouser-clad Hepburn full on the mouth. The sexual ambiguities are never resolved or met head on, and for 1930s audiences, the film was a disturbing and unpleasant experience.

A sneak preview of the film was held at a suburban Los Angeles theater, and though Kate usually avoided these Hollywood rituals, she agreed to accompany Cukor and Natalie Paley (the picture's second female lead) to the screening. After the credits were over, the trio entered the darkened auditorium and listened expectantly for the first audience reactions. There was nothing but coughing and a general air of restlessness.

"Why aren't they laughing?" Natalie whispered to Kate.

"Well, Natalie," Kate answered, "I suppose they don't think it's funny!"

Halfway through the movie, people began leaving in droves; they didn't walk, they *ran* up the aisles, Cukor remembered. Kate escaped to the ladies' room where she found a woman lying in a dead faint. "My God," she gasped, "the picture's killed her!"

Getting into Cukor's car, Kate hit her head on the door frame, and for a moment she thought people had started throwing things. Back at the director's home, a wake was held; Kate and Cukor made vain attempts to console producer Pandro Berman. They both promised to do another picture without pay if RKO would scrap *Sylvia Scarlett*. "I don't want either one of you ever to work for me again!" Berman screamed. (Later he changed his mind; both Cukor and Hepburn worked for him again, and all three remained good friends.)

RKO shelved *Sylvia Scarlett* for several months, but finally released it in January 1936—and lost over $200,000 on the film. Nearly all the reviews were poor, with *Time* magazine reporting, "Katharine Hepburn is better looking as a boy than as a woman." Only Cary Grant came out unscathed: up to this time, he had been floundering as a stiff-necked leading man, and the role of the Cockney ne'er-do-well was one of his first opportunities to play light comedy. He walked off with most of the good reviews, and the picture proved to be a major turning point in his career.

8

Flying Too High with Some Guy in the Sky

After *Sylvia Scarlett,* Kate decided she needed a vacation. RKO had nothing for her, though there was talk of a Hungarian play, *Marie Bashkirtseff*, and MGM wanted to borrow her for *The Gorgeous Hussy,* a biography of Peggy Eaton, Andrew Jackson's mistress. That part, however, went to Joan Crawford, so Kate decided to fly home to Hartford with Leland Hayward as her escort.

Reporters thought this might be the occasion for their long-awaited marriage, and all the time Kate and Hayward were in Hartford, newsmen kept a twenty-four-hour vigil outside the Hepburn home. Nothing happened during the holiday weekend, but a few days later Hayward entered Hartford Hospital and, with Dr. Hepburn in attendance, underwent minor surgery. Though the nature of his illness was never revealed, Hayward was possibly suffering from ulcers—an ailment that had begun, the agent claimed, when he took on Edna Ferber as a client.

Kate visited Hayward every day, and was usually tailed by reporters as she drove to and from the hospital. One evening, when she was returning home with her mother, she stopped for a red light and a car pulled up alongside her. Someone said, "Miss Hepburn?" She turned, and a flash bulb exploded in her face. She shifted gears, floored the accelerator, and raced to the Hepburn driveway. When their pursuers drove up to the curb, Kate jumped out of the car and yelled, "Grab the camera!" The two women kicked and scratched the photographer but failed to confiscate his camera. "My God!" he later told his colleagues. "The mother's as tough as Kate!"

As soon as Hayward was able to travel, the couple returned to the Coast, and Kate went to work on *Mary of Scotland,* an adaptation of one of Maxwell Anderson's blank-verse excursions into English history. During the making of the film, Kate almost had a nasty accident. One scene required her to ride sidesaddle, and she galloped off, oblivious to the fact that she was heading straight for a tree. At the last minute, director John Ford screamed, "Duck!" and Kate did—just in time. She missed a low-hanging branch by only a fraction of an inch.

It's too bad she didn't duck when RKO threw the script of *Mary of Scotland* at her. Despite its exalted Broadway reputation, the play is a long-winded bore, and while Ford tightened its action and heaved most of Anderson's poetry into the trash can, he couldn't breathe life into its wooden characters. As Mary Stuart, Hepburn is as haughty as a Bryn Mawr debutante—there's quite a bit of nostril flaring and far too much regal posturing. Her performance isn't really bad, just boring; the picture is a sure cure for insomnia.

Tedious as it was, *Mary of Scotland* was spellbinding compared to Hepburn's next film, *A Woman Rebels,* the story of a Victorian suffragette who bears a child out of wedlock, edits an advanced magazine, and then gives in to propriety and marries a dull and devoted suitor (Herbert

Marshall). Undoubtedly Kate was attracted to the subject because of her mother's feminist activities, but the script and direction were weak, and in the leading role Hepburn is more bluestocking than rebel.

Considering the fate of *The Little Minister*, *Mary of Scotland*, and *A Woman Rebels*, it should have been apparent to RKO and Hepburn that Depression audiences were not interested in high-flown historical romances, but Kate took on another Victorian heroine in her next film, an adaptation of James M. Barrie's *Quality Street*. Written for Maude Adams, this lavender and frayed-lace valentine is set in England during the Napoleonic Wars. Miss Phoebe Throssel is distraught when her fiancé, Dr. Brown, goes off with his regiment, and even more distraught when he returns ten years later and fails to recognize her. In the interim, poor Phoebe has faded into early spinsterhood, but her heart is still young and gay, and, masquerading as her young niece, she proceeds to regain Dr. Brown's affections. The rest of the film is a lighthearted treatment of what (to modern eyes) looks like a borderline case of schizophrenia.

Quality Street is handsomely designed (Walter Plunkett's Regency costumes are the best part of the movie), the supporting cast is excellent, and Hepburn gives a delicately stylized and elegant reading of the leading role. But George Stevens' directorial pace is so sluggish that the picture looks like a series of tableaux in a waxworks museum. The reviews were terrible, and Hepburn was unjustifiably ridiculed by many critics. "Such flutterings and jitterings and twitchings, such hand-wringings and mouth-quiverings, such runnings about and eyebrow-raisings have not been seen on a screen in many a moon," wrote Frank Nugent of *The New York Times*. The description is not inaccurate, but how else, one might ask, does an actress play a Barrie heroine?

At about the time she was making *Quality Street,* Hepburn's romance with Leland Hayward came to an abrupt and dramatic conclusion. One Sunday in November 1936, Kate was visiting George Cukor when news came over the radio that Hayward had just married Margaret Sullavan. It was a terrible moment and Kate was visibly shaken, but since the room was filled with Cukor's Sunday guests, she pulled herself together and acted as though nothing had happened.

She remained friendly with Hayward, and he continued to act as her manager until he sold his stable of talent to the MCA agency in the 1940s. Though Kate took no pleasure in their unhappiness, the Sullavan-Hayward marriage was very stormy; friends recalled that from the start, Miss Sullavan, an avid Hearts player, always hoarded the queen of spades—a penalty card—until she could discard it on her husband's winning trick. Hayward retaliated by pasting Miss Sullavan's picture over the face of the black queen.

A few months before Hayward's marriage, Kate had started seeing another passionate pilot, billionaire Howard Hughes, on an occasional, friendly basis. In the fall of 1936, the relationship became more intense—too intense to please many of Hepburn's friends. "One thing I'll never understand about Kate," said author and screenwriter Anita Loos, "is what she was doing with Howard Hughes. He had a whole stable of girls, and Kate simply wasn't the type to have anything to do with that kind of thing."

Others say Hughes appreciated Kate's wit and independence, and she admired his expertise at golf—he was the only man who coud out-putt her on every green. They also shared an enthusiasm for aviation—he taught Kate to pilot a plane. And while Kate was a startling about-face from the peroxide blondes and Follies cuties Hughes usually dated, he was not so different from her other beaus. From her father to Spencer Tracy, she has preferred men who are intelligent, successful, tough, individualistic. In short, she liked challenging, difficult men.

Whatever Hughes and Hepburn were doing together was interrupted when she decided to return to the theater in the late fall of 1936. A few months earlier, she had been invited to play Viola in Max Reinhardt's production of *Twelfth Night* at the Hollywood Bowl, but RKO had refused to give her time off; now the studio agreed that a stage success might bolster her sagging career. After reading several scripts, Kate selected an adaptation of *Jane Eyre,* which was being produced by the Theatre Guild.

This distinguished organization was managed by Theresa Helburn, the English-born Lawrence Langner, and his wife, Armina Marshall. Kate had known most of the Theatre Guild members for years, and was especially fond of the Langners, who soon became her closest friends on the East Coast. Hepburn had worked for the Guild once before as a maid in *A Month in the Country;* at that time she'd felt she'd been underpaid, so, with *Jane Eyre,* she decided to be tough about salary negotiations. The Guild offered $1,000 a week; Kate asked for $1,500. For a while, neither party would budge an inch, but eventually a compromise was reached—in Hepburn's favor.

As for billing, she wanted no preferential treatment. "I want it understood that I object to having my name in bigger print than the other actors'," she told Langner. "That's very generous of you," the producer replied. "Generous!" she said scornfully. "I just don't want to stick my neck out." Technically, she did not receive star billing in *Jane Eyre:* her name appeared below the title of the play.

Jane Eyre opened in New Haven on December 26, 1936,

and then moved to Boston. The notices were good, tryout audiences liked the play, but Kate was apprehensive. The script was weak and old-fashioned, a genteel condensation of Charlotte Brontë's psychologically tangled novel, and the production was unfocused. In Boston, *Stage* magazine reviewed the production and found it "healthily alive but still in an unfinished state." As for Hepburn, the critic admired "her style, breeding, gallantry, the pleasant crispness with which she speaks her lines, the luminous and disarming whiteness when she smiles." It was faint praise, and sounded as though Kate's dentist should take all the bows. The review ended by saying that only Dennis Hoey (as Mr. Rochester) "conveyed the splendid conviction of the story."

During the Boston run, the Guild announced that the Broadway premiere of *Jane Eyre* would be postponed while the play underwent "revisions" on the road. The next stop on the tour was Chicago, and it was there that the Hughes-Hepburn romance first made national headlines. According to contemporary newspapers, Hughes proposed to Kate after the opening night, and then disappeared and stayed in hiding until January 19, 1937, when he reduced the transcontinental flight record to seven and a half hours.

Two days later he was back in Chicago, inquiring about a marriage license. There was, of course, no marriage in Chicago, Pittsburgh, Cleveland, or any other city on the *Jane Eyre* itinerary, but the romance was good publicity for the show. The couple never traveled together, but there were rendezvous every few days, with Kate sprinting down a runway, waving excitedly as Hughes's plane came in for a landing. Crowds milled around stage doors hoping to catch a glimpse of the bashful lovers, and Kate often had to be smuggled in and out of the theater.

Meanwhile, *Jane Eyre* was still in trouble. In Chicago,

Brooks Atkinson, the all-powerful drama critic of *The New York Times,* dropped by to see the show, and turned thumbs down on both play and actress. "It is to be feared that the current play is only a pedestrian adaptation," he reported. "Miss Hepburn is not yet the sort of trouping actress who can mold a full-length performance out of scrappy materials. . . . Toward the end her personal reticence begins to emerge as monotony of voice and characterization. . . . When the play is finished, you have, accordingly, no feeling that anything vital has happened."

According to theater etiquette, Atkinson was stepping out of bounds. New York critics have no business reviewing plays during out-of-town engagements—unless, of course, they are invited to do so by the producers. Atkinson hadn't been invited, and the Guild resented his presence. So did Kate. After reading the review she decided to cancel the Broadway opening. "I told Armina, Terry Helburn, and Lawrence Langner that I would prefer not to take it to New York," she recalls. "I had been roasted in *The Lake* unmercifully and deservedly—and the next time I went to New York I wanted to feel, at least from my own point of view, that I was as good as I could be."

The Guild abided by Kate's decision. It was announced that *Jane Eyre* would not open on Broadway until the fall or winter of 1937 because Hepburn had film commitments that would keep her busy during the spring and summer. (In issuing this statement, the Guild was protecting Kate's reptuation: there were no film commitments and no thought of bringing *Jane Eyre* to Broadway in the fall.)

The show closed in Washington, after grossing $340,000 during its fourteen-week tour. The Guild made a tidy profit on the production and Langner expressed the hope that at some future time he could again work with Kate.

She agreed enthusiastically, but the Guild had nothing to offer her in the forthcoming season.

When *Jane Eyre* closed, Hepburn returned to New York. She spent the spring and early summer of 1937 on the East Coast, dividing her time between Manhattan, Hartford, and Fenwick. She read film scripts, considered appearing in a production of James M. Barrie's *Peter Pan* for Broadway producer Max Gordon—and entertained Howard Hughes.

Hughes's visit was shrouded in mystery. One July day, reporters learned that "KH" had left a cryptic message for "HH" at a Long Island airport. A few hours later, a limousine bearing a man who resembled Hughes drove up in front of Kate's home; he jumped out and ran into the house before a positive identification could be made. For the next twenty-four hours, newsmen prowled around East 49th Street, but no one was seen leaving or entering the premises except a waiter from a neighborhood French restaurant.

A few days later, the couple was spotted in Old Saybrook, Connecticut, where they were inspecting a million-dollar yacht that was up for sale at a reasonable price. The next evening, Hughes appeared at a dinner party held in one of Connecticut's Gatsby-like mansions. Reporters, who had been alerted to his visit, were disappointed when he drove in alone, but a few minutes later Kate walked up the driveway and feigned surprise when she caught sight of Hughes.

By the end of summer, the romance had ended as quietly as it had begun. There were no hard feelings—it was, friends said, just a case of two busy people following different careers; they had drifted apart. Probably the press had made too much of a fuss over the romance—it now seems highly unlikely that either Kate or Hughes ever seriously considered marriage as a possibility. (One Hughes biographer claims that the wedding-license episode was the fabrication of an overzealous journalist.) Outside of flying and golf, they didn't have much in common—Hughes was too rich and Machiavellian to fit into the pattern of Kate's life on a permanent basis.

A few years later, when some expensive jewelry given to her by Hughes was stolen, Kate called her father and told him what had happened. "Thank God," he said. "You have no right to have that kind of stuff anyway." Kate agreed; she had no taste for extravagant personal possessions.

9

Calla Lilies
and Peanuts

At the end of an unfavorable review of *Quality Street*, a critic for *Variety* added this postscript: ''Three short years ago, Katharine Hepburn rocketed to screen heights, but a succession of unfortunate selections of material has marooned a competent girl in a bog of box-office frustration. There probably is no one in pictures who needs a real money film as much as this actress.''

RKO was confident it could come up with a smash hit for Hepburn, and in the summer of 1937 offered her a new four-picture contract at $150,000 per film. With no theater projects to keep her in New York, Kate signed. It was announced that her first film under the new pact would be *The Mad Miss Manton*, the story of a madcap debutante who discovers a dead body during a treasure hunt.

The Mad Miss Manton was a bomb, but it exploded in Barbara Stanwyck's face, not Kate's. At the last minute, RKO gave Kate the leading role in *Stage Door*, an adaptation of a George Kaufman-Edna Ferber comedy that had been a smash hit in the 1936 Broadway season. In quality, *Stage Door* was several notches above *Miss Manton*, but it

93

was a setback for Kate: for the first time, she was co-starred with another actress, Ginger Rogers. And the supporting cast included such scene-stealing newcomers as Lucille Ball, Ann Miller, Eve Arden, Andrea Leeds, and Gail Patrick.

Ferber and Kaufman's play takes place at the Footlights Club, a boarding house for aspiring actresses. One girl (Jean Maitland) becomes a Hollywood star, but flops on Broadway; another (Terry Randall) turns down Hollywood and becomes a Broadway sensation. Besides being snobbishly partisan—it implies that only the dumb and untalented sell out to the movies—the play was a flat and formulaic piece of writing, coated with a slick professionalism but lacking charm or wit.

The premise of the play had been undermined by the presence of Margaret Sullavan in the role of Terry Randall, for Miss Sullavan, a stage actress, had gone to Hollywood and now was back on Broadway, a bigger success than ever before. But without her, the show would probably have folded after a couple of weeks. Five months after the opening, when she withdrew from the cast to await the birth of her first child by Leland Hayward, the producers decided to close the play rather than replace her with another actress.

RKO paid $130,000 for the screen rights to *Stage Door*, and then instructed screenwriters Morrie Ryskind and Anthony Veiller to scrap everything—first and foremost its virulently anti-Hollywood sentiments—keeping only the title and the characters' names. They did such a thorough job of renovation that on seeing the film, George Kaufman asked plaintively, "Why didn't they call it *Screen Door?*" He was out of order: the screen *Stage Door* is funnier and better plotted than the stage *Stage Door*.

In the picture, Terry Randall (Hepburn) is a wealthy

socialite-turned-actress with more ambition than talent. She checks in at the Footlights Club and exasperates everyone, most of all wisecracking Jean Maitland (Ginger Rogers), with her high-flown airs and unwarranted self-confidence. Her father pulls strings, and Terry wins a Broadway leading role that should have gone to talented Kaye Hamilton (Andrea Leeds), the darling of the Footlights Club. All through rehearsals, Terry is awful, and the show, *Enchanted April,* is headed for disaster. Then, on opening night, the disillusioned and half-crazed Kaye kills herself, and Terry, choked with emotion, goes out and wows the audience. At her curtain calls, she says, ''The person you should be applauding died a few hours ago. . . . I hope that wherever she is, she knows and understands and forgives.''

In outline, *Stage Door* sounds like another *Morning Glory,* but Kate is astonishingly moving in those final moments when Terry comes of age both as an actress and a woman. And it's only at the end that the movie dips into bathos. For the most part, it's snappy and bright and bristling with clever Broadway repartee. Next to *All About Eve,* it may be the best backstage film ever made—and it's never as pretentious or self-consciously bitchy as the famous Bette Davis comedy.

Director Gregory La Cava was usually pickled in alcohol, but whether sober or drunk, he had, according to W. C. Fields, the best comedy mind in Hollywood. He had started out as a cartoonist, and he worked quickly, improvised entire sequences of a film, and looked on his actors with a caricaturist's eye for absurd detail. Kate enjoyed working with him, which was fortunate, for *Stage Door* was a long series of inside jokes—most of them directed at her.

Like Hepburn, Terry Randall is rich, overbearing, and overconfident; like Hepburn, she has a father who disparages her ambitions and yet encourages them with financial support; like Hepburn, she receives leading parts before she is capable of playing them. Terry's acting coach is as fat and old-guard-theater as Frances Robinson-Duff; her director is as irascible as Jed Harris; *Enchanted April* is a dead ringer for *The Lake*.

Terry's great success is a devastating parody of Kate's notorious fiasco: wearing a filmy white dress, Hepburn floats listlessly across the stage, carrying a bouquet of over-sized wax flowers. "The calla lilies are in bloom again," she says in a flat, toneless voice. "Such a strange flower—suitable for any occasion. I carried them on my wedding day; now I place them here in memory of something that has died." She plays this scene without a trace of self-mockery, and it can be taken seriously (as perhaps was intended), but it's also a deadly accurate parody of everything wrong about *The Lake*.

The set of *Stage Door* was a happy place. All the actresses got along, and there were no temperamental clashes between Hepburn and Ginger Rogers, who had become her chief rival at RKO. A few years earlier, Miss Rogers had wanted to play Queen Elizabeth to Hepburn's Mary of Scotland; that request had been refused, but now the studio was grooming her for serious parts. Rogers, however, admired Hepburn, and was the soul of cooperation during their scenes together. She even cried on cue as she listened to Kate's curtain speech. La Cava was amazed. "Previously," he said, "the only way I'd ever been able to get her to cry was to tell her that her house was burning down."

For Kate, the most rewarding part of *Stage Door* was working with the legendary Constance Collier, who played Terry Randall's drama coach. Never well known to the general public, Miss Collier was an unparalleled celebrity to her colleagues. Even in her youth (a distant memory at the time of *Stage Door*), she had never been a beauty—"Constance comes toward you like a chest of drawers, and has a mouth like a galosh," said a contemporary rival—and yet until her death in 1955, she was the essence of theatrical glamour. A skillful actress as well as a witty and exuberant conversationalist, she was fanatically adored by nearly everyone who met her. Kate was no exception. The two actresses became fast friends, and later Miss Collier was to play an important part in Hepburn's Shakespearean career.

When *Stage Door* opened at the Radio City Music Hall in October 1937, it was a smash hit. The reviews were raves, with critics commending Kate for her "restraint and authority." The film, which cost $900,000, eventually grossed over $2,000,000—it was Hepburn's first big money-maker since *Little Women*. The actress and RKO were encouraged by this success, but their optimism wasn't entirely justified. Strictly speaking, *Stage Door* wasn't a Hepburn vehicle: she isn't the center of every scene, but shares the picture equally with Ginger Rogers, Andrea Leeds (who received a supporting Oscar nomination for her Kaye Hamilton), and the other members of the supporting cast. As a test of Hepburn's popularity, *Stage Door* was inconclusive.

While Kate was casting about for a new film, she met Garson Kanin, a recent addition to the RKO directorial staff. He had admired her since her first stage appearances, and once they had met face to face, his affection took a more personal turn. Kate wasn't really interested, but Kanin was an amusing and literate companion, so she saw him frequently over the next few months. They even appeared together in public—Kanin once managed to persuade Kate to have dinner at Chasen's Restaurant, a hallowed Los Angeles landmark. They arrived long before the fashionable dinner hour and enjoyed themselves so much that Kate didn't notice the patrons who were slowly filling the room to capacity. When she did, she jumped up in panic and raced out, Kanin following several strides behind.

Novelist John O'Hara happened to be in Chasen's that night, and later he tossed off an article for *Vanity Fair* implying that Hepburn was leading Kanin a merry chase all over Hollywood. There was no truth to the story—they were just good friends and would become even closer during the next two decades. They talked about collaborating on a film, but the time wasn't right. RKO had other plans for both of them.

Impressed by her flair for comedy in *Stage Door*, the studio next cast Kate as a dizzy heiress in *Bringing Up Baby*, now generally regarded as the best of all 1930s "screwball" comedies. As the picture begins, Susan Vance (Hepburn) meets absentminded paleontologist David Huxley (Cary Grant) at a country club dance: he steps on the hem of her dress, she keeps walking, and pretty soon she's lost the back of her skirt. At the film's end the couple are swinging precariously from a Brontosaurus skeleton. The rest of the plot is a wild goose chase involving a rare dinosaur bone, a wire-haired terrier named George, a crotchety collection of New England eccentrics, and a pet leopard who becomes a pussycat when he hears the tune "I Can't Give You Anything But Love, Baby."

Most screwball comediennes—Colbert, Lombard, Irene Dunne—were the last word in insouciance, and the heroines they played were dizzy young creatures who treated life as one long, crazy adventure. Hepburn's Susan Vance is the final evolution of this tradition; she's completely unhinged, so zany that at times she seems almost certifiably insane. It's a wonderfully witty performance, light, airy, physically agile, and totally deadpan—Hepburn never makes the mistake of finding herself amusing. Cary Grant is equally good, and director Howard Hawks piles up the absurdities with perfect control and balance.

Hawks was a tough, hard-cussing man's man of a director, but Hepburn admired him and was an apt pupil during his lessons on comic acting. *Bringing Up Baby* was made under relaxed, congenial circumstances—except when Nissa, the leopard that played Baby, was on the set. Practically everyone on the *Bringing Up Baby* set was terrified of the snarling, half wild beast. But Kate wasn't, and she doused herself with a perfume that made Nissa "playful." (Hepburn liked animals and maintained a private menagerie consisting of a Shelbourne terrier, a scottie, and a gibbon monkey called Amos.) Nissa's trainer, Mme. Olga Celeste, told a reporter, "I think if Miss Hepburn should ever decide to leave the screen, she could make a very good animal trainer. She has control of her nerves. . . ."

Bringing Up Baby is now considered a classic screen comedy, but on first release it was overlooked by both critics and the public. (Kate herself has no great admiration for it; she was surprised to learn that today it is considered superior to *My Man Godfrey*, the archetypal screwball comedy.) Perhaps *Baby* was too sophisticated, perhaps the timing was wrong—by 1937 the vogue for lunatic farce was coming to an end; or perhaps it was Hepburn's performance that put people off. And it's not difficult to see why audiences might be irritated by her Susan Vance. Headstrong, overpetted, triumphantly illogical, she undermines the paleontologist's neatly ordered existence and leads him by the nose until, by the middle of the film, he's running around in a marabou-trimmed negligee. He loathes her but can't escape, and at the end, when he surrenders, it's from exhaustion, not physical attraction. Hepburn's Susan

Vance was definitely not for people who liked their women sweet and pliant.

Under normal circumstances, RKO would probably have written off *Bringing Up Baby* as just another Hepburn failure, but shortly after its release, exhibitor Harry Brandt, president of the Independent Theatre Owners of America, published a list of stars who were "box-office poison." Kate headed the roster, which included Fred Astaire, Joan Crawford, Marlene Dietrich, Greta Garbo, Mae West, and Kay Francis. Brandt's slur, first published as an advertisement in a trade paper, was picked up by the national press and received enormous publicity. As a result, all the stars cited by Brandt lost prestige both with moviegoers and with their own studios.

"They say I'm a has-been," Kate commented. "If I weren't laughing so hard, I might cry." RKO was not so amused. The studio told Hepburn her next film would be *Mother Carey's Chickens*, a kind of cut-rate *Little Women* about a widow who struggles to keep a roof over the heads of her four teen-aged daughters. It was definitely a class-B project, and Kate refused to play one of Mrs. Carey's nestlings. Instead, she bought her way out of her RKO contract at a figure reported as somewhere between $55,000 and $200,000.

Once at liberty, Hepburn found it difficult to find a new job in keeping with her reputation. MGM offered her $10,000 for a one-picture deal, and though she had been earning $125,000 a film, Kate told them to send her the script. After reading it, she refused—not because of the money, but because she didn't like the material. She was unemployed until the spring of 1938, when she learned that Columbia Pictures had acquired the screen rights to Philip Barry's *Holiday*. Columbia was one of Hollywood's minor studios—it was only a few steps above the "Poverty Row" companies—and Kate had no difficulty in persuading studio boss Harry Cohn to hire her for the part of Linda Seton, which she had understudied ten years earlier on Broadway. She also convinced Cohn to hire George Cukor as director and Cary Grant as her co-star.

All three were ideally suited to their assignments, but the play wasn't geared to the interests of Depression audiences. A posh, Park Avenue comedy, it is the story of the black-sheep daughter of a wealthy New York family (Linda) who falls in love with sister Julia's fiancé, Johnny Case. He's a boy from the slums with a knack for making money. Julia expects him to become a Seton family banker, but Johnny has other ideas. He wants to take "a holiday" to find out exactly who he is, and then, with this voyage of self-exploration under his belt, he'll settle down to banking or some other nine-to-five job. Julia is horrified, but Linda gives him her full support.

"Oh, I've got all the faith in the world in Johnny," she says. "Whatever he does is all right with me. If he wants to sit on his tail, he can sit on his tail. If he wants to come back and sell peanuts, Lord how I'll believe in those peanuts!" Then she dashes off and joins Johnny on his European holiday.

Hepburn speaks these hypertense lines with such triumphant conviction that they achieve a kind of eloquence, and with that kind of faith behind him, Johnny might very well turn peanuts or sitting on his tail into a million-dollar proposition.

Depression audiences, however, didn't share her enthusiasm. For them, selling peanuts was no joke; many of the people who watched *Holiday* on its first release would have given their eyeteeth for the banking job Johnny so high-handedly refuses. And Linda Seton, the poor little rich girl who moons around her childhood nursery and denounces the philistinism of the filthy rich, seems to belong to an earlier, more innocent era.

Linda has rightly been called the archetypal Hepburn heroine; she's a tomboy, a rebel, a society girl with brains, beauty, and individuality; she's tough, yet vulnerable and unsure of herself. The part touches all sides of Hepburn's personality, and she plays it with the ease and authority of total identification. Linda Seton is one of Hepburn's most accomplished performances, but it failed to impress its first audiences. Despite generally favorable reviews, *Holiday* made little or no profit.

After finishing the film, Kate returned to Hartford and spent the summer playing golf and swimming at Fenwick. She was still vacationing at the Hepburns' summer cottage when, on September 21, a hurricane with winds blowing as high as one hundred eighty-six miles an hour buffeted the area. For a while Hepburn braved the storm, but when the Connecticut River began to overflow its banks, she decided to wade through the flooding tide. She reached safety just as the Fenwick house was totally destroyed by a tidal wave. A few weeks later the Hepburns began to construct a new summer place on the site of the demolished cottage.

All the time she stayed in Connecticut, Kate was thinking of the role of roles: Scarlet O'Hara in *Gone with the Wind*. She had first read the novel in 1936 when Lillie Messenger, the RKO talent scout who had directed her screen test, had brought it to her attention. She had adored the book and tried to persuade RKO to purchase the film rights. The studio raised several objections: the property was too expensive ($56,000); it was a period piece (costume epics were out); Scarlett was an unsympathetic role (and Kate was already alienating audiences in sympathetic roles).

A few months later, the screen rights were bought by

David O. Selznick, who hired George Cukor as director. Both men liked Kate, but neither could see her as Scarlett. "The part was practically written for me," Hepburn told Selznick. "I *am* Scarlett O'Hara!"

Selznick replied, "I just can't imagine Rhett Butler chasing you for ten years."

"Well, David," she snapped, "some people's idea of sex appeal is different from yours."

Some parts of Scarlett's character—her feistiness and courage—were well within Hepburn's range, but whether she could have handled Scarlett's greed and sexual allure, as Selznick apparently felt she could not, is debatable. Eventually Cukor decided she could, and many people, including Vivien Leigh, believed Hepburn was always his first choice for the role.

Part of the pre-production publicity for *Gone with the Wind* was a nationwide search for an unknown to play Scarlett, and after Cukor had finished this stunt, he tested nearly every star and starlet in Hollywood. According to newspaper reports, Hepburn made a screen test for the role in October 1938, but she says she didn't. "I told David that both he and George knew my work—so what was the point?"

A few weeks later, Selznick told Kate she had the part. She was suspicious. Believing that he was really committed to an unknown playing the part, she refused to sign a contract. She couldn't stand any more unflattering publicity at such a low point in her career. As a compromise, she told Selznick that if he failed to find his ideal Scarlett, she'd take the part at the last possible moment.

Kate's cautious attitude was well taken—Selznick still had strong doubts about whether audiences would accept her as Scarlett. In a memo to his staff, he wrote, "Hepburn has two strikes against her—first, the unquestionable and very widespread intense public dislike of her at this moment, and second, the fact that she has yet to demonstrate the sex qualities that are probably the most important of all the many requisites of Scarlett.''

The memo is dated November 18, 1938. Two weeks later, in a telegram to his wife, he lists Paulette Goddard, Jean Arthur, and Joan Bennett as the leading candidates for the role. He also mentions Vivien Leigh as ''the dark horse Scarlett.''

Hepburn was out of the race.

10

*Success
Story*

One late summer day in 1938, Philip Barry came to Fenwick and found all the Hepburns on the front veranda drinking tea, eating marmalade toast, and thrashing out the problems of the world. There was too much noise and too many people floating about for a private conversation, so Barry took Kate aside and said, "I want to talk to you alone." She jumped up and suggested a walk on the beach; as usual, the playwright was impeccably groomed in an expensively tailored suit, but he didn't mind a little sand in his shoes—not as long as there was peace and quiet.

As they walked along a deserted pier, Barry told Kate he was working on two plays that might suit her. One was *Second Threshold,* a drama about a diplomat on the brink of suicide. (Because of his troubled relations with his daughter, this was not to be produced until 1951, two years after Barry's death.) The second play was *The Philadelphia Story,* a comedy about Tracy Lord, a Main Line heiress whose wedding is disrupted by an unwelcome team of tabloid journalists. Kate found this intriguing and told Barry that she'd be interested in playing Tracy Lord—

provided that she wasn't tapped for the role of Scarlett O'Hara.

A few weeks later, Fenwick was washed away in the hurricane and Vivien Leigh was cast as Scarlett. While recovering from these calamities, Kate received the first act of *The Philadelphia Story.* "I loved it," she recalls. "But the second act didn't appeal, so I flew up to Maine to see Phil, and he agreed to change it."

Some say Kate really deserved a coauthor's credit for *The Philadelphia Story.* According to Broadway gossip, she peered over Barry's shoulder while he wrote, a blue pencil in one hand and a notebook full of suggestions in the other. He, in turn, painstakingly studied her every movement, "every little quirk of her head, every effective dart of the eye," and incorporated them into the character he was writing for her. Undoubtedly there is some exaggeration in all this, but it can't be denied that the role was meticulously tailored to show off Hepburn's talents to greatest advantage.

As Barry developed the play, it centered on Tracy Lord's transformation from "ice goddess" to "real woman." As one character tells her, "You'll never be a first-class human being till you learn to have some regard for human frailty . . . but your sense of inner divinity won't allow it. . . . You're a special class of American female— the Married Maidens—and of Type Philadelphiaensis, you're the absolute tops!"

Tracy's three-act crash course in humanity includes lessons in skinny-dipping, champagne-drinking, and flirtation. As the play begins, she is engaged to a pompous nonentity; in act two she falls in love with self-made, liberal Mike Conners, a reporter for *Destiny* magazine; at the end, she remarries her first husband, a smart-talking playboy named C. K. Dexter Haven. All these romantic upheavals

are amusing, but they're also contrived and sketchily motivated. Despite its great success, *The Philadelphia Story* is
second-rate Philip Barry—it's mechanical, unfelt, and
overstrident in its sophistication.

Part of the trouble was that Barry had started out with
a wispy idea—Tracy and the reporters—that wasn't as
easy to develop as he'd originally thought. At one point,
the play apparently concentrated on Tracy's intolerance
for her father, a financier with a taste for Russian balle-
rinas, but Kate felt this relationship was too heavy for a
drawing-room comedy, and steered the playwright in another direction. Perhaps she was right—Barry had had a
daughter who'd died in early childhood, and whenever he
tackled father-daughter relationships in his plays (as in
Second Threshold), his writing trailed off into vague and
unresolved introspection. But once the problems between
Tracy and Seth Lord were reduced to a few lines in the
second act, the play lost whatever purpose or point it might
have had.

Kate, however, liked the new second act, and agreed enthusiastically when Barry decided it was time to show the
unfinished manuscript to the Theatre Guild. Lawrence
Langner and his partners were enchanted with the comedy,
but they had just lost $60,000 on a Biblical extravaganza
called *Jeremiah* and couldn't afford to produce a new play
without outside backing. This was a problem: nobody
wanted to invest in a package that included Hepburn (box-
office poison), Barry (four flops in six years), and the
Guild (one hit in three seasons). Finally, Hepburn and
Barry both put up one-fourth of the production cost, the
Guild scraped up another quarter, and the rest of the
money was provided by Howard Hughes. In place of salary, Kate accepted 10 percent of the Broadway gross and
12.5 percent of the take of any subsequent road tours; with

shrewd foresight, she also acquired control of the screen rights.

While Barry set to work on the third act, the Guild lined up a topnotch cast and crew to support Hepburn. Robert Edmond Jones designed the sets, Valentina created Kate's simple, elegantly tailored costumes, and the supporting players included Joseph Cotten, Van Heflin, and Shirley Booth.

Hepburn had suggested Heflin and Cotten as her leading men. Three years earlier, she had brought Heflin to Hollywood to appear with her in *A Woman Rebels;* since then he had floundered through a series of RKO potboilers, and had been reduced to radio work when Kate rescued him for *The Philadelphia Story.* She had seen Cotten in Orson Welles' Mercury Theatre production of *Too Much Johnson;* the play had been a disaster, but Hepburn had liked and remembered Cotten, and recommended him to the Guild.

On her previous Broadway outings, Kate had been somewhat standoffish toward her fellow players, but this time she was warm and outgoing, and her spirit of camaraderie infected the entire company. Kate liked everyone and everyone liked Kate, particularly Van Heflin, who was to be her constant companion during the run of the play.

Just before rehearsals began, Barry turned in a third act that wasn't up to expectations. There was too much exposition and not enough comic momentum—the play became wordy and graceless as Barry tried to resolve the intricate relationships set up in the first two acts. With no time for revisions, the play was rehearsed and opened in New Haven with what theater people euphemistically call ''a third-act problem.''

Despite the weak finish, *The Philadelphia Story* pleased both critics and audiences on its first engagement. A week later, in Philadelphia, the reaction was even more affirmative. "To put it in a palindrome," wrote a local critic, "it's a wow!" That's only half a palindrome, and *Philadelphia Story* was only a partial wow—there were still problems with the third act. After a series of angry discussions, Barry secluded himself in his Florida home and went to work on a new finale. He completed his revisions just before the Washington, D. C., opening, and there, for the first time, *The Philadelphia Story* breezed along on a steady gust of laughter from start to finish.

The play looked like a shoo-in, but everyone was apprehensive about New York. For a while, the Guild thought of ducking Broadway, touring the show all over the country, and then bringing it to New York as an already profitable venture. According to Lawrence Langner's history of the Theatre Guild, *The Magic Curtain*, Kate wanted to stay in the provinces for as long as possible. "If I have a barrow and I'm selling my fruit very well on the side streets," she told Langner, "why should I go to the marketplace where all the other barrows are, and where I may not do nearly as well?"

Later she changed her mind—she couldn't close another play out of town without losing face, so she reluctantly agreed to face Broadway in *The Philadelphia Story*. She approached the opening night with fear and trembling (no star billing, she warned Langner), and her pre-premiere interviews were unusually candid and humble.

Questioned about her unflattering publicity, she told Douglas Gilbert of the *World-Telegram*, "I don't blame them [the reporters].... I never did cooperate.... I suffered the most idiotic interviews until I stopped them. They'd ask me the most personal questions, and I'd answer them idiotically, thinking they'd understand ... [but] they would print [whatever I said]. I made a lot of money, but in Hollywood you get nine million times what you're worth. I was never a great draw. I was overpaid."

On opening night—March 28, 1939—Hepburn walked around her dressing room in the Shubert Theatre and tried to quiet her nerves by chanting, "This is Indianapolis, this is Indianapolis." When the curtain went up, Kate was on stage dressed in slacks and a blouse, talking to two minor characters. Her appearance was greeted by a ripple of polite applause, but then an atmosphere of cold hostility fell over the auditorium. In the first scenes, Hepburn/Tracy Lord is astride her high horse and riding roughshod over everyone in sight. After her exit, the stage is left to Heflin and Shirley Booth, who warmed up the first-night crowd with tart put-downs of Tracy and her blueblood relatives. From then on, the play was off on a winning track as joke after joke was directed against Hepburn until, in the final hour, she discovers her "humanity." The curtain falls as Tracy and her father walk down the aisle to the strains of "The Wedding March." "How do I look?" she asks. "Like a queen—like a goddess," he answers. "Do you know how I feel? Like a human being!" Tracy exclaims. "And is that all right?" her father asks. "All right? Oh Father, it's heaven!"

And it was heaven for Kate, too. At the end, the audience applauded with real enthusiasm, and the critics turned in rave reviews the next morning. "A strange, tense little lady with austere beauty and a metallic voice, she has consistently found it difficult to project a part in the theater," opened Brooks Atkinson's appraisal of Hepburn's performance. "But now she has surrendered to the central part in Mr. Barry's play and she acts it like a woman who has at last found the joy she has always been seeking in the theater."

Richard Watts of the *Herald Tribune* spoke for many

people when he began his review with a tribute to Kate's pluck: "Few actresses have been so relentlessly assailed by critics, wits, columnists, magazine editors, and other professional assailers over so long a period of time, and even if you confess that some of the abuse had a certain amount of justification to it, you must admit she faced it gamely and unflinchingly and fought back with courage and gallantry."

There were a few nit-picking reviews here and there, but Kate's comeback was very close to a total triumph. For the next year, *The Philadelphia Story* played to packed houses on Broadway, and then went on tour. The overall gross exceeded $1,500,000.

"When I'm acting in a play," Hepburn once said, "I don't have energy for anything else." But during the run of *The Philadelphia Story*, she lived a full and active life. In California, her day had usually begun around 6:30 A.M.; in New York it started several hours later. Sometime after ten she got up, ate a hearty combination breakfast-lunch, spent a couple of hours on Joe Sawyer's East Side tennis courts, tramped around Central Park, studied with Frances Robinson-Duff, and kept a beauty appointment at the Ogilvie salon. Then she went home, rested, ate dinner (steak or chicken, vegetables, and a fruit), and arrived at the Shubert Theatre about an hour before curtain time. After the show, she entertained guests in her dressing room or at home, and, sometimes, the conversation went on until the early morning hours.

Her weekends were spent overseeing the reconstruction of the Fenwick house. Kate went to F.A.O. Schwarz, bought a box of building blocks, took them to Hartford, and started constructing a toy model of the new summer cottage. All the Hepburns were consulted—the blocks were shifted and rearranged until the house took on baronial proportions. Big but not pretentious, it would be an over-sized New England summer cottage with a private beach and a dazzling view of Long Island Sound.

A few weeks after the opening of *The Philadelphia Story,* Kate started receiving offers from Hollywood, but she wanted to return to the screen in the Barry play, and with the film rights in her pocket, she could afford to be choosy about selecting a producer. Failing all else, she was prepared to produce the film herself with Howard Hughes as a silent partner.

Warners came up with a high bid of $262,000, but Kate accepted MGM's offer of $250,000 because the deal gave her approval of her leading men and director. To bolster her pull at the box office, she decided to replace Cotten and Heflin with two established Hollywood stars. Her initial choices were Clark Gable and Spencer Tracy, but when they weren't available, she accepted Cary Grant and James Stewart. (To get Grant, MGM had to promise him first billing. Not since *Bill of Divorcement* had Kate been out-ranked by a leading man, but she didn't object—she knew that most audiences never pay much attention to the credits.) There was no question about the director—it had to be George Cukor, who was as expert at adapting stage material to the screen as he was at bringing out the best in Katharine Hepburn.

Cukor saw the show on Broadway and took copious notes, paying particular attention to those moments that showed Hepburn to greatest advantage. This groundwork was necessary, since Kate could spend only eight weeks in Hollywood—the picture had to be shot between the end of the play's New York run and the opening of the road tour in the fall of 1940. Cukor worked fast, keeping his retakes to a minimum, and sticking as close to the play as was possible.

One of the few additions to the original script is the famous opening scene: a door opens, Cary Grant walks out, Hepburn appears and heaves a bag of golf clubs after him; he turns around, pushes her in the face, and she falls backward like a tree that has just felt the axman's final blow. As an acrobatic feat, Kate's plunge is quite impressive, but the attitude behind it is not so pretty. The film tends to underline and overstress everything that worked in the play, including Tracy's comeuppance. It's a high-powered piece of picture making, as slick and polished and expensive as a Cadillac Eldorado. Except for James Stewart, whose yokel simplicity gets tiresome, all the acting is expert, and Cary Grant is especially winning in the not-so-winning role of C. K. Dexter Haven. Kate is a study in sheer professionalism. In her simple one-thousand-dollar Adrian frocks, she has never looked quite so glossy or self-assured: hands on hips, chin hoisted at a seventy-five-degree angle, she glides through the film, every gesture and movement programmed for maximum effect.

While the movie was being shot, Kate was polite and cooperative—"This is a new and mellow Hepburn," wrote Louella Parsons—but Hollywood was not yet ready to forget her reign as Katharine of Arrogance. When it came time to hand out the 1940 Oscars, James Stewart copped the best-actor award, but Kate lost to Ginger Rogers for *Kitty Foyle*. *Cue* magazine referred to Rogers' victory as "the revenge of the little people of Hollywood." Many commentators felt Hepburn had been deliberately slighted. After quoting an old theater adage—"Be nice to the people you pass on the way up; they're the same people you pass on the way down"—one writer argued that Kate was being rebuked for never learning this basic law of stage etiquette.

Even without the Oscar, Kate's return to the screen was an unqualified success. *The Philadelphia Story* grossed

$600,000 at Radio City Music Hall and then went on to break records around the country. There was no more talk of "box-office poison"—Hepburn was once again "top of the heap."

As soon as the film was finished, Kate went on tour with *The Philadelphia Story*, playing Dallas, Toronto, and practically every major city in between. The show closed, appropriately enough, in Philadelphia on February 15, 1941. At her final curtain call, Hepburn asked the backstage crew to join the cast on stage. "When I started this play," she told the audience, "these people knew I was on the spot. They could have treated me like a climber or a phony. Instead they treated me like an actress and a friend." It was a speech worthy of Tracy Lord, first-class human being, and cast, crew, and audience responded to Kate's gallantry by joining hands and singing a chorus of "Auld Lang Syne."

Later that evening, she threw a closing-night party at Philadelphia's elegant Barkley Hotel. Toward the end, when the guests had dwindled to Kate, Lawrence Langner, his wife, and a few stragglers, Hepburn asked, "What shall I do next?"

"Do something dangerous," Langner answered. "Do a play in which you'll aim high but risk falling flat on your face if you don't come through with a great performance." He suggested Shakespeare or Ibsen or Shaw.

Everyone nodded in agreement. Even Hepburn looked impressed. But a few weeks later, after a brief vacation with her family, she went off to Florida and listened while Philip Barry described a new comedy called *Without Love*.

11

Cutting Kate
Down to
Size

Without Love started as a comedy about a marriage of convenience. But 1941 was no time for comedy, and Barry wanted to write a play that would say something about the war effort. After casting around for a suitable subject, he settled upon the Royal Navy's need for Irish bases to combat the German submarines that were then sinking so many Allied ships. The hero of *Without Love* is an American diplomat who returns to Washington to try to persuade the neutral Irish to cooperate with Britain. He poses as an Irishman and gets a job as a butler in the home of a wealthy Washington widow. She soon learns his true identity and, for not very convincing reasons, they embark on a platonic marriage.

The romantic and political strands of the comedy never come together: inadequately explained characters enter and leave as if pulled by strings, and there's a feeling of manipulation about the plot that suggests that Barry didn't know where he was going or how he was going to get there. Kate recognized the problems, but she was indebted to the playwright for *The Philadelphia Story,* and she, too, wanted to support the war effort. She agreed to play Jamie Lee Rowan in *Without Love* as soon as Barry finished revising and polishing his script.

Meanwhile she returned to New York and started looking for a new film project. She turned down *My Sister Eileen* and a couple of other offers—she wanted something very special to cap her success in *The Philadelphia Story*. MGM and Cukor joined in the search, but found nothing suitable. Finally Garson Kanin came to Kate's rescue.

He had just received a script outline from a young writer named Ring Lardner, Jr., who was looking for a collaborator. Kanin liked what he read, but since he was about to join the Army, he couldn't work with Lardner; instead, he suggested that the writer collaborate with his brother, Mike, on developing the story (then called *The Thing About Women)* as a Katharine Hepburn vehicle.

The heroine of *Woman of the Year* (as Lardner and Kanin later named their script) is a celebrated political columnist, Tess Harding, a character modeled in equal parts on Dorothy Thompson, Clare Boothe Luce, and Tracy Lord of *The Philadelphia Story*. Tess entertains world leaders, influences international policy, speaks fluent Chinese, but can't tell a percolator from an egg cup. And she doesn't have much common sense when it comes to picking a husband. Of all the unlikely men in the world, she marries Sam Craig, a rough-edged Irish sportswriter who wants a woman, not a dictaphone, for a wife. "What do you know!" he snarls. "The Woman of the Year isn't even a woman!" They fight, separate, and then reunite on a tentative basis as the film ends.

Kate adored *Woman of the Year* and was determined to make the best possible deal for the unknown authors, neither of whom had ever earned more than $3,000 for their work. She removed the page listing the authors' names from the script and mailed it to MGM. A week or so later she wired Joseph L. Mankiewicz, executive producer of *The Philadelphia Story*, and told him to be in his office the next day at 3 P.M. She called and set up a meeting later on with Mankiewicz and the other MGM decision-makers.

At the conference, Hepburn did most of the talking. She said that she'd had several offers for *Woman of the Year*, but was giving MGM first refusal out of gratitude for *The Phildelphia Story*. Her terms were simple: $100,000 for her services, $50,000 for each author, plus $10,000 in agent's fees. She was also to have approval of her leading man and director. After stating her terms, Kate grew flustered and rushed out of the room. A few minutes later, Mankiewicz emerged and kissed her on the forehead. "Why did you do that?" she asked.

"I just wanted to kiss the blarney stone," he answered. MGM had accepted her proposal.

Louis B. Mayer, the head of MGM, was noted for his histrionic behavior during contract negotiations: he screamed, cried, fell on his knees, tore his hair, and generally carried on like a stock-company Shylock. The sight of Mayer hopping with rage intimidated most of the MGM stars—Greer Garson, Greta Garbo, and Katharine Hepburn were among the few exceptions. He rarely even tried to bargain with Kate: on both *The Philadelphia Story* and *Woman of the Year*, he gave her everything she wanted.

According to advertisements, MGM had "more stars than there are in heaven," and soon Hepburn joined Clark Gable, Robert Taylor, Fred Astaire, Lana Turner, Judy Garland, and Ethel and Lionel Barrymore in the studio's firmament. Beginning with *Woman of the Year*, Kate was to spend the next ten years at MGM. There was never a formal contract, only a verbal agreement that gave her story approval, choice of leading man and director, and time off for stage work. Though several of her MGM films were among the worst of her career, Hepburn was happy at the studio, which was noted for pampering and protecting its stars. The MGM ladies were dressed, lighted, and photographed with all the enhancing care that money could buy. As a result, in the early years of her MGM period, Hepburn looks sleeker and more sophisticated than before, but she also seems more synthetic, less individual. The glamour experts almost succeeded in streamlining her into high-fashion anonymity.

For director of *Woman of the Year* Hepburn wanted George Cukor, but he was working on another film, and as substitute, Kate selected George Stevens, the director of *Alice Adams* and *Quality Street*. On their last outing together they had clashed frequently, but in 1939, Hepburn and Stevens were romantically linked by the Hollywood columnists. Stories about their romance still circulate, possibly because in both personality and appearance Stevens bears a slight resemblance to Spencer Tracy, who replaced him in Kate's life. That makes a neat pattern, but there is no real evidence of a deep attachment between Hepburn and Stevens; they were close friends who dated frequently without giving any thought to a serious or lasting relationship.

At the time of *Woman of the Year*, Kate had never met Tracy, but she admired him greatly as an actor and chose him to play Sam Craig. Initially MGM said he wasn't available—Tracy was then on location in Florida shooting preliminary scenes for *The Yearling*. A few weeks later, that production bogged down in internal problems and was shelved indefinitely, and Spencer returned to Hollywood just in time to join Kate on the set of *Woman of the Year*.

At their first meeting, Kate was wearing platform shoes that added three inches to her height. That made her five foot ten; Tracy was five foot eleven. "I fear I may be a little too tall for you, Mr. Tracy," Hepburn said. According to most versions of the story, Tracy then shot back, "That's all right, Miss Hepburn, I'll cut you down to size." But as it actually happened, it was Joseph Mankiewicz, not Tracy, who outsassed Kate: "Don't worry," the producer said, "he'll cut you down to size."

"Cutting Her Down to Size, or The Taming of Hepburn" is a good alternate title for many of the Tracy-Hepburn comedies. Nearly all their pictures follow the same formula: a high-class or snobby girl meets a raffish or down-to-earth guy; they spar for a while, then he cuffs her with his big paw and she begins to purr with contented submissiveness. There's a sexist undertone to these films—which may explain why most Hepburn fans don't like them very much—and nowhere is it so flagrantly exposed as in the final scenes of *Woman of the Year*.

Louis B. Mayer didn't like the inconclusive ending written by Lardner and Kanin; he decided Tess Harding must put on an apron, invade the kitchen, and serve her husband breakfast in bed. This simpering domestic finale horrified everyone, and Joseph Mankiewicz worked out a compromise. Tess goes into the kitchen, but she makes a mess of everything—her waffles are too yeasty, the coffee perks over, the toast pops out of the toaster like a jack-in-the-box, the poached eggs turn into rocks. Even in 1941, this Mrs.-Newlywed-in-the-Kitchen routine was pretty tired stuff—it had been around since the silent days—and it was totally out of keeping with Tess Harding's character—it's hard to imagine a woman of her intelligence making the mistake of believing that the way to a man's heart is through the breakfast tray. And even if she did, it seems unlikely that she would be unable to master the use of electric appliances or the art of making a decent waffle.

Nearly all the Tracy-Hepburn films end with Kate placing a metaphorical hand under Spencer's foot, and the message is always the same: a woman who is really a woman always takes second place to the man in her life. And Kate always took second billing in her films with Tracy—his contract guaranteed him top spot in all advertisements and credit listings. (When Garson Kanin questioned him about his unchivalrous behavior, Tracy answered, "Listen, chowderhead, a film isn't a lifeboat!")

Kate made no objection to walking in Spencer's shadow. She thought he was the best actor she had ever seen, and envied the total concentration and unassuming self-confidence he brought to all his roles. "Spencer was as simple and unadorned as a baked potato," Hepburn once said, while she was "a dessert with lots of whipped cream." The description is clever but not accurate; Kate is too tart to be a dessert—she's the sour cream, chives, and crumbled bacon that gives the baked potato some sophistication.

Before starting *Woman of the Year,* Kate and Spencer spent several days studying each other's films in separate projection rooms. When shooting began, Kate's usually strident and clipped delivery was soft and mumbled, while Tracy sounded polished and overrefined. "My God," Joe Mankiewicz exclaimed, "they're imitating each other!"

After a few days they reverted to type and discovered they had a temperamental affinity that worked both on screen and off. Their rapport brought a touch of warmth and wit to the picture, and saved it from becoming just another ersatz-sophisticated Hollywood study of the battle of the sexes. For all their verve, it's still a pretty weak film, probably the most overrated of all the Tracy-Hepburn comedies (though *Adam's Rib* provides stiff competition).

Woman of the Year was completed by the end of 1941, and MGM considered rushing it into release as a possible candidate for that year's Academy Awards. Instead, the studio waited until 1942, and then opened it with great publicity and fanfare. *"Woman of the Year,"* said the ads, "is the picture of the year!" The critics didn't agree, but on the whole the reviews were good, business was excellent, the film brought Kate her fourth Oscar nomination (this time she lost to Greer Garson for *Mrs. Miniver*), and it won a best screenwriting award for Kanin and Lardner.

When she finished *Woman of the Year*, Hepburn returned to New York and began preliminary work on *Without Love.* The first obstacle facing Kate and the Theatre Guild, which was again acting as Barry's producer, was the choice of a leading man. Practically every Broadway star actor was approached, but no one wanted to take second place to Kate. Reaching close to the bottom of the list, Lawrence Langner suggested Elliott Nugent, a jack-of-all-trades with Broadway and Hollywood credits as writer, director, and actor. Blond, balding, and built like a Charles Atlas reject, he wasn't an ideal romantic lead, but his skill as a light comedian made up for his lack of physical presence.

Nugent was a manic-depressive who went through spells of heavy drinking, but on the night he had dinner at Kate's Turtle Bay home, he was on his best behavior. Hepburn agreed with Langner that he wasn't the worst of all possible choices.

On the first day of rehearsal, Nugent and Hepburn came to a scene that ended with a kiss. Most leading men duck the first embrace, indicating it with a light brush of the cheek, but Nugent zeroed in on target. Kate was taken aback. "Do you always kiss your leading lady at the first rehearsal?" she asked. Nugent nodded and explained that this was his way of breaking the ice. Kate smiled without looking totally convinced.

Later that day, Nugent drove Kate home, and, along the way, persuaded her to stop by his apartment for a drink with his wife Norma. Like her parents, Kate was a teetotaler, but she occasionally took a drink to be sociable, and, at the Nugents', she nursed a thimbleful of rum for an hour or so. Then she left, convinced that the Nugents were a happily married couple.

Without Love opened in New Haven on February 26, 1942, and then played one-week stands in Boston, Baltimore, and Washington prior to a Broadway premiere on March 25. On the road the show sold out on the strength of Hepburn's name. With *The Philadelphia Story*, people had waited to buy tickets until the reviews came out, but this time they rushed to the box office as soon as the posters were pasted on the theater billboards. The press agent for *Without Love* told Kate that, next to Gargantua, a circus gorilla, she was the greatest star attraction in America. For the rest of the tour, she referred to herself as Gargantua—ruefully perhaps, since the ape always got better reviews than *Without Love*.

Barry kept on writing and revising, but the play still didn't work. Shortly after the opening in Washington, the Theatre Guild announced that *Without Love* would extend its road tour and bypass Broadway until the fall of 1942. There was no mention of script problems—instead the announcement said Kate had a film commitment that would keep her busy for most of the summer.

This was, at best, a half truth. Once *Without Love* was postponed, Kate decided to return to MGM and Spencer Tracy, who, for the next twenty-five years, would be described as her "great and good friend."

12

Tracy

Any of the simple and pure things in life you can say about Spencer. He was like water, air, earth. He wasn't easily fooled—an unusual quality in the male. He was onto the human race—but with humor and understanding. Yet he was enormously complicated and tortured. He looked out from a terribly tangled maze, like a web. Yet from the center of this tangle would come the simple statement, the total clarity of his work.

—Hepburn, quoted by *Newsweek*

At the time of their first meeting, Hepburn was in her thirties, and Tracy was forty-one. He'd been born in Milwaukee to a mother whose "lineage went directly back to the settlers in the colonies before the Revolution" and a father "who was Irish with generations of good old Irish fighters behind him." His Irish blood, Tracy once said, gave him the "itch to wander" from his middle-class surroundings: a poor student, he quit school and enlisted in the Navy with his boyhood friend, Pat O'Brien. After his discharge, he entered college as a pre-med student, wandered into amateur dramatics, and finally came to New York and embarked on a professional career in the theater.

His progress was slow but steady, and after years of

stock, touring companies, and minor Broadway roles, he attracted the attention of George M. Cohan, then America's favorite song-and-dance man, who watched Tracy rehearse and advised him, "Spencer, you've got to act less." Soon Tracy was a model of economy and total concentration, but he never forgot another Cohan lesson: "Listen, kid," Cohan had said, "always serve it up with a little dressing." At first, there was too much dressing to suit some tastes. "He was too much the actor," wrote John Wexley, the author of Tracy's first great New York success, *The Last Mile*. "He was effective, but he played to the audience a good deal of the time and was, to that extent, self-conscious. He gave the character a sort of vanity or egotism that should not have been present."

Tracy was to become an actor's actor—his fellow professionals admired "the simplicity and reality of his acting"—but from a layman's point of view, he could be a terrible ham. Like his idol, George M. Cohan, he could wave a flag, tap dance, or lose his trousers and make it all look as natural as parading down Main Street on the Fourth of July with sparklers stuck in both ears. Alternately, he could be a dreadful bore—sometimes, particularly during his later career, an aggressive cockiness crept into his performances, and turned his easygoing approach to a role into an all-out assault. Pushed too far, simplicity can harden into a mannerism, and Tracy often went to extremes.

But, at his best, that tiny touch of Cohan flamboyance brought spice to his slice-of-life realism, and it called attention to his performance in *The Last Mile,* one of the big hits of the 1930 Broadway season. As soon as it opened Tracy was tested by most of the major film companies, but they were all put off by his mug of a face. Only director John Ford, who favored the hulking, leather-and-sweat kind of leading man, recognized Tracy's potential, and insisted that the Fox studio place him under contract.

Tracy jumped at the contract—he needed the kind of money that only Hollywood could pay. In 1923, while playing in stock, he had met a young actress named Louise Treadwell, whom he'd married a few months later. Within a year, their first child, John, was born, and when he was four months old, his parents discovered he was deaf. The expense of training a handicapped child was enormous, far greater than Tracy could afford on his small Broadway salary.

In California, the Tracys had another child—Louise, called "Susie" by her family—but by 1931 they had started to drift apart. He had "gone Hollywood" to the extent of playing polo with Will Rogers at the Riviera Club, and often he spent two or three nights a month with the "Irish Mafia," a group consisting of George Murphy, James Cagney, John Ford, Pat O'Brien, and several other Hollywood leprechauns who got together every so often to honor the memory of St. Patrick. Usually when he felt the thirst, Tracy went off alone—he had periodic spells of hard drinking and carousing, and then he would drop out of sight for days at a time. When he was off on a bender, he could wind up anywhere from a San Diego bar to a Denver saloon; his studio was forever ferreting him out, sobering him up, and sending him home to Louise.

"Most of the time, he was a gentle, quiet soul," remembered screenwriter and novelist Anita Loos, the author of *San Francisco*, one of Tracy's first movie hits. "But he wasn't easy to know. Around the studio, it was said that his periodic drunks were caused by his grief over his son. Like many parents with disabled children, he apparently felt he was in some way responsible for his boy's condition—it haunted him. Mrs. Tracy was the perfect mother—she gave up everything for her son and, when he was grown, she opened a clinic to help other deaf children. Her dedication, however, only added to Spencer's guilt."

It's a plausible explanation, except that Tracy was drinking heavily long before the birth of his son. He once told director Vincente Minnelli how, as a very young actor, he would buy a case of liquor and lock himself in a Broadway hotel room until he had drained the last bottle. Hepburn once said Tracy was tormented by his "Irish imagination," and from other reports he was a morbid worrier, given to fits of black depression and violent shifts of mood. Reporters always approached him warily; if he smiled, they went over and talked to him, but a scowl sent them scurrying in the opposite direction.

In the 1930s Spencer was called "Fox's bad boy." He was constantly at odds with the studio executives, who found him disobedient, irresponsible, uncooperative on the set—he never worked overtime and always took a two-hour lunch break, most of it spent relaxing over cocktails. The Fox producers couldn't see Tracy's sex appeal, and instead of playing romantic leads he was cast as convicts, gangsters, hobos, and cops in a string of B productions. Frustrated by his slow progress, he fought for better roles, and occasionally Fox assigned him to a class-A movie.

One of his better films of this period was *A Man's Castle*, a love story set in a Depression shantytown; it was directed by Frank Borzage and co-starred Loretta Young. Then only twenty years old, Miss Young was angelically beautiful and highly flirtatious—she made a habit of dating her leading men, and Tracy was no exception. By the end of the first week of filming, the two stars were knee-deep in a romance that caused a lot of talk and embarrassment on the set. Director Frank Borzage, who knew and liked Louise Tracy, was particularly upset, and other members of the cast felt they were "intruding or eavesdropping on a very private conversation" every time they approached Loretta and Spencer. Halfway through the production, Tracy left home and moved into a hotel suite. A few days later, Louise told the press that she and her husband were separating because of incompatibility.

Tracy often said the press made too much of this affair, but the facts say otherwise. Every day for four months there was a new picture in the papers of Loretta and Spencer: they were photographed at the races, driving in an open sports car, arriving at premieres, dancing at the Coconut Grove. And Tracy—who had never been a slouch when it came to dressing—now blossomed forth in dinner jackets, white ties, and top hats, all because of Loretta and her taste for expensive entertainment.

Eventually the gossip got out of hand, and in 1934, Loretta issued a statement that ended all speculation about a forthcoming marriage. "Since Spence and I are both Catholic and can never be married," she announced, "we have agreed not to see each other again." (Later, she referred to her breakup with Tracy as "a lesson in self-denial.") A few weeks later, Tracy went back to Louise, and for a while their marriage improved. At the end of 1935, he moved from Fox to MGM, and there came into his own as an offbeat, character-type leading man.

In 1937 he played a Portuguese fisherman in *Captains Courageous;* it was a part that required him to sing sea chanties and speak in dialect. "Do you say 'leetle feesh'?" he asked his dialogue coach, a real-life Portuguese fisherman. "No," his instructor answered, "I say 'little fish'." Tracy went right on saying "leetle feesh." This was to be not only one of his hammiest, but also one of his most joyous performances. It brought him his first Academy Award and also the undying admiration of Katharine Hepburn, who saw it again and again, always dissolving in tears when Tracy went to a watery death. A year later, Spencer won a second Oscar for *Boys' Town*, and these two trophies (one of them mistakenly inscribed "To Dick Tracy") established him as one of Hollywood's most gifted and popular stars.

As Tracy's career progressed, his marriage declined. By the beginning of the 1940s, Louise was totally immersed in her work with deaf children, while Tracy was seen around town with a strange assortment of young actresses, including Olivia De Havilland and eighteen-year-old Judy Garland. There was no official separation, but Tracy spent only weekends with Louise and his children at their ranch in the San Fernando Valley. Monday through Friday, he lived in a rented suite at the Beverly Wilshire Hotel.

Although it has been widely assumed that Mrs. Tracy refused Spencer a divorce on religious grounds, this is not the case—she is Episcopalian; it was Tracy who was a devout Catholic. No one really knows whether he ever asked for a divorce, but most people guess he didn't—not for Kate's sake, anyway. She had tried marriage once and found it not to her liking. On several occasions, she has said that actors are too involved with themselves to marry successfully, and generally she thinks only people who want children should wed. "When I realized I was going to lead a professional life," she once said, "I very quickly decided I would have no children."

From the start, the press treated the Tracy-Hepburn relationship with the utmost discretion. A few columnists hinted at the romance—Hedda Hopper reported that "the love scenes in *Woman of the Year* look like the real thing"—but otherwise it was, as Sheilah Graham wrote, "the greatest love story never told." It was a very private affair: Kate and Tracy never appeared together in public;

they barred interviewers and visitors from the set; they always stayed in separate hotels when they traveled together; they saw only a few close and trusted friends.

After meeting Hepburn, Tracy still went on binges in unpredictable rhythmic cycles (usually they occurred when she was out of town), but he gradually stopped seeing his Irish Mafia drinking buddies and eased his way into Kate's circle of friends. She introduced him to new intellectual and cultural interests, and, in exchange, he gave her a sense of humor about herself, laughed her out of her affectations, helped her to be more direct and human in her approach to life and other people.

Kate took on most of the grubby duties of a wife—she cooked for Spencer, nursed him through innumerable illnesses, drove him to the studio, dragged him out of bars, encouraged him when he became disgruntled about his career. In private as well as on the screen he cut her down to size, telling her to shut up if she interrupted one of his stories, ridiculing her mannerisms, calling her his "bag of bones." Occasionally she referred to him as her "dipsomaniac," but usually she accepted his jibes without comment or reproach. "Sometimes their bantering looked very cruel to outsiders," said a friend. "But it was all a big put-on. They loved to make people think they were having a fight."

"They couldn't live together, they couldn't be seen together, all they could do was work together," said Anita Loos. Even working together presented problems; there weren't many films with equal parts for two such disparate actors, and often either Kate or Spencer was miscast in their co-starring vehicles.

MGM had paired Garson and Pidgeon, Garland and Rooney, William Powell and Myrna Loy with happy results, and after the success of *Woman of the Year*, Louis B.

Mayer was eager to find another picture for Hepburn and Tracy. A few years earlier, the studio had bought an unpublished I. A. R. Wylie novel, *Keeper of the Flame,* that warned that fascism might one day come to America under the guise of jingoist nationalism. Apparently Mayer didn't realize that his good friend William Randolph Hearst was the model for Wylie's fascist hero, and he failed to grasp the full implications of the subject matter. To him, Wylie's novel was just a good Gothic melodrama with meaty roles for Tracy and Hepburn.

Donald Ogden Stewart, screenwriter for *Holiday* and *The Philadelphia Story,* went to work on *Keeper of the Flame.* As chairman of Hollywood's Anti-Nazi League, he was in sympathy with his subject and tried not to dilute Wylie's message. Kate, however, was not happy with his screenplay; she and Spencer both felt there was too much theme and not enough dramatics or characterization. (This is the only Tracy-Hepburn film in which there is no romantic relationship between the stars.) They complained to the front office, and MGM ordered Stewart to work on a rewrite.

Through the Hollywood grapevine, Kate heard that Stewart was very annoyed that she had passed him by and gone to MGM with her complaint. Kate never shied away from an argument, and, characteristically, she called Stewart and asked if she could come over and work out the misunderstanding. A few hours later, she agreed to do the film virtually as Stewart had originally written it.

Keeper of the Flame opens as newsman Steve O'Malley (Tracy) is writing a story about the life and death of an eminent American, Robert Forrest. During his research, O'Malley begins to suspect that there is some dark secret lurking in Forrest's past, and senses that the key to the mystery lies with his mysterious widow, Christine (Hep-

130

burn). After much prodding Christine reveals that her husband's patriotism was really a shield for his fascist activities. Forrest's private secretary overhears the confession, shoots Christine, and sets fire to the house. O'Malley rushes to the rescue, but arrives just as Christine dies. With her last breath, she gasps (with impeccable Bryn Mawr diction), "Write your story. Don't spare Robert. Don't spare me."

Keeper of the Flame is really Tracy's film. Kate appears only a few times during the first half of the picture. Though she wasn't needed every day, she was always on the set, meddling in everyone's business and annoying George Cukor with her advice on direction. One day she watched Tracy play a scene with another actor, and was displeased with Cukor's staging. "I don't think that was done correctly," she said. "I think Spencer should have been sitting when he spoke those lines." Cukor ignored her comment.

Then, after supporting player Audrey Christie did a scene with Tracy, Hepburn piped up, "Miss Christie should speak those lines more softly. It wasn't done properly." Cukor said nothing.

A week later, after a scene in which Tracy is talking to Christie and they are interrupted to be told that the house is on fire, Kate said, "I don't think they would have to be told about the fire. They would smell the smoke." Cukor turned to her and said, "It must be wonderful to know all about acting, *and* all about fires, too!" Tracy roared with laughter.

According to Hollywood gossip, Louis B. Mayer never saw *Keeper of the Flame* until it opened at Radio City Music Hall. Halfway through the film, he caught the political implications of the movie and stormed out of the theater in a rage. "I can't vouch for the story," said Donald Ogden Stewart, "but I'd be very happy if it were true."

The picture received cool reviews. *Time* was particularly harsh: *"Keeper of the Flame* is an expensive testimonial to Hollywood's inability to face a significant theme. . . . For stars Hepburn and Tracy and all concerned, it is the high point of a significant failure." Tracy's reviews were good, but Hepburn was roasted for her "arty acting" and "glamour-girl posturing." She comes on draped in yards of white chiffon and carrying a bunch of calla lilies, but this time, there's no intention of parodying *The Lake*—all the ethereal posturing is for real. Kate's major concern seems to be her cheekbones—she keeps flicking and tossing her head to find the right lighting to emphasize their dramatic contours. She seems to be suffering from Garbo-itis—possibly because William Daniels, Garbo's favorite cameraman, photographed the film. It's a classic of one woman's glamor being another woman's poison.

After *Keeper of the Flame,* Hepburn returned to New York and went into rehearsal for the revised *Without Love.* She was extremely apprehensive: Barry's script still hadn't jelled, Elliott Nugent was too meek for the dashing diplomat, and, to compensate for his deficiencies, Kate found herself overacting. Had she not felt obligated to the Theatre Guild, she probably would have canceled the engagement; instead, she limited the Broadway run to fourteen weeks.

After a brief tryout in Detroit, the play opened at the St. James Theatre on November 10, 1942, to lukewarm notices. The only outright pan came from Brooks Atkinson of *The New York Times:* "As the unloved wife, Miss Hepburn is giving a mechanical performance that is not without considerable gaucherie in the early scenes. In both the writing and the acting, *Without Love* is theater on the surface of a vacuum.'' The play did fair business and eventually showed a profit after MGM purchased the screen rights.

During the run of *Without Love,* Kate became very concerned about supporting the war effort. Earlier, at Eleanor Roosevelt's request, she had donated her services as narrator of an Office of War Information film, *Women in Defense.* Now, in the winter of 1943, she took an interest in the Stage Door Canteen, which was run by the American Theatre Wing in the basement of the 44th Street Theatre. Staffed by show-business volunteers, the canteen was a combination soup kitchen and nightclub where servicemen could relax and dance with the stars. Kate popped in and out occasionally, and when she learned that United Artists was planning a film about the canteen, with all profits going to the Theatre Wing, she agreed to participate.

More than sixty-five stars appeared in *Stage Door Canteen,* most of them in small cameo roles—Gracie Fields recites the Lord's Prayer, Katharine Cornell performs Juliet's balcony scene, Lynn Fontanne dishes out doughnuts. Hepburn, however, has quite a bit of footage; playing herself, she consoles a young girl (Cheryl Walker) whose fiancé (William Terry) is being shipped overseas. Her scenes were shot in New York while she was appearing in *Without Love.*

After the opening of the Barry comedy, Spencer came to New York and spent a few weeks with Kate. (To prevent gossip, he stayed at the Waldorf Towers.) It was a happy reunion, with therapeutic side effects: Hepburn was depressed about *Without Love,* but with Tracy's help, she relaxed and forgot her career problems.

This was Tracy's first long visit to New York in some

time. He liked the city, and, as the days passed, began to feel an itch to return to Broadway. Kate also talked about future stage appearances for the Theatre Guild, but she couldn't find a suitable script. When *Without Love* closed, she returned to Hollywood with Tracy, and both went back to work at MGM.

13

The Rugged Path

On their return from New York, Spencer started filming *A Guy Named Joe* while Kate slanted her eyes, sucked in her cheeks, and started work on Pearl S. Buck's *Dragon Seed* as Jade, an enlightened peasant who dreams of "a New China" and dreads the Japanese peril. It was an absurd role for Hepburn, but it was her way of making another contribution to the war effort.

She threw herself into the project, reading everything available on Chinese history and culture, and winding up with enough information for a doctoral thesis. Kate always did a lot of homework for her roles, and whatever information she culled from her reading was shared with her collaborators. She always had something to say about the decor, the costumes, the photography, the direction, and frequently played an active part in the writing or revision of the script. On *Dragon Seed*, she often sat in on story conferences, and watched with fascination as the art department began construction on the sets.

MGM hoped *Dragon Seed* would be as prestigious as *The Good Earth*, one of the studio's most honored productions of the 1930s. No expense was spared in making the physical production look authentic. Pearl Buck decided that sections of the San Fernando Valley bore a striking resemblance to the Chinese countryside, so MGM terraced the California earth, reterraced it, and finally painted it to bring out the contours. Pipelines were run across the valley, the land was flooded, and rice paddies appeared overnight. Farms and entire Chinese villages were erected in minute detail. MGM spent $2,000,000 on its Chinese Disneyland, and then populated it with (in the words of critic James Agee) "such distinguished Chinese as Walter Huston and Aline MacMahon and Akim Tamiroff and Agnes Moorehead and Turhan Bey."

Dragon Seed was nearly as long and reverential as *The Good Earth*, but critics didn't find it nearly as uplifting. The reviews were middling, with Walter Huston and Aline MacMahon as Mr. and Mrs. Ling Tan, Jade's in-laws, being singled out for praise. Kate was not so well received. James Agee decided he couldn't begin to describe how "awful and silly" she looked in "her shrewdly tailored Peck and Peckish pajamas," and Archer Winsten of the New York *Post* noted that "her memorable timbre defies all attempts at disguise."

While making *Dragon Seed*, Hepburn became fascinated with the idea of filming Eugene O'Neill's *Mourning Becomes Electra*. Lawrence Langner suggested the play—he wanted to help O'Neill, who was then pressed for money—and Kate, who had admired the playwright since she saw *Anna Christie* in 1924, responded enthusiastically. She wanted to make the picture with Greta Garbo playing her mother—a strange notion considering that Garbo is (at most) only five years older than Hepburn. At first, because of O'Neill's reputation, Louis B. Mayer was receptive, but when he learned that the play dealt with adultery, matricide, and incest, he shouted, "Over my dead body! This studio produces only wholesome family films!"

Instead of Garbo and O'Neill, Kate took on Tracy and *Without Love* as her next film project. Mayer didn't like the Barry comedy, but producer Lawrence S. Weingarten (an intimate of the Hepburn-Tracy-Cukor circle) convinced him that with a little editing, the play had the makings of a good picture. Donald Ogden Stewart turned in a screenplay that eliminated Barry's political message and kept only the romantic framework of the comedy. In the movie, the leading male character is a scientist who needs a place to work. He meets Jamie Rowan, a wealthy Washington, D.C., widow who feels guilty about living alone when there's a housing crisis in the capital. She offers him the basement of her mansion as a laboratory and they decide to marry "without love." Then, after months of batting eyes (Hepburn) and brusque put-downs (Tracy), they give up their bunk beds and kiss each other good night.

While the film was in production, director Harold S. Bucquet told a reporter, "Miss Hepburn requires direction, for she tends to act too much. Her acting is much less economical than Mr. Tracy's, but his style is rubbing off on her. The important thing is that I don't coach them on their scenes together—they know exactly what they want to accomplish when we begin a scene."

Left to their own devices, Spencer comes off as a brick while Kate is very mannered—little of his simplicity has rubbed off on her in this film. Every other line she exclaims "By gum!" and she romps about wearing polka dots, ostrich feathers, and a floppy leghorn hat larger than a family-sized pizza. She's rarely been so arch and girlish, and for a woman of her age, this kind of affectation seems a bit old-maidish. This is the beginning of that period when Hepburn became very self-conscious about her neck. She was right—it's not her most attractive feature—but no one paid much attention until she started clutching at her throat or covering it with scarves and high collars.

When *Without Love* opened in March 1945, it was a great success. Today, it seems the weakest of all the Tracy-Hepburn comedies, with nothing to recommend it but a pair of stylish, scene-stealing performances by Lucille Ball and Keenan Wynn.

In 1943 a gossip columnist reported that "Katharine Hepburn's romance with a well-known actor is just about over." If there really was a rift, it was soon patched up, and by 1945, the bond between Tracy and Hepburn was stronger than ever. With her aid, he had learned to control his drinking, but his health was permanently damaged—he suffered from insomnia, nerves, poor digestion, a weak heart, and a bladder ailment. Beyond that, he was also a hypochondriac. Hepburn mothered him, nursed him, fed him, cued him, lent him moral support, got him from one day to the next.

As a young girl Kate had been taught nothing about cooking or any other form of domestic science, but in later life, she never felt that housework was beneath her. A fanatic about cleanliness, she often scrubbed down her own dressing rooms, and sometimes washed walls and floors, an occupation she found relaxing and absorbing. She also enjoyed puttering around the kitchen, and by mastering one dish at a time, she soon built up a large culinary repertoire with special emphasis on baked goods—cookies, brownies (a specialty), cakes, and pies. There wasn't always time for her to cook, but when she was free, she took pleasure in preparing meals for her friends.

Besides keeping a watchful eye on Tracy's diet and health, Kate also advised him on his career. He always consulted her before making any decision, and Kate, who believed in taking risks, probably encouraged him to return to the stage. If so, she made a mistake. This unhappy chapter in Spencer's life began in early 1945 when he received the script of Robert E. Sherwood's *The Rugged Path*. Tracy liked the play, but was nervous about returning to Broadway after a fifteen-year absence. He mulled over the decision for several weeks, and then decided to go ahead with one contractual stipulation: if unhappy about his performance, he could give two weeks' notice at any time during rehearsals, tryouts, or the Broadway run.

In June, Spencer and his brother Carroll (who acted as his manager) came east by train and moved into a suite in the Waldorf Towers. A few days later, Kate arrived at her Turtle Bay townhouse. The couple spent a few weekends at Fenwick—Spencer was amused by the Hepburns' outspoken concern for "the Negroes, the slums, the Puerto Ricans, the homeless, the hungry"—but most of their time was spent on preliminary work for *The Rugged Path*.

One pressing problem was the choice of director, with everyone's top candidate being Garson Kanin. Kate's old beau had come up in the world—since 1937 he had directed several hit films and married Broadway actress and author Ruth Gordon. At the time of *The Rugged Path*, Kanin was in the Army, but as President Roosevelt's chief speechwriter, Sherwood had clout with the war office, and by pulling strings, he got the director a leave of absence.

When he checked in at *The Rugged Path*, Kanin was thirty-three, prematurely bald, and still dressed in his captain's uniform. All smiles on the day of his first meeting with Tracy and Sherwood, he told a reporter that he was very happy to be back in civilian life, but after a few days of rehearsals, he probably wished he had never left the service: Army life was a pushover compared to steering a diffident star through an indifferent play.

Sherwood's drama opens with a flashback into the not-so-distant past: newspaper editor Morey Vinion alienates his publisher by insisting that Hitler and fascism must be stopped, and that America must help in the battle. The first act ends as Vinion is fired from his post. In the next scene he is working as a cook on an American destroyer—he has decided it is action, not words, that counts. The destroyer sinks and Vinion makes his way to a Philippine island where he joins a guerrilla detachment. At the end of the play, he is killed, and Congress awards him a posthumous medal for conspicuous bravery.

The play has moments of excitement, but overall it is an interminable succession of speeches, all high-minded, incontrovertible, and intelligently simplified for the Broadway audience. Besides being long-winded and undramatic, Sherwood's lectures against isolationism were dated and irrelevant by 1945. And his idealistic protagonist is abstractly and illogically motivated: does a bad cook serve the cause of freedom better than a competent writer? Sherwood seemed to think so, but audiences were always puzzled by Vinion's change of profession.

Rehearsals began in August, and things went smoothly enough at first, though there were rumors that Kate was getting into everyone's hair—she washed down the dressing rooms, bossed, interfered, and protected Tracy until the producers talked about shipping her to Siberia. Later, they were glad she was around.

The trouble started on the opening night of the tryout engagement in Providence, Rhode Island. Just before the curtain went up, Tracy came down with a virulent case of the jitters. Kate nursed him and saw him through his first entrance; then she sneaked in the auditorium and watched the show from a front-row seat. At intermission, instead of heading for the lobby and lighting up for the cigarette break, the audience streamed down the aisles and gawked at Hepburn. It was a bad omen—Kate's presence was creating more of a furor than Tracy's performance.

As Spencer later said, "The reviews weren't mixed, they were *bad*." And they were even worse in Washington. An atmosphere of failure settled over the production as Tracy and Kanin came close to blows over differences of interpretation. Spencer couldn't gauge the impact of his performance; in the opening scenes his personality came across the footlights with the same force as from the screen, but later on, he overplayed as he struggled to make sense of Vinion's conversion from editor to cook. Kate knew he was in agony and wondered if he had the fortitude to face a Broadway opening. Taking aside one of the producers, she warned, "I think it will take a lot of courage to open in New York, and Spencer doesn't have that kind of courage."

From Washington, the show moved to Boston, where the reviews were so bad that Tracy decided to quit. It was too late to find a replacement, and the producers had just about decided to close the play when Spencer changed his mind. Kate convinced him that desertion would be far more damaging to his reputation than bad reviews from the Broadway critics.

When Tracy returned to the show, it was agreed that the New York opening would be postponed for a week of revision and rehearsal. All along the tour, Sherwood kept rewriting, and now, at Spencer's suggestion, he changed the framework of the play and scrapped two characters. Another Tracy suggestion, intended to ease the transition of Vinion between Acts I and II, was not followed, and without some correction in this area, the play was doomed to failure.

On November 10, 1945, *The Rugged Path* opened at the Plymouth Theatre. Backstage, Kate watched over Tracy, mopped his brow, and looked on from the wings as he made his first entrance. It was a long, tedious evening, but at the end, the audience rose and cheered Tracy.

After the premiere, Sherwood and his wife Madeline gave a dinner party for Spencer, his brother Carroll, Kate, the Kanins, and other close friends. It was a nice evening until the reviews arrived. There was praise for Tracy and Kanin, but the play was panned. "Spencer Tracy is one of the easiest, most effortless of all actors," wrote Lewis Nichols of *The New York Times*, "but an air of the lecture platform hangs over the evening." The weekly reviewers were equally harsh. "Mr. Tracy has a difficult assignment," wrote George Jean Nathan, "but he gave a performance that injected at least a superficial belief into the unbelievable materials provided him."

During the run, Tracy went to a few parties, visited some old Broadway friends, and saw Laurette Taylor, one of his idols, in *The Glass Menagerie*. (On his opening night, Miss Taylor sent Spencer a bouquet of flowers with a note that said he was one of her favorite actors.) But most of his offstage time was spent in seclusion with only Kate and Carroll for company. He was befuddled by the reaction to the play. "I can't say I'm enjoying it," he told an interviewer from *The New Yorker*. "I'm gratified at my personal reception by the critics, but I'm sorry they didn't like the play. I've looked up the records of plays that have been panned, plays with so-called stars in them, and I've never seen an instance of a serious play holding up under the kind of reviews we've had. . . . Still our audiences give us hearty, healthy applause. I'm frankly a little confused."

An actor makes a flop film and it takes six weeks of his life; on stage, he has to live with his flop as long as audiences fill the theater. It can be an enervating experience, and rumors abounded that Tracy wanted out as soon as possible. For the first week or so, *The Rugged Path* played to standing room only, then business began to dwindle. Trying to keep Tracy happy, the producers padded box-office statements and sent him every word of praise that could be culled from the press.

"I'll stay with the show until my boy John, who is flying from California soon, has seen it," Tracy told *The New Yorker*. "He wants to see me act on the stage." John arrived, saw the play, and then Spencer tendered his resignation. *The Rugged Path* closed in January 1946, after eighty-one performances.

"I'd like to come back in another play by Robert Sherwood," Tracy said, but around Broadway people shook their heads and predicted that he would never return to the stage. They were right.

14

Kate
the Red Menace

Every so often Kate decided it was time she found a permanent California home. Sometimes she wanted a piece of land, sometimes a house with a spectacular view, perfect plumbing, and absolute privacy. Enlisting the aid of realtors and friends, she'd scour the Los Angeles area, climbing hills, braving brambles and bumpy roads, peering into windows of vacant houses.

Perhaps if the right house had come her way, she would have bought it, but her friends suspect that she was too attached to New York and Connecticut to settle permanently on the West Coast. She wasn't, however, one of those transplanted Easterners who bolster their status by knocking Los Angeles. There were a number of things she disliked about Southern California—the sun was bad for her skin, the balmy weather became oppressive around the time the seasons were changing back east—but there were also many things she liked. Her work, for instance, and nostalgic memories, and most of all, the people she knew and loved. Tracy was based there, and for the next two decades, Kate began to spend more and more time in Hollywood.

Hepburn at age four.

Above left: The teenage Katharine Hepburn.
Above right: Shortly after her arrival in Hollywood.

Posing à la Garbo at the time of *Christopher Strong*.

With Adolphe Menjou in *Morning Glory*, the role for which she received her first Oscar.

Left: Hepburn as an Ozark mountain faith healer in *Spitfire*.

Right: With Cary Grant in *Sylvia Scarlett*.

Below: Cary Grant and Hepburn work together again in *Bringing Up Baby*.

In the stage production of *The Philadelphia Story*.

Above: With Spencer Tracy in their first co-starring film, *Woman of the Year*.

Below: Tracy, Judy Holliday, and Hepburn in *Adam's Rib*.

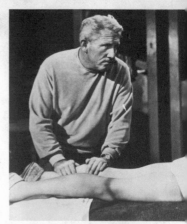

Above: Tracy and Hepburn in *Pat and Mike.*

Above left: Hepburn and Bogart in *The African Queen.*

Above right: With Montgomery Clift in Tennessee Williams's *Suddenly, Last Summer.*

Above: Guess Who's Coming to Dinner?

Right: Hepburn and Peter O'Toole in *The Lion in Winter*.

Below: John Wayne and Hepburn in their only film together, *Rooster Cogburn*.

Hepburn comforts Jane Fonda in *On Golden Pond*.

Two movie greats, Henry Fonda and Katharine Hepburn, in their only picture together, *On Golden Pond*.

As in the 1930s, she continued to move nearly every year. One or two of her rented houses were eyesores, but many were Hollywood landmarks. Of the latter variety, there was the former John Gilbert home and a mansion built by Charles Boyer, a sprawling place with terrazzo floors, low ceilings, beautiful terraces, and a dining room that could seat three hundred people. Later on, she lived in the Birdcage, a converted aviary on the Tower Road estate once owned by John Barrymore.

Tracy also moved a couple of times, finally settling in one of the three cottages on the grounds of George Cukor's home in the Hollywood Hills. Kate spent part of nearly every day with him; sometimes they went for picnics or for a drive or a long walk in the hills above the Sunset Strip. Both were passionate amateur artists, Kate having taken up painting during a dull stretch of her life in the 1930s; since then, she had turned out a steady stream of vividly colored pictures, many executed in a primitive style, which she hung on her walls or occasionally gave away as gifts. Spencer was more secretive about his paintings, showing them to only a few close friends.

Tracy and Hepburn also enjoyed reading, and in the early 1940s, they discovered *The Sea of Grass*, Conrad Richter's novel about a New Mexico cattle baron and his uppity, citified wife. They fell in love with the story, and Tracy asked MGM to buy it as one of his future vehicles. The studio complied, and in 1945 announced that *Sea of Grass* and Sinclair Lewis' *Cass Timberlane* would be the next two Tracy films, the order of production to be determined at a later date. On his return from New York after *The Rugged Path*, Spencer decided to lead off with the Richter picture, and requested Hepburn as his leading lady.

The Sea of Grass is a delicate and elusive novel with

very little dramatic potential. The narrator of the book is a young man who draws on foggy childhood memories to tell the story of Colonel Brewster and his wife, Lutie; his narrative is riddled with gaps, particularly about the history of Mrs. Brewster, who appears only at the beginning and end of the novel. To make the role worthy of Katharine Hepburn, the screenwriters invented a gloomy love affair to fill in Lutie's missing years, thereby turning Richter's Chekhovian Western into a romantic horse opera.

To direct, MGM hired the young Elia Kazan, a New York actor and director whose only film credit was *A Tree Grows in Brooklyn*. That picture, one of the top successes of 1945, had skillfully reproduced tenement life in 1910 Brooklyn, and MGM was probably hoping that Kazan would be equally imaginative in creating the Old West backgrounds of *Sea of Grass*. There was, however, a disagreement about how the film should be produced. Kazan envisioned the picture as a Russian-type epic with the grasslands of New Mexico sharing equal importance with Lutie and Colonel Brewster. He wanted to work on location, but MGM had ten reels of background footage in the can, and insisted Kazan use it for whatever local color he needed. The rest of the film was to be shot in the studio.

"I was too dumb to quit," Kazan later said. "I was in a mechanism called Metro-Goldwyn-Mayer, which was run . . . oddly enough, not by L. B. Mayer, but by the head of the Art Department, Cedric Gibbons. He ran that damn studio. There was a rigid plan about how every film was going to be made, and this film was going to be made in front of a rear projection screen. So what it ended up, to my vast humiliation, was that I never saw a blade of grass through that picture."

Kazan admits that he was intimidated by Tracy and Hepburn. On the set, they were surrounded by friends and long-term co-workers (Pandro Berman, who had recently come to MGM from RKO, was producer of *Sea of Grass*), and as a result, he often felt left out of their conversation and coffee klatsches. (Tracy was a connoisseur of coffee, and there was always a steaming cup waiting for him when he finished a scene.) Kazan insists that Hepburn and Tracy were never intentionally exclusive or rude, but other sources say there was frequent friction between Spencer and the director.

Kazan was an advocate of the Stanislavsky method, which emphasized psychological motivation, "emotional recall," "sense memory," and several other soul-probing exercises that Tracy dismissed as a lot of high-flown mumbo jumbo. Spencer had only one rule of thumb about acting: "Memorize your lines," he said, "and don't bump into the furniture." Obviously he and Kazan didn't speak the same language, and while Hepburn tried to act as translator and mediator, there were many tense moments on the set of *Sea of Grass*.

Kazan was also uncomfortable with Hepburn, whom he considered "a very cool person." To break down her reserve, he asked her to cry in one scene, and Kate was happy to oblige. After *Alice Adams*, tears had become her forte—she wept with such abandon that George Cukor and other directors urged her to keep her eyes dry. Not Kazan: he didn't know her crying jags were a joke around the studio, and was surprised when no one shared his enthusiasm for Kate's tears in *The Sea of Grass*.

"She's terrific!" Kazan told Pandro Berman. The producer gave him a pained look and said, "Mr. Mayer doesn't think so." Kazan made an appointment with Mayer to discuss his objections to the scene. "The channel of tears is wrong," Mayer said, "they go too near her nostrils." Kazan tried to explain that Kate's face was made that way, but Mayer shouted him down. "Some people cry with their voice, some with their throat, some with their eyes, but she cries with *everything,* and *that* is excessive.

Mayer wanted the scene reshot, but Kazan refused. *Sea of Grass* was shelved for several months, then released in February 1947, with Kate's crying scene intact. To no one's surprise, the picture was a box-office and critical disaster.

Around this time, Hepburn became interested in filming *Happy Birthday,* a Broadway comedy written by Anita Loos and starring Helen Hayes. "I had written the play for Helen," Miss Loos recalled, "but when Kate wanted to make it into a movie, I was enthusiastic. I thought she was perfect for the part." Kate peddled the idea in Hollywood, and was surprised when the censorship board of the Motion Picture Association of America turned thumbs down on Miss Loos' script.

Happy Birthday is a romantic trifle about a prim librarian who gets tipsy on her birthday, and winds up the next morning with a husband instead of a hangover. "What's objectionable about the story?" Miss Loos asked Kate. "I don't know," Hepburn answered, "but come out here and we'll find out."

The two women met with Eric Johnson, then head of the Motion Picture Association, who informed them that *Happy Birthday* was pro-alcoholism. "The message seems to be get drunk, lose your inhibitions, win a man, and forget your troubles," he said. Hepburn and Loos were dumbfounded: they couldn't imagine how anyone could interpret this lighthearted comedy as a plug for the distillery industry. "We argued, but it did no good," Miss Loos recalled. "Johnson was convinced we wanted to turn all the spinsters in America into alcoholics."

When *Happy Birthday* fell through, Kate went on to make two flops in quick succession: first came *Undercurrent*, a Dorothy Eden-type thriller about a mousy girl who marries a homicidal psychopath; and then, *Song of Love*, a schmaltzy biography of Clara and Robert Schumann. Both were dreadful, and the kindest thing that can be said about Kate's performances is that she failed to rise above her material.

Hepburn had coasted through the early 1940s on the goodwill built up by *The Philadelphia Story* and *Woman of the Year*, but with *Song of Love*, her career dipped to its lowest point since the mid-1930s. MGM was nearly as bungling as RKO when it came to supervising her career, but Kate rarely complained and always expressed admiration for Louis B. Mayer. Sometimes her friends urged her to break loose. "How can you stay at that studio?" Garson Kanin once asked. "They're giving you such lousy parts and such stinking pictures." Kate shrugged and replied, "Oh, yes, but they're marvelous when you come through Chicago, and have to change trains."

Few of Kate's MGM films lost money, but none registered as a box-office champion. Outside New York and the other big cities, she remained a minority or acquired taste, rarely appealing to Southern or Midwestern audiences. People couldn't identify with her. She wasn't marketing sex or wholesomeness or penthouse glamour, the commodities most leading ladies dealt in, and her singular beauty wasn't the sort that triggered fantasies in the minds of shopgirls and adolescent boys. Kids laughed at her tony diction and aristocratic airs—she reminded them of their maiden aunts or their English Lit teachers. Hepburn's fans came from the middle-aged, sophisticated portion of the moviegoing public, but even this group was frequently put off by the fluttery mannerisms and deadly pretensions of the worst of her MGM films.

Hepburn was a luxury for MGM. She was a prestige star, and the studio treated her like royalty, never badgering her about interviews or photographs, never forcing her to attend premieres or to make publicity tours. All her pictures were made on closed sets. On the first day of one production, she called over the unit publicist and said, "If you want to get along with me, keep the god-damned press off the set. Otherwise I'll make your life absolute hell."

For most of the 1940s, the press kept hands off Kate's private life, and it was not friendship for Tracy, but political controversy that brought her back into the gossip columns in the late 1940s. This was the beginning of the Hollywood witch hunts, and for a time, rumors circulated about Hepburn's "pink" sympathies. The stories were nonsense, but they damaged her career far more than the string of rotten films she had made at MGM.

"I'm not very political," Hepburn once said, "I just believe in being liberal and affirmative." During the 1930s Kate steered clear of political issues, though in 1934, when Upton Sinclair was a candidate for governor of California, her name was mentioned in a list of prominent actors who were being pressured into contributing funds to an anti-Sinclair campaign. Kate wasn't pro-Sinclair, but she refused to be intimidated into lending her name or money to his opposition.

During the war years, Kate was a Roosevelt partisan, supporting him in his campaign for a third term, but losing faith in the Democratic party at about the time Truman inherited the office. In 1947, she switched allegiance to Henry Wallace who was campaigning for the presidency on a third-party, Progressive ticket. At this time, Wallace was under heavy attack: his outspoken criticism of the

American "get tough" policy toward Russia had cost him his job as Secretary of Commerce and brought him to the attention of the House Committee on Un-American Activities (HUAC). In one session of the committee's hearings, he was labeled "a Communist dupe," and the conservative press immediately picked up the phrase and applied it to his followers or to anyone who criticized HUAC.

In May 1947, when Wallace was barred from using the Hollywood Bowl for a political address, Kate agreed to participate in an anti-censorship rally held at Los Angeles' Gilmore Auditorium. Her speech centered on the role of the artist, but she found space for a few comments about HUAC's chairman and chief investigator. "J. Parnell Thomas," she said, "is engaged in a personally conducted smear campaign of the motion picture industry. He is aided and abetted in his efforts by a group of super patriots who call themselves the Motion Picture Alliance for the Preservation of American Ideals. For myself, I want no part of their ideals or those of Mr. Thomas. The artist since the beginning of time has always expressed the aspirations and dreams of his people. Silence the artist and you have silenced the most articulate voice the people have."

Kate's speech was impressive and carefully prepared, but she had been negligent about her clothes. "At first, I was going to wear white," she recalls. "And then I decided they'd think I was the dove of peace, so I wore pink. Pink! How could I have been so dumb?" The pink dress was just the frosting on the cake. As far as her enemies were concerned, she could have whistled the "Internationale" or performed eurhythmics with the Russian flag and no one would have been surprised.

In the late 1940s, HUAC turned its attention to Hollywood in an attempt to prove that Communists had been spreading propaganda by infiltrating the film industry.

Kate was never officially investigated, but her name did crop up in the HUAC hearings. Directors Leo McCarey and Sam Wood both testified that she had helped raise $87,000 for a "very special" political party, which, McCarey added, "certainly wasn't the Boy Scouts." (He was probably referring to Wallace's Progressive Party.) This kind of innuendo was enough to get people blacklisted, and soon Kate found herself unemployed for several months.

Kate was one of the lucky ones; she had enough money and prestige to ride out the storm, but she was deeply concerned about the welfare of friends whose lives had been disrupted by the hearings. Ring Lardner, Jr., author of *Woman of the Year*, went to jail rather than cooperate with the Thomas committee, and Donald Ogden Stewart moved to London when he was unable to find work in Hollywood.

In 1947, Kate joined George Stevens, David O. Selznick, John Ford, Humphrey Bogart, and three hundred other independent producers, actors, directors, and writers to form the Committee for the First Amendment, a group dedicated to combating "the unfavorable picture of the film industry arising from testimony before the House Committee on Un-American Activities." Soon Hollywood was divided into two enemy camps—romances broke up and long-standing friendships came to an end as people declared themselves for or against the Thomas committee.

Tracy shared Kate's contempt for HUAC, but stayed on the sidelines of the battle. When asked about politics, he often remarked, "Remember who shot Lincoln," which was his way of saying that, like John Wilkes Booth, actors often went to extremes when they got mixed up in world events. There were a few references to Tracy in the HUAC hearings, but nothing damaging was said against him; consequently, he had no problem finding work during this black period of American film history.

It was through Tracy and a whim of his temperamental co-star that Hepburn found her next part. In the fall of 1947, Spencer signed for Frank Capra's *State of the Union*, the story of a presidential candidate, Grant Matthews, who throws over the nomination rather than betray his ideals. Originally Claudette Colbert was cast as Matthews' estranged wife, but three days before production she dropped by Capra's office and announced that, for reasons of health, her doctor and her agent had forbidden her to work past 5 P.M. (Her doctor was her husband; her agent was her brother.) When Capra refused to accept this stipulation, Colbert handed him her unsigned contract and walked out of the room.

Capra was over a barrel: a $15,000 wardrobe had been designed and tailored for Colbert, the entire production crew was to go on salary the following Monday, *State of the Union* had a big budget, and any delay would result in skyrocketing, possibly unrecoupable, costs. Capra called Tracy and told him the problem. "Do you have any girl friends that aren't working?" he asked. "Well," Tracy said, "Kate hasn't been hamming it up much lately. . . ." He passed the phone to Hepburn, who said yes—without quibbling about salary or billing or costume fittings.

Three days later, the crew of *State of the Union* was surprised to see Hepburn, not Colbert, on the set with Tracy, and to at least one member of the cast, her appearance came as a shock. Witty, debonair, and ultra-conservative Adolphe Menjou had been one of HUAC's "friendly" witnesses, and, during his testimony, he'd named so many famous names that one show-business wit suggested a revised title for his autobiography. Menjou had called it *It Took*

Nine Tailors; the next edition, it was suggested, should read, *Nine Tailors and a Helluva Big Mouth.*

Menjou never mentioned Kate while he was on the HUAC witness stand, but in private he had been heard to mutter, "Scratch a do-gooder like Hepburn, and they'll yell 'Pravda.'"

To cool tempers, Capra closed the production to reporters who were itching to start a feud between Hepburn and Menjou. Too professional to allow personal differences to interfere with their work, they kept their distance and rarely spoke except when they were in front of the camera. Then the sparks flew. The script gave Kate several opportunities to lace into Menjou, and in these scenes, her eyes narrowed into slits and her voice became as abrasive as sandpaper.

Today it seems hokey and naïve, but in 1948, *State of the Union* was considered a controversial, even dangerous, film. It suggested that there was corruption in high political places. Vaguely pro-liberal in tone, it spared neither the Republicans nor the Democrats, and many of its sharpest jibes were aimed at President Truman. Capra was alarmed when he learned that the president had decided to attend the film's Washington premiere, but Truman loved it and later arranged a private screening for his staff and friends. His endorsement quieted all rear-guard criticism of the picture, and also helped squash stories of Kate's red sympathies.

Despite Truman's support and generally favorable reviews, *State of the Union* did only moderately well at the box office. The political subject matter scared off most audiences, but those who did see it enjoyed the glossy professionalism of Tracy's and Hepburn's performances. Both are upstaged by Angela Lansbury as a predatory Washington hostess (a sketch for her later performance in *The*

Manchurian Candidate), but they make the most of their lackluster roles, and Kate looks very handsome in Colbert's hand-me-down wardrobe.

Despite the mixed reception, *State of the Union* further established Tracy and Hepburn as the screen's foremost acting team. The magic of their partnership had vanished in *Sea of Grass*, but now MGM was encouraged to reunite them in a new film, preferably a comedy with no political controversy, but lots of *Woman of the Year*-type skirmishes.

15

With a Little Help from Their Friends

In the winter of 1948, Kate accompanied Spencer to London for the filming of *Edward, My Son*. Originally she was cast in the picture, but the role didn't suit her, and she relinquished it to Deborah Kerr. Tracy would have done well to follow her example—he was badly miscast as a ruthless, self-made millionaire, and despite George Cukor's sympathetic direction, his performance is one of the weakest of his career.

Tracy was miserable for most of the production, and Kate had her hands full in keeping him distracted. London helped her out. Unlike Kate, Spencer wasn't an enthusiastic sightseer, he wasn't keen about visiting museums, he didn't enjoy poking around in moldy antique shops and secondhand stores. He was an avid theater fan, but neither he nor Kate wanted to be seen together in public, so playgoing was out of the question. Instead, the stars of the English stage came to visit Tracy. While in London, Tracy and Cukor stayed with Laurence Olivier and Vivien Leigh (Kate took a suite at Claridge's, London's most elegant hotel), and with them Spencer spent most of his happiest hours while making *Edward, My Son*.

Hepburn had known the Oliviers since their Heathcliff and Scarlett O'Hara days. Back in 1940, when the couple had been secretly wed in Santa Barbara, she had acted as Miss Leigh's bridal attendant—an act of love on Kate's part, since the ceremony took place at midnight, several hours after her regular bedtime. On the night of the marriage, she and Kanin drove the Oliviers up the coast to Santa Barbara, stood by during the brief service, and were startled when a half-crocked justice of the peace concluded the ceremony by shouting, "Bingo!" Later that night Kanin and Hepburn drove the newlyweds to a secluded spot where they boarded Ronald Colman's yacht and sailed off on a honeymoon voyage.

Tracy and Olivier were as different as two actors can be, but both were masters of their own style, and on first meeting they formed a mutual admiration society. All the great English actors admired Tracy—his soft-spoken, off-the-cuff manner was a wonder to actors trained in the classics-conscious British drama academies—and their esteem helped him through the trial of making *Edward, My Son*.

Back in Hollywood, Kate and Spencer were disappointed to find that MGM had nothing lined up for them. The studio had fallen on hard times. Following an anti-monopoly suit, the major film companies had been ordered to divest themselves of their theater chains, and this loss, combined with the emergence of television as America's favorite pastime, undermined the prosperity of the entire industry. All the studios suffered, but the prodigally staffed and heedlessly managed MGM was struck particularly hard—in the 1947–8 fiscal year it lost $6,500,000. The company cut back on production, pink-slipped many of its employees, and pinched pennies wherever possible. No longer were films rushed before the cameras just to keep a contract player gainfully employed, and even the most resplendent of the stars began to feel the red carpet slipping beneath their feet.

This transitional period was traumatic for many old-time contract players. The studio system, with its paternal guidance and mother-hen protection, was coming to an end, and the road ahead looked dim and threatening. Hepburn and Tracy, of course, had too much intelligence to wallow in nostalgia, but they both felt a twinge of regret about the passing of the old regime.

While waiting for a new assignment, Kate had plenty of time to satisfy her appetite for ''violent'' exercise. Several hours a day, she played tennis with Bill Tilden, the former Wimbledon champion who then was working as a pro on the staff of the Beverly Hills Hotel, and she also played golf and went for daily tramps around the Los Angeles reservoir. Wearing knee socks and heavy boots to protect her legs, she brushed aside brambles and tangled bushes until she came upon a clearing where she could sit and read the books and scripts she had brought along for company.

Nearly every summer she rented a small cottage next door to Spencer's close friends, Sally and Chester Erskine, in the resort village of Trancas. Whenever they needed outside distraction, she and Spencer called upon a small but choice circle of trusted companions that included the Erskines, the Minnellis, George Cukor, Lawrence Weingarten, and two great ladies of the American theater, Ethel Barrymore and Fanny Brice. For both actresses, Hepburn felt something close to idolatry. She called on Miss Barrymore every day, and Fanny became her professional advisor. ''I brought all my scripts to her and read them aloud,'' Kate recalls. ''If Fanny didn't like a script, I was frightened.'' Spencer was also very fond of Fanny—she suggested painting, her favorite pastime, as therapy for his melancholy and hypochondria. The prescription didn't cure the disease, but it helped, and for this and many other reasons he was indebted to Miss Brice.

One former friend was missing from the Tracy-Hepburn circle in the late 1940s. Spencer and Garson Kanin had never patched up their differences during the tryouts of *The Rugged Path*, and afterward, they had let things ride, neither willing to take the first step toward reconciliation. For a while, they were a continent apart—after *The Rugged Path,* Spencer returned to Hollywood while Kanin went on to write and direct his biggest Broadway hit, *Born Yesterday.* Two years passed and there was no direct communication—no letters, no Christmas or birthday cards, no first-night telegrams. By 1948, when Kanin and his wife, Ruth Gordon, visited Hollywood, the feud had dwindled to a point of honor—who was going to make the initial bid for a peace conference? Goaded on by a mutual friend, Kanin called Tracy and invited him for dinner at a posh Los Angeles restaurant. Spencer accepted, but Kate sent regrets—her distaste for eating in public kept her at home.

At first Tracy was cool and reserved, but Kanin won him over with a little flattery. After talking about his misadventures with Florence Eldridge and Fredric March, the stars of his latest Broadway play, he said, "You know, Spencer, there were times when I wished I had you and Kate back instead of those two." Tracy looked jubilant. A few minutes later they were on their way to Kate's house. She was thrilled to see them. For most of the night, they sat up reliving every moment of *The Rugged Path* and its painful journey to Broadway. This time there was only laughter, no recriminations, and, by dawn, their friendship was closer and stronger than before.

It was through the Kanins that Kate and Spencer found their next film. A few months earlier, Ruth Gordon had had an idea for a screenplay about two lawyers, man and wife in private life, who wind up on opposite sides of a court case. For a while, the idea remained dormant, but after their reunion with Kate and Spencer, the Kanins began to develop it as a vehicle for their friends. Eventually called *Adam's Rib,* their script begins as Amanda Bonner (Hepburn) agrees to defend a dumb blonde who has tried to murder her two-timing husband. Adam Bonner (Tracy) becomes the prosecuting attorney. In her overzealous attempt to debunk the double standard, Amanda turns the courtroom into a three-ring circus and publicly humiliates her husband. She wins the case, but almost loses a husband, regaining his affection only when she admits that there may be "a little difference" between the sexes.

Kate and Spencer were enthusiastic about the screenplay. So was MGM. The studio paid the Kanins $175,000, and the film went into production in the spring of 1949, with George Cukor as director. It was partly shot in New York—a treat for Kate, who could walk from her Turtle Bay home to many of the locations chosen for the film. She also enjoyed working with the group of up-and-coming stage actors (Judy Holliday, David Wayne, Jean Hagen, Tom Ewell) who made up the supporting cast of *Adam's Rib.*

Judy Holliday had just scored a major Broadway triumph in Garson Kanin's *Born Yesterday,* and was eager to star in the movie version that was soon to be filmed by Cukor for Columbia Pictures. Cukor wanted her, so did Kanin, but Harry Cohn, the head of Columbia, thought she was fat and dumpy and too plain to appeal to film audiences. He wanted Rita Hayworth, Lucille Ball, or a Marilyn Monroe-type starlet for the part. With Kate's help, Cukor and Kanin decided to use *Adam's Rib* as an elaborate screen test for Miss Holliday: she was to be shown to such advantage that even Cohn couldn't miss her star potential.

Kate's part in this plot was to fade into the background whenever she was on screen with Miss Holliday. Hepburn couldn't have been more generous: in most of their scenes together, she is photographed from behind or in close profile, while Holliday plays straight into the camera. Later, when the film was in the editing stage, Kate made sure that no one tampered with the footage, and as a result, a year later Holliday went on to win an Oscar for *Born Yesterday*.

When it opened in December 1949, *Adam's Rib* was enthusiastically received by both critics and the public. Perhaps the best-loved of all the Tracy-Hepburn movies, it definitely established the stars—in the words of *Time*—"as the ideal U.S. Mr. and Mrs. of upper-middle income." It's a smart and sassy comedy with first-rate acting from all the players (except Tracy, who often mugs outrageously), and for those who don't notice a certain slick, smug tone about the writing and direction, *Adam's Rib* is a complete delight. For those who do, the picture isn't such a pleasant experience—it pushes too hard for its laughs, it's cocky about its own cleverness, and the slapstick manner in which Kate is cut down to size is too mocking and absurd to be enjoyable. Like *Woman of the Year*, *Adam's Rib* is fun while it lasts, but it leaves an unsavory aftertaste.

Despite the success of *Adam's Rib*, MGM had nothing lined up for Tracy and Hepburn in the immediate future. Discouraged by the studio's decline, Kate began thinking about the stage, and in 1949, she discussed a number of ideas with the Theatre Guild. After several months, the field narrowed to two plays—*Hedda Gabler* and *As You Like It*. Hepburn as Hedda is an intriguing idea, but the role is perhaps too neurotic and decadent for her to have handled with ease, and instead she chose Rosalind in *As You Like It*.

Theater people admired Kate's courage, but wondered if she wasn't biting off more than she could chew: she had no training in the classics and her personality seemed too robust to fit any role that hadn't been artfully designed to reflect her own image. Kate knew she was asking for trouble. "I realize I'm putting my head on the line," she told a reporter, "but for me, the personal satisfaction justifies the risk. . . . The part of Rosalind is really a good test of how good an actress you are, and I want to find out."

To get in shape for the role, Hepburn went into training with Constance Collier, the celebrated British actress who had played a small role in *Stage Door*, as her coach. Every afternoon for six months, the two women worked together, and after the play opened, Miss Collier continued to watch Kate's performance and suggest ways of improving it. The show went into rehearsal in November 1949, with Michael Benthall, a prominent English director, in charge of production. At Kate's request, the Theatre Guild arranged a nine-week pre-Broadway tour, which was a great critical and financial success. In every city, reviews expressed admiration for Kate's buoyancy and grace, while the public was astonished at how trim and shapely she looked in Rosalind's doublet and hose.

When the play opened on Broadway in January 1950, the New York critics were sharply divided on the virtues of Kate's performance. She captivated many reviewers, but there were a few who, while admiring her personality and pretty legs, felt that neither the charms nor the legs belonged to Rosalind. "Miss Hepburn's legs are always poetry," wrote John Mason Brown. "Even so . . . I cannot

help feeling that she mistakes the Forest of Arden for the
Bryn Mawr campus.''

Audiences, however, were not so finicky: they were
charmed by Kate's magnetism and personal beauty, and if
she wasn't Rosalind—well, so much the worse for Rosalind.
Kate's legs became the talk of New York and every night
there were gasps and applause when she appeared in tights.
A great popular hit, the production established a long-run
record for *As You Like It,* chalking up one hundred forty-
five performances before closing in early June.

Playing Rosalind eight times a week was a grinding
schedule, but Kate found time and energy to keep up her
physical-fitness program. On weekends, she skied or played
golf; during the week she bicycled and jogged around Central Park, usually with her chauffeur, Charles Newhill, following her in a limousine. (If she spotted a photographer,
she'd duck into the car and they'd drive off with lightning
speed.) During her hikes, she noticed a man observing her
with a curious and dubious look; after several days of
watching her from a distance, he approached stealthily and
whispered, ''If you have such fabulous legs, why don't you
show them instead of wearing trousers?''

After the Broadway run, Kate toured cross-country with
As You Like It, and then returned to Hartford for a short
vacation. While she was there, on March 17, 1951, Mrs.
Hepburn died in her sleep at the age of seventy-three. Kate
was hit hard by the death—she had adored her mother,
and was pained at the thought of never again having the
benefit of her friendship or comforting presence. There was
one small consolation—Mrs. Hepburn had been passion-
ately fond of Shakespeare and she had lived long enough to
see Kate play Rosalind. ''I suppose that's why I took on
the role,'' she once said. ''I really did it for her.''

Only a few months after his wife's death, Dr. Hepburn married Madelaine Santa Croce, a nurse who had worked with him for many years. All the Hepburns knew and liked Miss Santa Croce, and they accepted the marriage with equanimity—especially Kate, who was happy her father had found someone to share the last years of his life. After the marriage, she continued to visit her family as frequently as in the past, usually flying in for Thanksgiving and Christmas, and nearly always spent a few days of every summer at Fenwick.

16

Cherce
Meat

While touring in *As You Like It*, Kate talked to the Guild about another Shakespearean revival, possibly *The Taming of the Shrew*. Before she had committed herself, she heard from director John Huston, who was planning a screen version of C. S. Forester's novel, *The African Queen*. He wanted to know if she would be interested in starring in the film with Humphrey Bogart. Yes, Kate replied, she was definitely interested.

The African Queen is the story of a missionary and a riverboat skipper who fight the Germans during World War I. She's a psalm-singing, skinny old maid; he's a gin-soaked Cockney: they're the most unlikely of odd couples, but during their journey down an African river, they fall in love and wind up as man and wife. The novel was an actor's dream: Rosie Sayer and Charlie Allnut are color-ful, richly detailed characters, and they dominate the ac-tion—the rest of the people in the story are no more than bit players. Many stars had toyed with the idea of filming Forester's tall tale—Deborah Kerr wanted MGM to buy it for her, and, for a while, there was talk of a British production with John Mills and Bette Davis in the leading roles. Huston also thought of Miss Davis as Rosie Sayer, but for Allnut, he had only one choice—Humphrey Bogart—and, to get him, he agreed to change Allnut from a Cockney to a Canadian.

After this was settled, both Huston and Bogart had the same idea: Hepburn would be the perfect Rosie Sayer. "John and I went to see her, entertaining righteous skepticism," Bogart later told an interviewer. They had heard that she was "difficult," that she drove "hard Yankee bargains," that she insisted on "editing and cutting her films." Huston told her *The African Queen* would be made in an inhospitable part of Africa and that there might be all sorts of hardships and deprivations. Kate wasn't intimidated. She adored the book, liked Bogart and Huston, and, as for Africa, that was a bonus—she had always wanted to explore the Dark Continent.

There was only one drawback—Tracy. She hated leaving him for such a long period, and since he was about to start work on a new film *(Father's Little Dividend)*, he wouldn't be able to join her. But the offer was too tempting to refuse—Kate agreed to play Rosie Sayer and, in mid-April 1951, she flew to London for costume fittings and pre-production conferences.

As her companion in London, Hepburn took along Constance Collier. They checked in at Claridge's, where Kate's wardrobe raised eyebrows. For the African jaunt, she had bought several unusual safari outfits, including a gabardine slacks suit, mannish in cut, with ballooning trousers and a lounge jacket with padded shoulders. The hotel manager took one look at her pants and informed her that ladies were not permitted to wear trousers in the lobby. Kate didn't take offense; from then on she used a side door whenever she entered or left the hotel.

Prior to leaving London, Kate filled her luggage with lots of toothbrushes and all sorts of pills, medicines, and disinfectants. This was standard procedure: whenever she traveled, she went prepared for any emergency, and always compiled a list of the best doctors and dentists in each city on her itinerary. The African jungle, however, was not noted for its medical conveniences, so Kate went prepared to doctor herself and any other member of the company who fell ill.

In early May, Hepburn, Bogart, and Huston started on their journey to Africa, stopping off in Rome before flying to their final destination, Ponthierville in the Belgian Congo. There Hepburn was assigned a native guide, a little man named Tahili Bacomba who spoke no English, just a little broken French that Kate could hardly decipher. For real conversation, she had to depend upon Lauren Bacall, who had come along on the journey with her husband, Humphrey Bogart. The two women got along beautifully, but at first Kate was less than popular with the men.

"She talked a blue streak," Bogart later recalled. "We listened for the first couple of days, and then began asking ourselves, 'How affected can you be in the middle of Africa?' She used to say that everything was 'divine.' 'Oh, what a divine native!' she'd say. 'Oh, what a divine pile of manure!' You had to ask yourself, 'Is this really the dame or is this something left over from *Woman of the Year?*'"

Hepburn informed Huston that she couldn't begin work until she had a dressing room and a full-length mirror. "There we are," Bogart said, "a million miles from nowhere, sleeping in bamboo huts, and she wants a dressing room with ankle-deep rugs and a star on the door." To keep her happy, Huston had the natives construct a crude shack, placed it on floatable oil drums, and pulled it up and down the Lualaba River as the company moved from one location to the next.

While Kate studied the local plant and animal life, Huston and Bogart boozed it up and cracked dirty jokes. Most of their double-entendre witticisms went over her head, but their drinking was something Kate understood only too well. "You boys think you're awfully wicked, don't you?" she asked. "Well, you're not. You don't know what the word 'wicked' means." Bogart was bewildered. "Now what the hell do you think she meant by that?" he asked Huston.

Bogart and Huston had a lot of fun at Kate's expense, but they both became very fond of her. "She's actually kind of sweet and lovable," Bogart later said. "And she's absolutely honest and absolutely fair about her work. None of this late on the set or demanding close-ups. . . . She doesn't have to be waited on, either. You never pull up a chair for Kate. You tell her, 'Kate, pull up a chair, willya, and while you're at it, get one for yourself.'"

Once shooting started, Hepburn became apprehensive about her characterization. She sensed that her playing was flat, and though she tried several different attacks, Rosie's personality continued to elude her, and she asked Huston for help. He listened to the problem and said, "I don't know what to tell you, Kate, but when you're serious, you look *very* serious. Why don't you play it like Eleanor Roosevelt? Smile, pour out the gin, smile. Whatever you do, *smile.*"

This inspired piece of advice gave Kate everything she needed. From then on her acting had spirit, and the scenes she played with Bogart were wittier than anyone had imagined. "Katie and he were just funny together," Huston later wrote. "The combination of their two characterizations brought out the humor of dramatic situations which originally none of us thought existed. Basically the humor underlines the story. . . . But it didn't come out of the printed page. It was the surprising combination of Hepburn and Bogart which enabled it to emerge.''

What went on behind the cameras was not so amusing. The sun was brutal; the air swarmed with pestiferous insects; the natives went on strike for higher pay; hungry-looking crocodiles crawled along the banks of the Lualaba; Kate found a black snake in the portable ladies' toilet. The script called for Hepburn and Bogart to submerge themselves in the river, but these scenes were shot later in studio tanks and at other locations—the water of the Lualaba was infested with a parasitic form of bacteria that caused an incurable blood disease.

The heat was too much for Bogart; he was all for packing up and returning to the air-conditioned comforts of a Hollywood or London sound stage. Kate was more resilient, but when an army of man-eating ants invaded the campsite, she agreed that it was time to move on. From Ponthierville, the company traveled to an area outside Entebbe in Uganda, and though the air and water were clean, there were heavy rains, and several members of the crew contracted malaria. Kate brushed her teeth four or five times a day, bathed just as frequently, and swallowed all kinds of pills, but she too became seriously ill. She brought the sickness on herself. Disdainful of Huston's and Bogart's boozing, she self-righteously drank nothing but water, and promptly came down with one of the world's worst cases of dysentery. For weeks, she never left her bed except to work, while Huston and Bogart glowed with good health and Jack Daniels bourbon.

Eventually so many members of the crew were disabled with either malaria or the African trots that Huston decided to finish the film in an English studio. Kate got off the plane in London carrying a spear and an oversized archer's bow—just two of the many souvenirs she brought back from her African adventure. She looked drawn and emaciated, but sported a big grin, which was more than the Bogarts could manage. They both looked as though they had just been roughed up by King Kong.

Kate was still in poor health when she returned from Africa. Her dysentery continued to flare up occasionally, and she was suffering from a severe complexion problem, which she correctly diagnosed as skin cancer. A short while later, she underwent surgery, and a cluster of skin cancers were removed from her chin. While there were no serious repercussions, her complexion in recent years has taken on a permanent spotted or blotchy appearance, the result of overexposure to the sun of California and the Belgian Congo.

After a brief vacation, the *African Queen* company went back to work on an English sound stage, and the rest of the production went smoothly. Once finished, the picture was edited and rushed into release in Los Angeles in time to qualify for the 1951 Academy Awards. (The rest of the United States didn't see *The African Queen* until early 1952.) No one really expected the film to win many Oscars—1951 was the year of *A Streetcar Named Desire, A Place in the Sun,* and *An American in Paris*—and, as predicted, Hepburn lost to Vivien Leigh. Bogart, however, won a surprise victory over Marlon Brando as best actor.

When it opened around the country, *The African Queen* received love letters instead of reviews—deservedly so. In spite of an abrupt and unsettling ending, it's nearly perfect, one of the most charming and entertaining films ever made. Many critics ranked Hepburn over Bogart, but their performances can't be parceled off so easily; practically all of the movie's warmth and humor comes from the obvious enjoyment they found in playing off each other. With the possible exception of Cary Grant, Bogart was the most satisfying of all Kate's leading men. Their interplay wasn't quite so polished as her teamwork with Tracy, but it had the bite and spice that was missing from the synthetic he-hates-her-she-loathes-him-but-there's-a-happy-ending-in-sight skirmishes of the Tracy-Hepburn films.

Hepburn was now past forty, a traditionally awkward age for any female star, but in *The African Queen* she made a daring and triumphant leap into middle age. Wearing little if any makeup, and outfitted in ill-fitting dresses and a large-brimmed hat, she looks like a scarecrow. The picture spares her nothing—her face is pinched and bony, she's smudged with mud and dirt, her freckles and scrawny neck are cruelly exposed. She has never looked so unglamorous—or so womanly. This is one of Kate's most appealing performances: her offbeat love scenes with Bogart glow with tenderness and the sort of open emotion she checked or stylized in many of her earlier films.

The African Queen was the best thing that had happened to Hepburn since *The Philadelphia Story*. It won her many new fans and also brought her a lot of money. She had made the film on loan-out from MGM, and, instead of a flat salary, she accepted a percentage deal. The United States gross exceeded $4,000,000, allowing a handsome profit for everyone, Kate included.

Returning to New York, Hepburn spent a few weeks resting and relaxing. Then, loaded down with masks, archer's bows, and other assorted pieces of African memorabilia, she took a train to the West Coast with the Kanins, who had written a new picture for her and Tracy. Called *Pat and Mike* and designed as a showcase for Kate's athletic prowess, it was about an all-around woman athlete who falls in love with her raffish sports promoter. There wasn't much of a plot, but the dialogue was witty, and the leading roles were perfect for Tracy and Hepburn. Kate was especially excited about the picture since it gave her a chance to play golf and tennis with such pros as Gussie Moran and Babe Didrikson Zaharias, who were scheduled to appear in cameo roles.

During Kate's absence, Tracy had started to drink, partly out of loneliness, partly (according to one report) because he was depressed by the continuing HUAC investigations of Hollywood. After her return, his spirits lifted, and by the time the picture went into production, he was once again on the wagon. With George Cukor directing, shooting started in early 1952 at a Los Angeles country club where most of the sport scenes were staged. The picture was made under friendly, relaxed conditions, with many lines and bits of business being improvised at the last minute. The biggest laugh in the film was a sudden inspiration on the part of Garson Kanin who was unhappy about a line in which Mike (the sports promoter) discusses Pat (the lady athlete) with one of his cronies. The line was supposed to be a tribute to Pat's physical charms, but Kanin kept running up against the fact that Kate's vital statistics were too puny to send the average American he-man into ecstasy. At the last moment, he came up with a new quip and handed it to Tracy who walked in front of the camera and said (in the Brooklyn accent he had adopted for the role), "There's not much meat on her, but what there is, is cherce." As a one-line comment on Katharine Hepburn, it's as perfect as anything that can be imagined.

Pat and Mike is the most engaging of the Tracy-Hepburn comedies. It's very low-pressured and not as clever as the best of *Adam's Rib*, but it doesn't fight for its laughs, and Tracy and Hepburn's teamwork has never been better.

Their Punch-and-Judy sparring bouts are so beautifully coordinated, so graceful and easy that they're almost a complete show in themselves. The film got good reviews and it did nicely at the box office, but for some reason, it is not as fondly remembered as some of the earlier Tracy-Hepburn films.

Hepburn's pact with MGM ended with *Pat and Mike*. A few months earlier, Dore Schary had replaced Louis Mayer as head of the company, and his policy was to black out many of the stars in the MGM firmament. Not very happy about the new regime, Kate decided to go her own way. Tracy stayed on for another three years, working out the tag end of his contract in a series of undistinguished films.

Once liberated from MGM, Kate entered the most exciting period of her career since the 1930s. Traveling far and wide, she played a number of challenging stage and screen roles that extended her talent and enhanced her reputation as an actress. There were to be a few flops and misguided performances, but, by the time of her semi-retirement in 1962, her position as the foremost film actress of the sound era was secure.

Pshaw and "Summertime"

During the early 1950s, Hepburn was courted—in a courteous and professional fashion—by Hugh "Binky" Beaumont, England's leading theatrical producer, who was so eager to sponsor her London stage debut that he was willing to put on any play she selected. The idea appealed to Kate—the West End was a new world to conquer, and she was eager to work again with Michael Benthall, the director of *As You Like It*. One night in Los Angeles, shortly after she returned from making *The African Queen*, she picked up a volume of George Bernard Shaw plays, and read *The Millionairess*, a late Shavian comedy, which had not yet received a major New York or London production.

It seemed inevitable that at some point in her career, Kate would play Shaw. Her parents had both been influenced by Shaw and his Fabian friends, and many of Kate's views on life were modifications or extensions of Shavian philosophy. Like Shaw, she believes there is a natural antagonism between man and woman that makes it difficult for them to live together under one roof; that domesticity can become a form of bondage for the creative person; that the primary function of marriage is child-rearing. In giving up all thoughts of having children when she decided to pursue a career, she was following in the footsteps of many emancipated Shaw heroines.

In the past Kate had talked about appearing in a number of Shaw's plays, including *The Millionairess*. Shortly after *The Philadelphia Story*, she had discussed it with the Theatre Guild, but at that time, it didn't interest her. A few years later Gabriel Pascal (producer of the screen versions of *Pygmalion* and *Major Barbara*) wanted her to star in a film adaptation, and again she refused. But in 1952, it was a different story; she was dazzled by the play's wit and wisdom, and convinced Michael Benthall and Binky Beaumont that *The Millionairess* was the ideal vehicle for her London debut.

Hepburn asked Constance Collier to come to London and help her prepare her new role. Miss Collier accepted with the provision that she could bring her devoted secretary-companion, Phyllis Wilbourn. Kate agreed, but in one of her periodic spells of Yankee thrift, she cashed in the first-class air ticket Beaumont had sent her, and booked passage for three on a small Dutch liner, the *Nieuw Amsterdam*. The crossing was rough, and the three travelers were sick for most of the journey. By the time they reached England, Kate was very contrite. It wasn't in her nature to be stingy or unfeeling; she was always picking up thoughtful and imaginative gifts for her friends—Ruth Gordon once received a miniature painting of the Haymarket Theatre when she was playing there in *The Matchmaker*, and Anita Loos was sent an eighteenth-century print of her favorite Italian resort, Montecatini. To make up for the cheerless crossing, Kate moved Constance and Phyllis into a plush suite at Claridge's, and there the three of them went to work on Shaw's millionairess, Epifania Ognisanti de Parerga Fitzfassenden.

In the play, Epifania has inherited from her father thirty million pounds sterling and one piece of advice : she must not marry until she finds a man who can turn one hundred fifty pounds into fifty thousand pounds within six months. Eventually she meets a mysterious Egyptian doctor who falls in love with her pulse—this is one of Shaw's coyest plays—and challenges her to go out in the world with two hundred piastres and earn her living for six months. She agrees, and before the time is up, she has amassed another fortune. As the curtain falls, she is about to marry the Egyptian doctor.

Epifania is perhaps the most vigorous of Shaw's "superwomen," a human hurricane with so much energy and strength that she crushes chairs merely by sitting on them. A judo expert, she floors one of her suitors and sends him to the hospital for several weeks. The part highlighted the most disagreeable side of Hepburn's personality, and yet it's easy to see why she wanted to play Epifania. The role provides a field day for an actress who's bold, intelligent, and endowed with great vitality.

The Millionairess appeals mainly to Shaw fanatics. It's a talky and badly constructed play, and to disguise its weaknesses, Michael Benthall mounted a posh and very glamorous production. Pierre Balmain designed Hepburn's costumes, and one of his dresses, a jewel-encrusted organdy ball gown, became the talk of London and New York. The distinguished supporting cast included Robert Helpmann as the Egyptian doctor and Cyril Ritchard who played the judo-thrown suitor. Rehearsals went smoothly, though once or twice Kate came dangerously close to injuring Ritchard as they played the wrestling scene. She also had trouble with her voice. The longwinded lines and peculiar rhythms of Shaw's dialogue can be treacherous, and the role of Epifania, which demands an all-out vocal delivery, is particularly difficult. Kate had trouble pacing herself, and throughout the run she suffered severe attacks of laryngitis.

After a tour of the British provinces, *The Millionairess* opened at the New Theatre in London on June 27, 1952. That night, Kate whipped through the play like a whirlwind, sweeping Shaw and everything else before her, electrifying the audience with her energy and magnetism. The next day, one London newspaper carried the headline HEPBURN PLAYS SHAW—AND WINS, and most critics agreed: it was nip-and-tuck for several scenes, but by the time the curtain fell, Kate had scored a TKO victory over Shaw's play.

Kate's personal reviews made the show a sellout for the rest of the summer, and immediately there was gossip about a forthcoming Broadway engagement. Soon after the opening, an American fan visited Kate's dressing room and asked if she was going to take the play to New York. In Epifania's stentorian voice, Kate responded, "Good God, man! We've just opened here!" Kate had doubts about how well the play would travel. "I think it went over so well here because American vitality has a great appeal for the British," she told a London reporter. "But back home, vitality is not so bloody unique." Despite reservations, she finally agreed to take the play to New York for a limited ten-week run.

Kate's London triumph had received extensive coverage in the theatrical pages of all the New York papers, and by the time *The Millionairess* opened at the Shubert Theatre in early October, it was one of the most oversold shows of Broadway history. To have lived up to advance reports, Kate would have needed the combined talents of Eleanora

Duse, Jesse Owens, and Wonder Woman. She didn't entirely disappoint—most critics echoed the opinion of one reviewer who described the evening as "a track meet." Kate had been right—calisthenic acting wasn't enough to turn *The Millionairess* into a Broadway smash. The show finished out its ten-week engagement and closed with only a small profit.

Many people admired the bravura dynamics of Kate's performance and felt she had been treated unfairly by the New York critics. Hepburn seemed to share their opinion. She was so pleased with her portrayal of Epifania that she decided to make a film version of the play. No one in Hollywood was interested in the project, with good reason: none of the Shaw films had made much money, and *The Millionairess* hardly seemed likely to prove an exception. Kate was not discouraged; using her own money, she obtained the film rights, and hired director/writer Preston Sturges (*The Lady Eve; Hail the Conquering Hero*) to fashion a screenplay out of Shaw's verbose comedy.

For several months, they spent four or five hours a day working on the script in Hepburn's Turtle Bay house. Sturges had the reputation of being erratic and undisciplined, but Kate kept him on a strict schedule, and for her pains, received a well-crafted and inventive screenplay. For the next year she peddled it around Hollywood and England, but found no buyers. Finally, she made an uncharacteristic move: she admitted defeat and went on to the next project.

All during her tribulations with *The Millionairess*, Kate kept an ear open to other film offers. At one time she was scheduled to appear in John Huston's adaptation of *Miss Hargreaves,* an English novel about a seventy-year-old woman who scandalizes a conservative cathedral town. When this fell through because of script problems, Hepburn found nothing that interested her until the end of 1953, when English director David Lean invited her to star in *Summertime*. Lean had made *Brief Encounter, Great Expectations*, and *Oliver Twist*, all films that Kate admired, and the leading role in his new picture was ideal for her. She accepted the offer at once.

Hepburn's suitability to the role was not immediately apparent—in fact, when the film was first announced, many people thought she was badly miscast. *Summertime* was based on a Broadway play called *The Time of the Cuckoo*, which had starred Shirley Booth, a soft and motherly actress whose appeal was far different from Kate's. Written by Arthur Laurents, the play is about a Midwestern secretary who vacations in Venice in hope of finding "a wonderful mystical magical miracle;" instead she meets a middle-aged, married Italian shopkeeper who can't afford the price of a drink at Harry's Bar. He offers her the pleasure of his company, and, though she's tempted, her romantic notions and middle-class American morality won't allow her to accept.

In the play the secretary is named Leona Samish; she's a regular Miss Lonelyhearts, a good sport who's too ingratiating, too quick with the smart remarks and Gilbey's gin, too glib to be quite as sophisticated as she pretends. And with two or three martinis under her belt, she turns nasty, bitter, and self-pitying. In the film she's called Jane Hudson, and though the outline of the role remains the same, the details are quite different. Hepburn brings strength and dignity to a role Miss Booth played as an emotional cripple. Both interpretations were effective, but Hepburn's was the more attractive since it cut away some of the embarrassment implicit in the character as originally written.

The film was shot in Venice in the summer of 1954. Kate

arrived with Constance Collier and Phyllis Wilbourn as her companions and moved into a handsome *palazzo* on the Grand Canal. She was enchanted by the city's fantasy setting, appalled at its filth, and constantly annoyed by the *paparrazzi* and tourists who followed her everywhere. The making of the film received extensive publicity; Hepburn cooperated to the extent of talking to columnist Art Buchwald, who was so enthralled by the meeting that he later immortalized Kate's cheekbones with the famous quip, "They are the greatest calcium deposit since the white cliffs of Dover."

During production, the scene that aroused the most curiosity was one in which the secretary takes a snapshot of an antique shop and, while backing up to find a suitable angle, slips and falls into a canal. Later it was to become the most famous sequence in the picture, but for Kate, it holds only unpleasant memories. The Venetian canals are the city's unofficial garbage dump—the water is brackish and filled with rotted fruit, wine bottles, condoms, and every other form of human refuse that can be imagined. Kate was very apprehensive about diving into such filth, but since there was no way to fake it, she agreed to perform the stunt. Before and after the scene, she covered herself with all sorts of lotions and disinfectants, forgetting only her eyes, which immediately became inflamed and watery. From that day on, they have rarely been dry. The infection, which proved incurable, saddled Kate with one of her most notorious mannerisms: the weepy look she wears in so many of her later films is not an artistic miscalculation, it's a souvenir from her swim in a Venetian canal.

A slow and methodical worker, David Lean spent most of the summer of 1954 shooting the picture, and then took another six months editing and polishing it. *Summertime* was first shown at the Venice Film Festival on May 29,

1955. Less than a month later, it opened in New York to generally enthusiastic reviews, though a few critics complained that Lean had taken the bite out of Laurents' original play.

The film does come dangerously close to being a picture-postcard tearjerker. Jack Hildyard's color photography is several shades too touristy, Rossano Brazzi turns the shopkeeper into a matinee idol, and Lean overplays the fireworks and Venetian waltzes. Kate, however, manages to steer the film away from the Ross Hunter school of filmmaking. Dresssed in crisp shirtwaist dresses, a little ribbon stuck jauntily in her hair, she might be Alice Adams grown old as an aging spinster, desperately lonely but still bravely hoping that someone will come along and fulfill her dreams. *Summertime* marks the final evolution of the heroines Hepburn started playing in the 1930s, and by this time, the characterization was perfection—nothing was superfluous or overwrought or unfelt.

18

Down Under

After finishing *Summertime*, Kate stopped off in London on her way back to the States and spent a few days with Ruth Gordon (who was then rehearsing for the West End production of *The Matchmaker*) and several English friends, including Michael Benthall, Noel Coward, and Hugh Beaumont. Benthall was then preparing an Australian tour for the Old Vic Company, which was to star Robert Helpmann, the goblin-faced actor-dancer who had played with Kate in *The Millionairess*. On the spur of the moment, he asked Kate to join the tour. She was apprehensive about another long absence from Tracy, but the temptation of playing Shakespeare was irresistible. Before leaving for Los Angeles, she and Benthall had chosen *The Taming of the Shrew, Measure for Measure,* and *The Merchant of Venice* as her repertoire for the 1955 Australian tour.

Back in the States, Hepburn studied her new roles with her great friend, Constance Collier, who died on April 25, 1955, only a few weeks before the start of the Australian tour. Kate was deeply saddened by her death, but, in losing

one friend, she gained another—she inherited Phyllis
Wilbourn as a secretary-companion. Miss Wilbourn, described by Garson Kanin as "a treasure," and by Anita
Loos as "a Jane Austen character," is a reserved and
quiet-spoken Englishwoman who abandoned a stage career
to serve Miss Collier. When death ended that relationship,
Phyllis was besieged with offers, all of which she refused
in favor of carrying on Miss Collier's work as a drama
coach. But when Kate made a bid for her services, she was
content to resume her old duties as a combination housekeeper, secretary, traveling companion, and confidante.
Since 1955, Phyllis's loyalty and devotion have seen Kate
through many bad periods, particularly those difficult
months preceding and following Tracy's death.

Phyllis was unable to join the Australian jaunt. Kate
went off alone, joining the other members of the Old Vic
troupe in London, and then flying to Sydney in early May
1955. The tour was sold out in advance, and the reviews
were excellent, although Kate was worked over by some of
the local critics. While her reviews ranged from very good
(Taming of the Shrew) to poor *(Measure for Measure)*, she
was severely rapped for the Yankee intonations and peculiar speech patterns she brought to Shakespeare's verse.

Kate's voice had never been particularly flexible, and as
she grew older, its timbre became harsh, flat, and coppery.
This metallic quality was particularly pronounced on the
stage where the need for projection caused her to force and
push her voice beyond its limitations. While in *The Lake*
and *The Philadelphia Story,* she required vocal coaching;
during *The Millionairess,* she had frequent bouts with
laryngitis; and whenever she played Shakespeare, she frequently found herself winded before she had finished one
of the long speeches. Part of the problem, she decided, was
her heavy smoking, a habit she had acquired when she was

asked to light up a cigarette for one of her screen roles. From then on she'd been hooked, and she had thought nothing of it until she had trouble catching her breath after a strenuous soliloquy or a fast volley on the tennis courts.

Too health-conscious to ignore these warning signals, she tried to cut down on her smoking, but discovered that the first cigarette invariably set off a chain reaction—once she started, she couldn't stop. So she delayed her first cigarette. She had never smoked before breakfast, and with a little willpower, she was able to hold off until lunch. Once that goal was achieved, she pushed on and stayed clean until after tea. The next stop took her past dinner, and finally, by inching ahead, she was able to reach cold-turkey day. At the time of her Australian visit, she was smoking only in the evening, sometimes waiting until after the show before taking her first puff.

Despite the mixed reaction, Kate thoroughly enjoyed the Old Vic tour, taking equal pleasure in playing Shakespeare (''a thrilling experience'') and exploring a new continent. From May to November, as the company trouped through Perth, Adelaide, Sydney, Melbourne, and Brisbane, Hepburn spent many hours sightseeing and touring the surrounding countryside. Later she told a reporter that Australia was just as exciting as Africa, and it was much more comfortable for the tourist—there were no invader ants or debilitating diseases to spoil one's pleasure.

Before leaving for Australia, Kate had committed herself to starring with Bob Hope in a Ben Hecht film called *The Iron Petticoat*. Shot in London, the production was overrun with difficulties and conflicting interests, and it turned out to be the worst film of Hepburn's career. Making it was an ordeal for Kate, who was preoccupied with bad news about Tracy. During her absence, he had started work on a Western called *Tribute to a Bad Man,* which had been shot on location in the Colorado Rockies. Lonely and suffering from the high mountain altitude, Tracy had begun drinking and had disappeared from the production for several days. Director Robert Wise stopped filming, and after a series of arguments and hurried conferences, MGM decided to replace Spencer with James Cagney. The studio also terminated Tracy's contract and gave him a pension.

A few weeks later, Tracy signed on for a Paramount movie that presented similar problems. *The Mountain,* the story of a plane crash in the Alps, was filmed on location near Chamonix, France, and once again Spencer suffered severely from the high altitude. He got through the production without any mishaps, but both he and Kate were happy to return to Hollywood in early 1956. From then on, Hepburn usually traveled with Tracy whenever he went on location; she stayed in the background as much as possible, but was always close at hand in case of emergency.

This arrangement started in the spring of 1956 when she accompanied Spencer to Cuba for the filming of *The Old Man and the Sea.* The picture was the brainchild of Leland Hayward, who had left the agency business in the late 1940s to become one of Broadway's most successful producers—his list of hit productions included *Mr. Roberts, South Pacific,* and *Call Me Madam.* In 1952 he visited Ernest Hemingway in Havana, and was one of the first to read the manuscript of *Old Man and the Sea.* Enormously impressed by the novel, Hayward arranged for its publication in *Life,* and later sold the screen rights to Warner Bros. for $175,000. The studio hired him as producer, and, as star, he chose Tracy.

From the outset, the making of *The Old Man and the Sea* was a nightmare. The flight to Havana was very choppy, and Spencer, who had never been keen on flying, was shaking by the time the plane landed. His first meeting with Hemingway was a fiasco; he couldn't adjust to the discomforts of the small Cuban village chosen as the film's chief location; he suffered terribly from the heat; he was upset by the long delays caused by the changeable weather conditions; he was unhappy with his director, Fred Zinnemann.

Tracy had worked compatibly with Zinnemann on an earlier film *(The Seventh Cross)*, but on this occasion, as the picture went way over its schedule and budget, he became disgruntled and difficult. Kate knew he was miserable and urged him to speak to Leland Hayward, who was also disturbed by the constant delays in production. After conferences with Tracy and Hepburn, Hayward approached Zinnemann, who withdrew from the film. A few days later, it was decided to finish *The Old Man and the Sea* in a tank on the Warner Bros. lot with John Sturges directing.

While Tracy went to battle with a rubber marlin in the Warner Bros. tank, Hepburn was working at Paramount in *The Rainmaker*, an adaptation of a Broadway comedy about a con man who brings rain to Kansas and romance to the parched heart of a twenty-seven-year-old spinster named Lizzy Curry. The play is cornbelt James M. Barrie, but it's sweet, palatable corn, and the film version, despite garish color photography that makes Kansas look like Munchkin-land, is far better than the original stage version. The entire cast is excellent, with the best moments coming from Burt Lancaster who plays Starbuck, the rainmaker, as a clownish and exuberant Elmer Gantry. Hepburn isn't quite so good—her performance can't really be faulted, but she's too mature and wordly for Lizzie Curry, and by this time her plain-Jane spinster act was a little stale. Lizzie is a country cousin of Jane Hudson in *Summertime,* and Kate had already made the definitive com-

186

ment on this character in the earlier film. *The Rainmaker* was too poky and whimsical for most audiences, but critics liked it, and Hepburn's personal reviews were nearly as good as for *Summertime*. Both films brought her Oscar nominations; both times she lost, but the way she racked up nominations in the 1950s was just as impressive as winning the award itself.

Tracy and Hepburn began 1957 on a low note. Spencer was exhausted from the extended production schedule of *Old Man and the Sea*, and Kate worried about his poor health and glum spirits. Then , at the end of January, they were saddened by the death of Humphrey Bogart. While making *The African Queen*, Kate had become very fond of Bogart, whom she once described as "a total gentleman, one of the few men I've ever known who was proud to be an actor." In the 1950s she and Tracy had been occasional guests at the Bogarts' parties, and, at the end, when Bogie was resting at home after an unsuccessful cancer operation, they spent part of every evening with him. At the close of one visit, Spencer said, "Good night," and Bogart answered, "Good-bye." Tracy was shattered. Outside the house, he turned to Kate and said, "Bogie knows he's going to die tonight." The next morning he was gone.

At the time of his death, Bogart was close to fifty-eight; Spencer was then almost fifty-seven, but he looked (according to how he felt or was photographed) five to ten years older—his face was crevassed and unhealthily pink, his hair was snow white, and he had lost his lifelong battle with overweight. Feeling his age, he became grouchier than before, and was subject to spells of brooding and depression when he wasn't working. Kate decided he needed a job that would be a happy experience, something light and physically undemanding, possibly a co-starring vehicle so that she could watch over him on the set. She found what she wanted when Twentieth Century-Fox offered her the film version of *The Desk Set*, a light-weight Broadway comedy about a woman whose job as head of a TV research library is threatened by a computer named Emmy.

The original script needed a complete overhaul before it suited Tracy and Hepburn, and though the film was an improvement on the play, it just squeaked by with the critics and public. Despite the lukewarm reviews, Tracy and Hepburn were pleased with *The Desk Set*, and had no regrets about making it. Spencer had perked up as soon as filming started, and as usual, Kate drove nearly everyone wild with her helpful hints and picky objections. This time she made a great fuss over a monster philodendron plant that climbed up the walls and bookshelves of an important set. Hepburn took one look at the vine provided by the Fox prop department, and said, "That's not a philodendron." The prop man said it was; she insisted it wasn't. The studio gardener was called in. He said it was a philodendron; Kate said he was wrong. During a lunch break, she disappeared and came back with a twenty-year-old rented philodendron that was too big for the elevator and had to be carried up the stairs to the set.

"Now," she exclaimed, "that's a philodendron!" She was right, and her rented plant added a touch of authenticity to the picture.

19

Much Ado
About Nothing

In the summer of 1957, Hepburn decided to return to the stage. In doing so, she was helping her friend, Lawrence Langner, who a few years earlier had realized a lifelong dream by establishing an American Shakespearean theater in Stratford, Connecticut. This theater, built at great expense and opened with fanfare and dignified civic ceremony, proved to be something of a headache for Langner and his associates. American actors and directors weren't trained in the classical tradition, and the first productions at Stratford were overburdened with gimmickry and growing pains. Business fell off during the second season, and the management decided to add a few "guest artists" to its resident company for the third year. Out of loyalty to Langner, Hepburn and Alfred Drake agreed to spend the summer at Stratford, each appearing in two plays for $350 a week.

Hepburn made her debut with the company as Portia in *The Merchant of Venice*, and later appeared with Drake (best remembered for his performances in the original productions of *Oklahoma!* and *Kiss Me, Kate*) in *Much Ado*

About Nothing, staged by John Houseman against a nine-teenth-century Texas setting. Kate had very definite plans about how she was going to play her two roles, and, according to cast members, there were some bumpy moments during rehearsals since not all her ideas were exactly first-rate. (She insisted, for reasons known only to herself, on reading ''The Quality of Mercy'' speech at top speed, as though she were a schoolgirl reciting a lesson at an oral exam.) She clashed with Drake, Morris Carnovsky (Shylock in *Merchant*) and her two directors, Houseman and Jack Landau. But all hard feelings were forgotten once the plays became popular and semi-critical successes. (There was some quibbling about Houseman's Tex-Mex *Much Ado* and Kate's alternately aggressive and coy approach to roles that needed lightness and wit more than calculation and belligerence.)

Kate endeared herself to the company with her simplicity and boundless energy. That summer she lived in a ramshackle fishing hut clinging precariously to the banks of the Housatonic River; the house had been remodeled, but it was still crude and probably no star except Hepburn would ever have agreed to live there. She found it delightful, even when the high tide crept up and soaked its wooden floors. The cottage was only about a hundred yards from the Festival Theatre, and on matinee days she bicycled to the theater with a metal lunch pail slung over her wrist. Her wardrobe rarely varied; most of the time she wore white slacks and a Brooks Brothers shirt, changing to a Mexican embroidered blouse and a sombrero for dressy occasions. All members of the Stratford company were forbidden to swim in the treacherous waters of the Housatonic, but Kate broke the rule; much to the management's consternation, she went for an early morning dip several times a week.

She could often be seen walking or jogging along the banks of the river, sometimes stopping to chat with one of the local fishermen. People came to the theater early on the chance of catching a glimpse of her, and if they kept their distance, she would occasionally nod brusquely and snap out a flat "hello." Inevitably there were some confrontations with her fans, one of which took place during a performance. A lady in the front row started taking snapshots and, after a few flash bulbs interrupted the show, Hepburn walked to the edge of the stage, and laced into the amateur photographer. By the time she had finished, the entire audience was quaking, but Kate walked blithely back to her place and resumed the play as though nothing had happened. Reminded of this incident many years later, she laughed and said, "It brought out the schoolmarm in me."

When the summer season closed, Kate agreed to tour with *Much Ado* during the winter and spring of 1957-58. The itinerary included Philadelphia, Detroit, Cleveland, St. Louis, Washington, and Boston, with the possibility of a limited Broadway run as the last engagement. About halfway through the tour, Hepburn came down with pneumonia, but never missed a performance, sometimes going on stage with a temperature of 103 degrees. The illness left her exhausted, and she decided to forgo a Broadway engagement.

Much Ado was a cumbersome and expensive production to move from city to city, and though business was good, the tour wound up slightly in the red. Kate did her part in making up the deficit. At the end of the run, Lawrence Langner asked why she hadn't cashed her pay checks. She told him she had torn them up as her contribution to the American Shakespeare Festival.

On her return to California, Kate began reading film

scripts, but came across nothing that gave her a burning itch to get back to work. She was, she once said, a "dedicated," not a "sublimated" actress—she didn't depend upon acting for personal fulfillment, at least not in her later years. A creature of habit, her life went through few outward changes over the years—she remained a private person, she retained her taste for violent exercise, for eating at home, for the same people she had known and loved when she was thirty. She continued to move from one California house to the next, to tramp around the Los Angeles reservoir, to return to her family whenever possible.

The changes came from within. As she grew older, Hepburn stripped her life to essentials; she became more disciplined, and achieved a deeper understanding of herself and those around her. Her life revolved around whatever she happened to be doing at any given moment, and she committed herself wholeheartedly to any activity she undertook. "Whatever I'm doing I like enormously," she said. "I don't yearn for something I haven't got." She was equally absorbed by acting or washing ceilings or observing the blue herons that nested around the Los Angeles reservoir. And she found great satisfaction in looking after Tracy.

Shortly after Kate's return from Stratford, Spencer began filming *The Last Hurrah* under the direction of his good friend and former Irish Mafia drinking buddy, John Ford. The picture went smoothly and it brought Spencer a collection of fine reviews, but once it was finished, he started talking about retirement. Out of concern for his declining health, Hepburn was thinking along similar lines, and, in the next few years, she became more selective about her roles, choosing only parts that promised her some kind of inner satisfaction.

As it turned out, neither Hepburn nor Tracy was ready

to retire in 1958. Spencer was idle for the next year, but Kate, after much deliberation, accepted an offer to co-star with Elizabeth Taylor and Montgomery Clift in an adaptation of Tennessee Williams' one-act play, *Suddenly Last Summer*. In the picture, she was to play the vampirish and very rich Mrs. Venable, an aging New Orleans socialite who tries to bribe a hospital into performing a lobotomy on her emotionally disturbed niece. As it turns out, the girl isn't mad—she's been traumatized by witnessing the death of Mrs. Venable's homosexual son, a poet who had been murdered, dismembered, and devoured by a group of street urchins he had molested.

This elaborate homosexual nightmare is too garish and guilt-ridden to be taken as seriously as Williams intended. At first Kate loathed the play. After reading through Williams' early works, she came to appreciate his talent, but she never shared his destructive view of human relations. She accepted the role of Mrs. Venable as a challenge, and also as an opportunity to work with two old and trusted colleagues, producer Sam Spiegel and director Joseph Mankiewicz. (Shortly after producing *Woman of the Year*, Mankiewicz had left MGM and gone to Twentieth Century-Fox, where he directed such successful films as *A Letter to Three Wives* and *All About Eve*.)

Though Williams' play is set in New Orleans, the picture was made for reasons of economy at the Shepperton Studios in England. Spencer wasn't ready for another flight, so Kate and Phyllis Wilbourn set off together, and arrived in London in the spring of 1959. Once the film went into production, Kate began to have misgivings: the role of Mrs. Venable and the subject matter of the play continued to make her uneasy; she admired Elizabeth Taylor's professionalism, but couldn't make contact with her at a personal level; she was deeply disturbed by Montgomery

Clift's physical and mental deterioration. A few years earlier, Clift had been in a car crash that had shattered his jaw; plastic surgery had repaired some of the damage, but had left his face with a permanently immobile expression—registering the smallest emotion, even the flicker of a smile, seemed to cost him incredible pain. After the accident, he had begun to rely heavily on drugs and alcohol, and by the time of *Suddenly Last Summer* it was impossible for him to get through the day without the help of artificial stimuli. On the set he mumbled, forgot his lines, walked through his scenes mechanically, and seemed incapable of relating to the other actors.

Mankiewicz was sympathetic up to a point, but when Clift's performance failed to improve, he talked about finding a replacement. Kate argued him out of this step, and for the rest of the production she nursed and protected Clift, doing everything in her power to make him comfortable. She became increasingly disenchanted with Mankiewicz, who continued to drive Clift mercilessly at times when, in her opinion, a little kindness and understanding might have produced happier results.

On the last day of shooting, Kate decided to show Mankiewicz how she felt. She went up to him and asked, "Are you finished with me?" He nodded. "You're quite sure you won't need me for retakes or dubbing or additional close-ups?" He shook his head. She glared at him, then threw back her head and spat. A few minutes later, she marched into Spiegel's office and spat at him. Exactly where she spat has never been determined. Some witnesses say her target was the floor, others say she aimed for Spiegel's eyes.

Another version of this incident presents a different motive for Kate's unseemly behavior. Throughout the film, Mankiewicz had photographed Hepburn with loving care—

her face is a chalky white mask, ghostly-looking but handsome and free of wrinkles or splotches. At the end of the film, when Mrs. Venable is forced to face the truth about her son, Mankiewicz wanted the mask to crumble so that Mrs. Venable would be revealed as a pathetic and wretched woman. This meant that Hepburn would have to be photographed harshly, without benefit of gauze or filters or flattering lights. Hepburn wasn't vain—growing old was a fact of life she accepted with resignation—but she saw no reason why her wrinkles should be put on public display, especially when there were equally effective ways of making the same dramatic point.

Mankiewicz decided to shoot the scene on the sly, forgetting that Hepburn knew as much about the camera as he did. When she saw the cinematographer making some last-minute adjustments, she knew what was going on, but made no comment until the day she spat at Mankiewicz. Whichever version of the story is true (and it's possible that both are true), the end result was the same: Hepburn never worked again with Mankiewicz or Spiegel.

Suddenly Last Summer received excellent reviews on its release in November 1959, but it's an absurd film, so self-conscious and overemphatic that it ends up as a straight-faced parody of the Williams style. Hepburn won an Oscar nomination for her performance, and she's quite good in an impossible role: Mrs. Venable isn't drawn from life, she's a literary artifact made up of snips and scraps of Oscar Wilde, Beatrice Lillie, Daphne Du Maurier, and early Tennessee Williams.

Williams didn't like the film, but he admired Kate, and later had her in mind as he wrote *Night of the Iguana*. Kate was flattered when he offered her the leading role, but, after long consideration, she decided the subject matter was too unsettling and gamey to live with for eight performances a week. Instead of Williams, she chose Shakespeare for her next stage appearance. In the summer of 1960, she returned to Stratford, Connecticut, and played Viola in *Twelfth Night* and Cleopatra in a production of *Antony and Cleopatra* that co-starred Robert Ryan. The critics turned thumbs down on the productions, but, for Kate, the season wasn't a total bust—playing Shakespeare always gave her personal satisfaction and her performance as Cleopatra aroused genuine enthusiasm among some critics and theatergoers.

Nonetheless, this was her final summer at Stratford and her last stage appearance for nine years. By 1960 Broadway was in a state of decline, and the best of the new playwrights were turning out the kind of seamy and depersonalized dramas that offended Kate both professionally and personally. When Lawrence Langner died in 1962, she lost her greatest friend in the theater, and though she continued to receive tempting Broadway offers, she turned them all down with polite regrets. For the next few years she was content to stay in Hollywood and look after Spencer Tracy.

20

"Long Day's
Journey"

Between *Suddenly Last Summer* and her final season at Stratford, Kate had returned to California and watched over Spencer, who was making a new film, *Inherit the Wind,* a fictionalized account of the Scopes trial. In the past, Hepburn had rarely visited the set of Tracy's films, but this time, she was always sitting on the sidelines, trying to look inconspicuous as she knitted and cheered Spencer on. A few months later, while he was filming *The Devil at Four O'Clock* on location in Hawaii, she kept up her vigil. "Oh, look at these pictures," she exclaimed while leafing through a batch of publicity stills. "Aren't they marvelous character studies?" Spencer glanced at the candid shots and shook his head. "They're not character studies. They're just pictures of an old man."

On his return from Hawaii, Tracy once again announced his retirement, and this time Hollywood was inclined to take him seriously. He was so obviously tired and ill that most producers doubted whether he could endure the work load of a major production. Stanley Kramer disagreed. He had directed Spencer in *Inherit the Wind,* and their relationship was so rewarding that he was willing to take any risk to repeat the experience. Kramer had first come to public attention in the late 1940s as the producer of a series of low-budget, crusading films that were admired by middlebrow critics and dismissed by intellectuals as self-righteous and opportunistic. In the 1950s he started directing extravagant star-studded pictures *(Not as a Stranger, On the Beach)* that diminished his reputation, although around Hollywood he continued to be respected for his courage in tackling daring or offbeat subject matter.

In 1961, Kramer was preparing his biggest and most controversial film, *Judgment at Nuremberg,* a fictionalized account of four suspected Nazi war criminals who are being tried by a U.S. military court. He had lined up an all-star cast including Marlene Dietrich, Judy Garland, Montgomery Clift, Richard Widmark, Burt Lancaster, and Maximilian Schell, and for the role of the humane, patriarchal judge who presides over the hearings, he wanted Tracy. Spencer admired the script and was pleased with his role, which was prominent without being overtaxing; the only drawback was Kramer's decision to make the film on location in Nuremberg and Berlin. The thought of a transatlantic journey gave Tracy nightmares, but when Kate agreed to go with him, he signed for the film.

Kate and Spencer left for Germany in early 1961. The first leg of the trip went smoothly, but during a stopover in New York, Tracy got cold feet and refused to continue. Kate was equal to the emergency: with a kiss and a few words of encouragement, she got him on the plane and kept him happy for the rest of the flight. At the airport in Berlin, a limousine was waiting to drive them to their hotel. Two blocks from their destination, Kate jumped out of the car and walked the rest of the way, entering through a back entrance and taking the freight elevator to her suite. All during the production, there were rumors of her presence, and the German press tried to track her down, but she remained elusive.

Making *Judgment at Nuremberg* was a happy experience for Tracy. Once he exploded at a fellow actor who was munching a pastrami sandwich during one of the courtroom scenes, but usually he was even-tempered and pleasant. He was particularly considerate toward Montgomery Clift, who had the shakes and couldn't remember his lines. Tracy grabbed him by the shoulders and said, "Don't bother about the lines. Just look at me and tell it to me." This piece of advice pulled Clift through the film, and though his performance is nerve-wracking, it brought him an Oscar nomination, an honor of which he was very proud. (Tracy was also nominated, but lost the award to another *Nuremberg* co-star, Maximilian Schell.)

When the picture was finished, Tracy and Hepburn stopped off in Paris to visit the Kanins who were vacationing at the Hotel Raphael, and then returned to California where they learned that Kramer expected Tracy to attend the German premiere of *Judgment at Nuremberg* in December 1961. Spencer didn't want to go, and Kate concurred; she despised premieres, and she felt the journey would be a needless waste of Tracy's time and energy. Kramer, however, kept after them until they reluctantly agreed to return to Berlin and Nuremberg.

Between these two trips, Tracy and Hepburn received a phone call from Ely Landau, a rotund and jovial TV producer who had put together the highly praised "Play of the Week" dramatic series for NET television. Kate knew him only by reputation. "What are you considering?" she asked.

"A film of *Long Day's Journey into Night*," he replied. "I've been interested in the play for years," Hepburn said. "Who will do the screenplay?" "Eugene O'Neill," Landau answered. There was a long pause. "That's marvelous. When do you plan to do it?" Landau took a deep breath and said, "Next month." There was a gasp from Kate. "Mr. Landau, I think you're nuts," she exclaimed. "We don't do things that way!"

Nevertheless, when he said he was coming to the Coast, she agreed to see him. And by the time of their meeting, she had read *Long Day's Journey* several times. Her admiration for O'Neill was unbounded, as was Spencer's—in the late 1940s he had seriously considered returning to Broadway in *A Touch of the Poet*, but the project fell through when O'Neill decided his script wasn't ready for production.

Long Day's Journey is O'Neill's greatest achievement, a sprawling, self-pitying, obsessive masterpiece that makes arduous demands on both actors and audiences. Kate wondered if she could measure up to the part of Mary Tyrone, perhaps the most challenging role for a woman in all of modern American drama. O'Neill's play seems to give equal weight to each of his four major characters, but Mrs. Tyrone is the pivotal figure, and if she is weak (as was the case in the first New York production), the play loses intensity and seems more diffuse than it actually is.

On the day of her first encounter with Landau, Hepburn was still scared of the part. Landau had nothing much to offer her as an incentive—the film would be made on a tight schedule and a limited budget. He could pay her no more than $25,000 and a percentage of the net profits—if there were any. Salary wasn't important to Kate. "I've never been much interested in money," she once said. "I don't give a damn about clothes and I don't care about possessions. I've gotten tremendous fees when the material was boring, and the only time I've ever kicked myself is when I've done something just because of the money involved.''

Mary Tyrone was just about the best role she had ever been offered, and she knew that someday she'd kick herself if she refused. Once she was set, Landau went after Tracy, but he refused on the grounds that the pay was too low. Though he never said so, it is also possible that he feared the role might be too exhausting. The ghosts and devils that haunted O'Neill's Irish imagination were probably not so very different from those that plagued Spencer, and bringing them out into the open might have cost him more than he could afford to expend at this late stage of his life. That he did not play James Tyrone, Sr., is a great misfortune—this might well have been the crowning achievement of his career.

Long Day's Journey went into production in the fall of 1961 with Jason Robards, Dean Stockwell, and Ralph Richardson playing the other major roles. Director Sidney Lumet spent three weeks rehearsing his cast in New York, then shot the picture in thirty-seven days, working first in an old Victorian summer cottage on City Island in the Bronx, later moving to Production Center Studio in lower Manhattan for the interior scenes. Making the film was an exciting and exhausting experience for Kate. To play Mary she had to wallow in self-pity and other dark, ugly emotions that were alien to her personality; she wasn't accustomed to giving so much of herself, and, by the end of the day, she was mentally and physically fatigued.

''I look terrible in this film,'' she told a *New York Times* reporter. ''You know, I progress to the nether reaches of insanity in the course of a day—but I've never had such a part.'' She made no objection to being photographed unbecomingly—there were no filters, no artful lighting, no flattering angles. She groveled on the floor, wrenched her

body into ungainly postures, disheveled her hair, made no
attempt to hide the telltale traces of age.

Lumet pruned the play slightly, but for the most part he
stayed close to the original script, and shot in strict continuity out of consideration for the actors. There were a
few shifts in locale and one or two fancy cinematic flour-
ishes, including the controversial reverse tracking shot that
ends the film. Otherwise, Lumet was content to walk in
O'Neill's shadow, risking everything on the chance that the
play and the actors would be enough to sustain audience
interest. The gamble paid off. One can peck away at some
of the performances—Dean Stockwell doesn't entirely remove the curse from the thankless role of the younger son;
Ralph Richardson is physically miscast as the father;
Jason Robards is not quite as forceful as he was when he
created the older son on Broadway—but it's petty to look
for minor flaws in the face of such brilliant ensemble playing.

At first, Kate seems too intelligent and highborn for
Mary Tyrone, the convent-educated daughter of a parvenu
shopkeeper. But by the time she comes to the scene in
which the audience first discovers that Mary Tyrone is a
drug addict, Hepburn is in total, triumphant command of
the part. Circling around the room, clasping, rubbing, and
worrying her hands like a latter-day Lady Macbeth, she
starts to come apart at the seams, and the anger, violence,
and self-disgust that pour out of Hepburn are nothing
short of electrifying. Most actresses have played Mary
Tyrone on an extended note of fragile self-pity; Hepburn
knows better—this woman is strong; she's an emotional
vampire who uses her addiction to subjugate and terrorize
her family.

Kate never shies away from the ugly realities of the role.
She goes through a series of extraordinary transforma-

tions, looking young and spiritual in one shot, ravaged and ready for death in the next. In the closing sequences of the film, she floats through the Tyrone house like an apparition of fog, and by the time she speaks Mary's final lines, she has gone beyond tears, beyond chills on the spine, and achieved true tragic grandeur.

"The play is so brilliant," Hepburn later said. "I wanted to play it without really acting it. I did not want to be fascinating or colorful or exciting. I just wanted to keep out of its way and let it happen." She succeeded. Mary Tyrone is her greatest performance to date.

Long Day's Journey was first shown at the 1962 Cannes Film Festival, where the four principals were awarded a joint "best acting" award. Five months later, in October 1962, it opened in New York to fine reviews and poor business. Feeling that the original 174-minute running time might be too much of an endurance test for some customers, distributor Joseph E. Levine cut an hour out of the picture. This butchered version, used mainly for second-run engagements, was also a commercial failure. Hepburn won a ninth Oscar nomination for her performance as Mary Tyrone, but lost the award to Anne Bancroft for *The Miracle Worker*.

During and after the shooting of *Long Day's Journey*, Kate spent many weekends in Hartford, visiting her father who was in poor health. Several times she shuttled between the East and West coasts, watching over her father for a few days and then returning to Spencer, who was suffering from a respiratory ailment. This was a bad period for Hepburn—she was worn out from the strain of making *Long Day's Journey*, saddened by her father's steady decline, and enraged by an article in *Look* magazine that had openly discussed her relationship with Tracy. The story was sympathetically written and only confirmed what most people already knew or suspected, but Kate thought writer Bill Davidson had exceeded the bounds of good taste. More than ever before, she fiercely guarded her privacy, refusing all interviews and making fewer and fewer appearances in public.

On November 20, 1962, Dr. Hepburn died at the age of eighty-two. Kate was there at the end, and she stayed on in Hartford until after Thanksgiving, consoling her brothers and sisters and answering sympathy notes from her friends. Nearly all her friends had met Dr. Hepburn, and practically everyone found him every bit as remarkable as his famous daughter. Kate accepted her father's death stoically. He had led a rich, productive life, and his last years had been vigorous and happy. When he was eighty, he decided to visit Kate, who happened to be vacationing in Greece. As soon as he stepped off the plane, he said, "Well, let's go and see the Acropolis." Kate suggested he take a rest after his long flight, but he said that he hadn't flown thousands of miles to stare at the walls of an air-conditioned hotel room. Ten minutes after his arrival, he and Kate were on their way to the Acropolis.

After her father's death, Kate returned to California and devoted all her time to Tracy, who was about to embark on a new Stanley Kramer film, *It's a Mad, Mad, Mad, Mad World*. Spencer was so seriously ill during the making of this elephantine comedy (which ran for more than three hours and also starred Ethel Merman, Sid Caesar, Milton Berle, and a host of other famous comics) that Kramer limited his shooting schedule to six hours a day and relieved him from all location work. Even with these dispensations, Tracy was exhausted by the time the film was completed; his color was bad, he had no stamina, he was once again talking of retirement.

The summer of 1963 was set aside for rest and relaxation. Nearly every day Kate would pick him up at his house on the Cukor compound and they'd go for a drive or a walk or a picnic. On July 21, 1963, she had planned a trip to the beach and she had a basket lunch ready when Spencer arrived at her house in his Thunderbird. They drove off towards Malibu, and along the way Tracy started gasping for breath. Kate brought the car to a halt, jumped out, and called the local Fire Department. While waiting for an ambulance she also called Carroll, Tracy's brother, and Louise, his wife, to tell them what had happened. On the way to the hospital, Spencer looked up and said, "Kate, isn't this a hell of a way to go on a picnic?" Kate smiled and replied, "Next week."

At first everyone thought Spencer had suffered a heart attack, but after a careful examination, the doctors diagnosed his illness as pulmonary edema. Kate waited around the hospital until Louise Tracy arrived, then she went home. Two weeks later Tracy left the hospital, weak, still sick, and badly in need of rest and constant attention. Kate moved from a house near Malibu to Beverly Hills to be close to him and started refusing all offers that came her way. She never said she had retired—it was always "I don't think so" or "Not at this time"—but around Broadway and Hollywood, when Hepburn's name was mentioned, the advice was, "Forget it, she won't leave Tracy."

21

Tracy's
Last Film

For the next three years, Tracy and Hepburn lived in virtual seclusion. She visited him daily, and when they weren't in direct contact they talked by phone. If they couldn't eat together she sent a hamper of nourishing, home-prepared food to his cottage. Spencer made a slow recovery, but his health remained precarious: an oxygen tank was installed in his bedroom and his physical activity was limited to a short ride on an Exercycle or a walk with Kate in the Hollywood Hills. On mild, breezy days, they could often be seen on a high, grassy slope, gazing at the sky as they pursued a new pastime—kite-flying.

They saw only a few trusted friends, including George Cukor, the Erskines, director Jean Negulesco and his wife, Phyllis Wilbourn, Stanley Kramer, and their agent, Abe Lastfogel. These friends were Tracy's lifeline to the outside world. Although he zealously guarded his own privacy, he adored gossip, and as soon as a visitor came through the door, he started digging for the latest dirt, his face crinkling with mischief as he caught up on who was doing what with whom. One of his last public appearances was made at the Mia Farrow–Frank Sinatra wedding; he had known Sinatra for years, but several people suggest that it was curiosity as much as friendship that brought him out for this highly publicized event. Kate, of course, stayed at home.

Another way Tracy coped with the boredom that occasionally engulfed him during this spell of enforced inactivity was to flirt with the idea of returning to the screen. He read scripts, talked to producers, and came close to signing a contract for *The Cincinnati Kid,* a 1965 film about a group of New Orleans card sharks that starred Steve McQueen. At the last minute, he backed out and was replaced by Edward G. Robinson. A few months later, Stanley Kramer asked him to play the ship's doctor in his screen version of Katherine Anne Porter's best seller, *Ship of Fools,* and, though Tracy refused, he frequently dropped by the set and looked on as Kramer tried to keep his star-heavy Noah's Ark afloat. Before his illness, Tracy had left work as early as possible, but now that he was a spectator and not a participant, he was fascinated by every aspect of film production and watched intently as the director and technicians went through the familiar and tedious business of readjusting lights, striking sets, blocking new scenes.

Kramer admired Kate as much as Spencer, and while casting *Ship of Fools,* he offered her the role of Mary Treadwell, a society matron who bludgeons a masher with the point of her stiletto-heeled pump. Hepburn declined and the role went to Vivien Leigh.

Every so often there was a press release about a forthcoming Hepburn film. At one time, she and Shirley MacLaine were scheduled to star in a George Cukor adaptation of a 1944 Broadway musical called *Bloomer Girl* in which Kate was to play Amelia Jenks Bloomer, an 1850s feminist who'd advocated trousers for women. Sartorially, Kate was perfect for the part, but the original material was second-rate, and Cukor abandoned the project. Later she considered a film version of *A Very Rich Woman*, a 1965 Broadway comedy written by the Kanins, and though she liked the script, she wouldn't commit herself to any project at this time. In the fall of 1965, Tracy was once again seriously ill.

During the first week of September, he had entered the hospital for a prostatectomy, a fairly common operation for men of his age, and one that rarely causes complications—unless the patient is in poor health. Tracy almost died on the operating table. After several days on the critical list, his health began to improve, and he seemed out of danger when, on September 17, he suffered a complete relapse. At one point, his condition was so grave that a priest was summoned to the hospital. For over a month, as Spencer hovered between life and death, Kate and Louise Tracy watched over him, one replacing the other in alternating day and night shifts. By the beginning of November, he was well enough to leave the hospital, but far too ill to think about returning to his career.

Tracy's only job in the next year was narrating a short documentary about his alma mater, *The Ripon College Story*. He was virtually unemployable. All major film productions were insured against a star's death or illness, and no insurance company in the world was ready to stand behind a movie starring Spencer Tracy. Kate tried to keep him amused, but most of their friends sensed that Spencer was unhappy at being banished from the screen. He lacked Kate's total absorption in the daily routine of life, and the long, idle days made him moody and restless. Hepburn encouraged him to get out, but he rarely went anywhere except for an occasional visit to see Louise and his children.

He entertained few guests besides Kate, his brother Carroll, and Stanley Kramer, who was concerned by Spencer's retreat into a state of semi-vegetation.

Once again, Kramer came to Tracy's rescue. In November 1966, he had dinner with William Rose, the author of *It's a Mad, Mad, Mad, Mad World,* who mentioned an idea for a screenplay about a young white girl who shocks her liberal, socialite parents by announcing her engagement to a black doctor. Rose wanted to treat the story as a comedy, an approach that appealed to Kramer, who had already produced two serious films about racial problems. Both agreed that Sidney Poitier would be ideal as the black fiancé, and, for the white parents, Kramer immediately thought of Tracy and Hepburn.

During the next two weeks, Kramer and Rose worked out a verbal outline for the film as they strolled through Beverly Hills and sat over coffee at the drugstore of the Beverly Wilshire Hotel. Then Rose went off to write the script at his home on the Isle of Jersey while Kramer opened negotiations with Tracy, Hepburn, and Sidney Poitier. Of the three, Poitier was the most important from a commercial standpoint: in 1966, he was the only black actor who could conceivably woo a white girl without alienating a large portion of the American film public. At a meeting in New York, Kramer described the film, and then asked Poitier, "Will you play the part? Do you think it's right?" Poitier nodded. "Of course; my God, it's beautiful."

Back in Hollywood, Kramer called on Hepburn and Tracy and told them his "dream." (He referred to each new production as his "dream.") They were excited by the idea, and wanted to know how the plot would be developed. Kramer ad-libbed scenes, made up funny bits of business, and eventually convinced them his "dream" was a workable project. Tracy left the decision to Kate. She was torn between her admiration for Kramer's theme and her concern for Tracy's condition. For the last three years she had devoted nearly all her energy to keeping Spencer alive, and now she was being asked to endorse a project that might further impair his health. Kramer argued that Tracy would be better off working than sitting at home and brooding, and Kate knew he was right—Spencer was itching to make one last film. She continued to vacillate for a few days, but finally consented. "All right," she told Kramer, "we'll do it."

Columbia Pictures agreed to finance *Guess Who's Coming to Dinner?*, as the film was now called, provided that Hepburn and Tracy accept percentage deals instead of salary, and that Kramer personally guarantee the studio against loss if Tracy died or was unable to finish the production. Spencer didn't want Kramer to take the risk, but the director had no alternative; he agreed to the stipulation, fully aware that he would face financial ruin if anything happened to Tracy. The odds were not in his favor. Only a few weeks before the film was to go before the cameras, Tracy suffered an attack of lung congestion. A local rescue squad was called to give him oxygen, and for several days, his condition was serious.

As soon as he was up and around, Spencer told Kramer he didn't think he should go ahead with the picture—he couldn't sleep nights worrying about the risk Kramer was taking. "Okay, Spence," the director replied. "Nobody wants you to do it if you're not up to it. There are no obligations. It isn't too late to call the whole thing off, and I will, if you can't make it. I'm not going to make the picture without you, and that's final."

Tracy gave him a long, thoughtful look. "Okay," he said quietly. "Let's do it."

On the first day of production—February 15, 1967—
there was a brief press conference at which Kate and
Spencer talked to reporters for the first time in many
years. "Most people get grumpier in their old age," she
explained. "I get nicer." Then (and this was the real
reason for the conference), she introduced Katharine
Houghton, the girl selected to play her daughter in the picture. Miss Houghton's previous experience was negligi-
ble—a few stock appearances and a small Broadway role in
the Garson Kanin–Ruth Gordon comedy *A Very Rich
Woman*—but she was eager and talented and very pretty.
She was also Katharine Hepburn's niece, the twenty-three-
year-old daughter of Marion Hepburn Grant. Without
pushing, Kate had suggested Kathy for the part, and
Kramer, who had heard about Miss Houghton from other
sources, had set up an audition and been impressed by
what he saw and heard. He gave her the part without a
screen test.

As soon as shooting began, everyone realized that this
was going to be a strenuous and difficult production. Tracy
was ill and couldn't work more than four hours a day. He
came in at about ten and left shortly after lunch, and during that period, all the other actors and technicians were
keyed up, painfully aware that any blunder on their part
was a waste of valuable time. Tracy rarely flubbed a line.
Nearly every day, Kate would arrive at his house at 5 A.M.
and they would rehearse until it was time to leave for the
studio. Often, when he had finished a scene that was satisfactory from his viewpoint, Spencer would yell to the
cameraman, "Did you get that, Sam?" and wait apprehensively until Sam (Leavitt) waved him a sign of approval.

As usual, Kate prowled around the set, making suggestions, finding fault with the ashtrays and the way the pictures were hung—too much exposed wire, she complained.

Some days she drove Kramer nearly crazy, but Spencer cut her down to size. Once, when she was arguing about the interpretation of a scene, Spencer scowled and said, "Why don't you just mind your own damn business, read the lines, do what he says, and let's get on with it!" Kate pulled a funny face, and then looked contrite and did exactly what Kramer had suggested.

A few days later, Kate finished a scene and went to her dressing room to change from skirt to slacks. She returned to the set and sat in the director's chair, waiting to "feed" lines to Tracy during a close-up. He was on camera, she was off, and, to make herself comfortable, she propped her feet on an adjacent table. Tracy couldn't see her but he knew what she had done. In a deathly quiet voice, he asked if she intended to stay in that position. Kate took a deep breath and her legs quivered, but she made no answer. There was a long, hushed pause, and then Tracy said they would begin as soon as she lowered her "goddamn feet" and started acting "like a lady." Kate stuck out her tongue, wrinkled her nose, and crashed her feet against the ground with a dramatic thud. A moment later she assumed a demure posture, and Tracy spoke the opening lines of the scene.

By shooting around Tracy as much as possible, Kramer managed to stay on schedule. In the afternoon while Spencer rested at home, Hepburn, Poitier, and the rest of the cast played their scenes with him to blank space, and though this is a nerve-wracking form of film-making, no one complained. Spencer was pleased with the progress, but privately he worried about whether he would make it through the production. About a week before the end, he took Kramer aside and said, "You know, I read the script again last night, and if I were to die on the way home tonight you could still release the picture with what you've got.''

Four days later—on May 26, 1967—it was all over. Kramer jumped out of his chair, hugged Tracy, and started to cry. Spencer's eyes moistened, and soon the set was overflowing with tears. The emotional display was too much for Tracy—he got out of the studio as quickly as possible and was soon sitting at home, enjoying the one bottle of Danish beer he allowed himself each day. The other members of the cast and crew went to an on-set party, where there were many heartfelt tributes to Tracy. Near the end of the evening, Kate stood up and made an impromptu speech. ''I don't think you people realize how dependent we are on you for the encouragement you give us,'' she said. ''These are the things that make up our lives. You are the people who make an actor able to act, and I don't know how many of you realize that. But I know that your help made a hell of a lot of difference to Spence.''

Tracy's health continued to decline after the conclusion of *Guess Who's Coming to Dinner?*. He had no regrets about making the picture; on the contrary, he was proud that he had come through it on two feet and with all his acting faculties intact. Kate shared his pride, but she was also alarmed at his worsening physical condition. Extremely knowledgeable in the area of medical science, she must have known that the end was near; she rarely left his side, watching over him more zealously than before and making his final days as comfortable and peaceful as possible.

On the morning of June 10, 1967, she arrived at Spencer's cottage, and found him slumped over a kitchen table. She knew instantly that he was dead. After the first wave of shock had passed, she called George Cukor and the Chester Erskines, and they rushed to help her. By noon, the first announcements of Tracy's death came over the radio: the body, it was incorrectly reported, had been discovered by Ida Gheczy, Spencer's housekeeper, and the cause of death was described as heart failure.

The question of whether Kate should attend Tracy's funeral was a subject of considerable debate—some said she must go, while others warned that her presence would provide a field day for reporters and photographers. Kate stayed at home, and, after the services, a small group of mourners stopped by and kept her company. Later she took over Tracy's cottage on the Cukor estate, and for several weeks she rarely ventured outside except to see Cukor, the Erskines, and the Kanins. Several industry observers speculated that she would now permanently retire from the screen, but they had failed to consider her Yankee upbringing; Kate's Puritan temperament wouldn't allow her to surrender to grief, and she turned to work as an antidote for her pain. "I don't want to think at all for two years," she said. "I'm going to work hard. When I can think again, I'll retire."

22

Woman
of the
Year

Within weeks of Spencer's death, the offers started trickling in, tentatively and tactfully at first, then with increasing urgency as it became known that Hepburn was once again available for stage and screen work. Nothing appealed to her, so she went off with Phyllis Wilbourn and the Kanins to Martha's Vineyard, a section of New England she had never visited. It turned out to be a perfect holiday—Kate loved the island, and as she walked along the sandy beaches, tingling from the salt air and the warm rays of the sun, she felt refreshed and invigorated. She enjoyed the simple accomodations, the plain food, the company of her good friends, and the natives, who made a point of not recognizing her.

While on vacation, she received the script of James Goldman's *The Lion in Winter*, a historical comedy about Eleanor of Aquitaine and Henry II, which had been unsuccessfully produced on Broadway in 1966. Despite its financial failure, a young producer named Martin Poll thought it had the makings of a splendid film, particularly if Hepburn would play Eleanor opposite Peter O'Toole's Henry.

Kate fell in love with the script, and looked forward to working with O'Toole, whom she admired. (After seeing him in an English play, *The Long and the Short and the Tall*, in 1959, she had recommended him to David Lean for *Lawrence of Arabia.*) O'Toole called from London and urged her to accept the part but she needed no encouragement: she had already accepted Poll's offer.

Much to everyone's surprise, Poll had difficulty in arranging financing and distribution of the production; prospective backers were put off by Goldman's script, which was considered "too special" for the general public. For a while it looked as if the film would never get off the ground, so Kate agreed to appear in a screen adaptation of Jean Giraudoux's play, *The Madwoman of Chaillot.* She wasn't at all sure she could play Giraudoux's heroine—a dotty countess who single-handedly saves Paris from falling prey to the forces of greed and corruption—but she admired the play, and was eager to work again with her old friends, producer Ely Landau and director John Huston.

Shortly after signing for *Madwoman*, she learned that Poll had arranged financing for *Lion in Winter*. If the latter film was rushed into production, she could make both, shooting them back to back, but that meant almost a year of steady work outside the United States—*Madwoman* was to be shot in France, *Lion* in France, Wales, and Ireland. It was a grueling schedule, but Kate decided she could handle it, and, in early 1967, she and Phyllis Wilbourn left for Europe, where they remained until the late summer of 1968.

Before she left, Hepburn attended to one piece of unfinished business. Some weeks earlier she had reluctantly agreed to launch the publicity campaign for *Guess Who's Coming to Dinner?* with a New York press conference. Ostensibly the meeting had been arranged so that Kate could

introduce Katharine Houghton to the local reviewers and
entertainment reporters, but most of the guests ignored the
niece and directed their attention to her famous aunt. Kate
swept in wearing the latest version of her truck-farmer
outfit—dark slacks, fatigue jacket, heavy walking shoes,
peaked cap—and she was as slim and straight as ever. But,
though the cheekbones were glorious, her eyes were watery,
her hair had lost its auburn glow, her complexion was
blotchy from the California sun. There was no attempt to
create the illusion of eternal youth. Kate carried her years
handsomely and honestly, refusing to pickle herself like so
many movie queens whose beauty had passed its prime.

At first, Kate answered questions tersely, and it seemed
as if the conference would be very brief. But soon she relaxed, opened up, and began to enjoy herself. Two hours
later when the meeting ended, Hepburn and the press had
formed a mutual admiration society. All the questions had
been tactful and intelligent, with no one asking Kate to
comment on the intimate details of her personal life. From
this time on, she stopped looking on the press as her "natural enemy," and became more accessible for interviews. As
for the newsmen, they hadn't realized how much they had
missed Kate during her absence from the screen; now that
she was back, they rushed to their typewriters and tapped
out nostalgic tributes to her talent and her legendary partnership with Tracy.

This wave of sentiment carried over to the first reviews
for *Guess Who's Coming to Dinner?* in December 1967. The
picture was almost universally dismissed as slick and sim-
plistic, with only Tracy and Hepburn being singled out for
praise. Appraised coolly and calmly, their performances
aren't first-rate—she plays most of her part through a veil
of tears; he is very tired—but in some peculiar way, they
are both beyond criticism. In the final scene, when Tracy is

accused of being too old to remember what love and desire are really like, the movie drops all pretense of being fiction and becomes a private moment in which Spencer Tracy talks about Katharine Hepburn—or so it seems to the audience. Tracy says very slowly, each word weighted for emphasis, that he has not forgotten, and the camera pulls back to show Hepburn, her head trembling and her eyes shining with pride and suppressed tears.

The scene is too much—it borders on the embarrassing, it might even be called exploitative since it draws on the audience's knowledge of the performers' private lives. But these objections don't register until the film is over—at the time, that exchange of glances between Tracy and Hepburn seems reason enough for weeping and lumps in the throat. During the first Broadway engagement, the theater resounded with mass sobbing unequaled in intensity until the opening of *Love Story*, and, at the end, people walked out with Tracy and Hepburn enshrined in their hearts. As the living member of the partnership, Kate had to carry the weight of this adoration. No longer just an actress, much more than a star, she was now a national institution.

Long before the opening of *Guess Who's Coming to Dinner?*, Kate had taken off for Europe with an armful of books on Eleanor of Aquitaine. On her arrival she traveled through France, visiting the castle and monument connected with Eleanor, who had spent the later years of her life imprisoned by edict of her husband, Henry II, the first Plantagenet king of England. Out of all this research came a very personal interpretation of a woman whose life has aroused considerable controversy among historians. "For all her political manipulation and power struggles, Eleanor loved Henry," Hepburn said. "I think a lot of [*Lion in Winter*] touches on something that everyone in the world has been through—the desperation that two people experience when they try to get together satisfactorily. It starts with a dream and no matter how impossible the circumstances become, the dream remains.''

This is a rather somber view of an entertaining little comedy that burlesques the Shavian concept of history as repetition without much progress. ''The year is 1183,'' one character says, ''and we are all barbarians.'' Goldman's clan of Plantagenet barbarians might very well be a contemporary, upper-class American family—their greed and bickering, sexual hangups, and love-hate relationships are emphatically modern in feeling and depiction. The play is glib and occasionally vulgar but, camped up a bit, as it was on Broadway, it can be fun. On stage Rosemary Harris purred and scratched her way through the role of Eleanor, and her elegant scenery-chewing approach set the tone for the entire production. This interpretation was too broad for the screen, and a whole new approach was needed if *Lion in Winter* was to work as a film.

During their first conversation about the picture, Peter O'Toole told Kate about a young English director named Anthony Harvey who had made only one picture, a film version of Le Roi Jones' *Dutchman*. At O'Toole's request, Hepburn saw the film in Los Angeles, and agreed that Harvey was the perfect choice for director of *Lion in Winter*. The two films were as different as night from day, but *Dutchman* showed that Harvey was adept at turning stagebound material into a fluid and visually interesting movie.

Harvey's first decision as director of *Lion in Winter* was to rehearse his cast for two weeks at the Haymarket Theatre in London. The supporting players were all young and unknown, and several were intimidated by the presence of Hepburn. Harvey shared their nervousness, but Kate soon put him at ease. ''Working with her,'' he later said, ''is like going to Paris at the age of seventeen and finding everything is the way you thought it would be." Dressed in a hastily put-together mock costume (flannel headdress, crinoline skirt), she strode through the rehearsals with such enthusiasm that soon everyone was relaxed and on the friendliest of terms. "By the time shooting began," Harvey recalls, "we felt we were a family."

In late November 1967, the company moved from London to Ardmore Studios in Ireland. On the first day of filming Kate left her hotel and bicycled over four miles of bumpy Irish roads, reaching the studio at 8 A.M. The set was dark and deserted, and it wasn't until 11 A.M. that Peter O'Toole arrived. European film production often starts late in the morning as a convenience to the stars, but Kate let it be known that she worked on the American plan. O'Toole bowed to her wishes: he arrived on schedule, was always letter perfect in his lines, and never complained until the last day of shooting. Then he said half jokingly, "Kate was sent by heaven to make my life a hell."

Their only major collision occurred late in the production. Once Kate asked for the makeup man and was informed that he was unavailable; he was working with O'Toole. Kate saw red. She went straight to O'Toole, read him the riot act, and slapped him across the face. Still in a state of high dudgeon, she stomped out, and then, on the way back to her dressing room, she started to laugh at her absurd display of temperament. O'Toole accepted the incident good-naturedly, and promised that from then on the makeup man would always be at Kate's disposal.

After eight weeks in Ireland, the company moved to Montmajour Abbey near Arles, France, and then to Chateau du Roi Rene at Tarascon, where Hepburn's final scenes were shot. A few days after she left the cast, the production came to a three week halt while Anthony

Harvey recuperated from an attack of jaundice and Anthony Hopkins (playing Richard the Lionhearted) recovered from a bad riding accident. At the time, it seemed as if fate was on Kate's side—had either mishap occurred earlier she would have missed the March 1968 starting date for *Madwoman of Chaillot*, which was filmed at the Victorine Studios in Nice.

As it turned out, she would have been luckier if she had missed the entire production of this unhappy film. Just before filming started, John Huston became dissatisfied with the script and withdrew as director. He was replaced by Bryan Forbes whose interpretation of the script did not always meet with Kate's approval. There were violent arguments that led nowhere. Unsure of the material and her director, Kate fell back on her personal charm and well-known mannerisms to see her through the production. She clenches her teeth, smiles bravely, flutters her hands and head, and sheds enough tears to flood the Gobi desert.

Despite the problems with the production, Kate enjoyed herself while making the film. She lived in a rented villa near Cap Ferrat, and bicycled to the set wearing trousers, sneakers, and the madwoman's net and egret-feathered bonnet. The Mediterranean is often icy until late spring, but Hepburn went for a daily swim even when the water was so cold that it chilled the blood of the people who stood onshore and watched her. She and Phyllis entertained frequently, usually at dinners Kate prepared herself, and when she wasn't cooking or cycling or swimming, she was out seeing the local tourist sights or boning up on her French while bargaining with the neighborhood shopkeepers. She loved Nice and the Provençal region she had visited during *Lion in Winter*, and when *Madwoman* was finished, she stayed on in France, ending her year abroad with a brief and well-deserved vacation.

While in France, Hepburn received word that she had won the 1967 Academy Award as best actress for *Guess Who's Coming to Dinner?* The news came by transatlantic phone, and Kate immediately asked, "Did Spencer win, too?" Informed that he had not, she said, "Well, that's okay. I'm sure mine is for the two of us." Most people agreed—if Tracy had lived, he probably would have won, but no matter which member of the team received the Oscar, it was still a sentimental gesture on the part of the Academy voters. It was also a way of making amends— Hepburn had lost the award so many times when she'd deserved it (*Long Day's Journey* being a prime example) that by 1967 it was time to pay tribute to all the fine performances she had given since 1933—the year she'd won the Oscar for *Morning Glory*.

Financially *Guess Who's Coming to Dinner?* was the greatest success of Kate's career, grossing over $25,000,000 in the United States alone. *Lion in Winter* took second place with a gross of $9,000,000, but, in terms of prestige, it was a far greater triumph for Kate. Many critics thought Eleanor of Aquitaine was her finest performance in recent years, and the picture was also lavishly praised. Later there was a backlash of negative comment, with Anthony Harvey and Hepburn being accused of softening and sentimentalizing Goldman's original script. Kate's characterization is not immune to criticism—she rarely gets through an important scene without weeping, her head trembles whenever she comes to an emotional passage, and she speaks Goldman's epigrams as though they were gems of weighty wisdom. She turns Eleanor into a tragedy queen, a gallant and half-defeated old lady who bemoans her fading beauty in long, maudlin monologues. The interpretation may be overly sentimental, but it works within the framework of the film, and Kate carries it off with great panache.

Lion in Winter brought Kate her eleventh Academy Award nomination—an all-time record. No one thought she could possibly win the award two years in a row, particularly since she was up against stiff competition. (Most forecasters favored either Barbra Streisand for *Funny Girl* or Joanne Woodward for *Rachel, Rachel.*) On the night of the ceremony, Ingrid Bergman presented the best actress award; after reading the list of nominees, she ripped open the Price-Waterhouse envelope and gasped, "It's a tie!" Hepburn and Streisand shared the award. This was another record-breaking event—Kate was the first person ever to win three Oscars in the leading actor-actress category.

In terms of popularity, the late 1960s were Kate's greatest years. At an age when most actresses were reduced to playing Grand Guignol murderesses in shoddy horror movies, she was still playing leading roles in prestigious films. Nearing the end of her fourth decade as a movie star, she captured the public's imagination in a way she had never done earlier in her career. She was now a member of that select group of film favorites who are mythic embodiments of certain values treasured by American audiences.

Usually these values are subversive—for instance, Bogart's cool, Harlow's platinum-plated sexuality, Brando's repressed violence, Streisand's nose. Kate is one of the few exceptions. In 1970, *McCall's* magazine elected her "Woman of the Year," a title that suggests Eleanor Roosevelt or Golda Meir rather than a movie star, but it was indicative of the way people felt about Hepburn. She represented what was best about the American way of life, a Yankee independence and integrity that nearly everyone could respect. In the crazy, compromising, circus world of show business, she had done things her own way, never accepting defeat and never pandering to success. She had valued fame and fortune, but had never stooped to achieve them. She had pursued her career on her own honorable, dignified and exacting terms, and made it work. ''Go out and make life interesting,'' her father once said, and Kate had followed his advice with such success that she was now venerated for her individuality and strength of character.

23

"Coco"

At the end of the 1960s, Kate often juggled two or three projects at once, trying to fit them all into a neat pattern, but sometimes losing one along the way. Shortly after Tracy's death, lyricist and writer Alan Jay Lerner had approached Hepburn about playing the title role in *Coco*, a Broadway musical based on the life of the famous French couturière, Gabrielle Chanel. At first, Kate thought Lerner was crazy—she couldn't sing, she couldn't dance, she had never seen a stage musical. On second thought, the idea appealed to her, and she told Lerner that if he was willing to wait until she had finished *Lion in Winter* and *Madwoman of Chaillot*, she might be available.

On her return from Europe in the fall of 1968, Kate took up another project. She announced that she would soon direct a film called *Martha*, an adaptation of two related novels by Margery Sharpe *(Martha, Eric and George; Martha in Paris)* about the unusual career of a gifted girl who goes to France to become a painter. "This isn't a fantasy," Kate told a reporter from *The New York Times*. "The fact is I've always been interested in directing. Louis B. Mayer quite seriously asked me to direct films twenty years ago, as did John Ford, but I've never had a real opportunity to do so before this."

The opportunity came from Irene Mayer Selznick, the daughter of Louis B. Mayer and first wife of David O. Selznick, who had produced several Broadway hits, including *A Streetcar Named Desire* and *Bell, Book and Candle*. She and Kate had been close friends for many years, and together they were a powerhouse combination of brains, energy, and resourcefulness. They worked hard to get the film off the ground, but script problems defeated them. After several months' work, *Martha* was indefinitely shelved, and Kate returned to *Coco*.

Producer Frederick Brisson and lyricist-writer Alan Jay Lerner had been working on their musical biography of Chanel since the early 1960s. Originally Rosalind Russell (Mrs. Frederick Brisson) was announced as star of the show, but later she withdrew for unspecified reasons. It was then that Lerner thought of Hepburn, and, though he knew she could handle the dramatic side of the role, he was apprehensive about her singing. To set his mind at ease, Kate croaked her way through a chorus of "Auld Lang Syne," a song she had sung in *The Little Minister*. Lerner was delighted; Hepburn's voice was not secure and it certainly wasn't conventionally pretty, but, with the right kind of material, it would pass muster.

Kate decided she needed a few singing lessons. During the winter and spring of 1969, she stayed in California, playing tennis in the morning and rehearsing every afternoon with Roger Edens, a highly regarded vocal arranger and coach who had worked extensively with Ethel Merman, Kay Thompson, and Judy Garland. After several weeks of study, Kate and Edens went to New York and gave a concert in Irene Selznick's apartment at the Pierre Hotel; for an audience that included the Kanins, Brisson, and Lerner, Hepburn performed "Camelot" and three Cole Porter songs—"Just One of Those Things," "Miss Otis Regrets," and "Mrs. Lowsborough, Goodbye." The recital was a huge success.

Before the show went into rehearsal, Hepburn and Lerner went to Paris to visit Chanel, who was then in her late eighties. Kate was terrified at the prospect of being inspected by this legendary designer who had dedicated her life to making women beautiful. Dressed sprucely in her best trousers and jacket, she marched into Chanel's apartment in the Ritz Hotel, and watched apprehensively as the great lady appraised her from head to foot. Coco smiled, and immediately put Kate at ease. Her only comment on Hepburn's appearance was made in private to Lerner. "She's too old for the role," Chanel complained. "Why, she must be close to sixty!"

Perhaps Chanel thought the musical was going to concentrate on the early chapters of her life story—a natural assumption, since the 1920s and 1930s were her most exciting and colorful years. Instead, Lerner's script opens in 1953, when Coco, in her seventies, has been in retirement for over a decade. As the curtain goes up, she is bored and thinking about a comeback; for most of the first act, she wavers—it's yes, no, yes, no, and, finally, yes. As the curtain falls, she is putting together a new collection. The second act begins with the Paris fashion world dismissing Chanel as a has-been—her collection has been a fiasco. Then the buyers from Ohrbach's, Bloomingdale's, and Saks arrive, and snatch up everything in sight—her collection is a success. Curtain.

There are two subplots—one revolves around a scheming homosexual designer who tries to sabotage Chanel by adding frills to her basic black dresses, the other concerns a model who brings out "maternal" urges in Coco—but they don't help. The basic concept was unworkable—an entire show can't be built around the success or failure of a fashion show. This fatal flaw was not, however, apparent to the people involved in the production. Kate loved Lerner's script and her enthusiasm and energy spread a contagious excitement among the company during the first days of rehearsal. She arrived early, left late, and pushed herself harder than anyone else. At her request, the theater was kept at sixty degrees, a temperature she felt was conducive to good work. Soon there was an epidemic of the sniffles that infected everyone except Kate, who arrived one day with a big box of sweaters, announcing they were for anyone who felt cold. She rarely left the theater for lunch, but munched on fruit, cheese, and packaged meat as she watched the intricate production start to take shape.

Budgeted at $900,000, *Coco* was one of the most expensive musicals in Broadway history up to that time. *(Dreamgirls* in 1981 cost nearly $4,000,000 and the 1982 New York production of *Cats* exceeded that.) It was also one of the most elaborate: Cecil Beaton had designed only two sets, but they split apart, twirled around, and rearranged themselves on a turntable that could barely carry their weight. Because of the bulkiness of the production, Brisson and Lerner decided to forgo out-of-town tryouts and play five weeks of previews in New York. The preview tickets were snatched up as soon as they went on sale: *Coco* had generated an enormous amount of public interest, and all the smart people in New York were clamoring to have the first word on the show's status. The audience at the initial preview was a glittering array of Broadway, the fashion world, and what was once known as café society. Before the curtain went up, there was an atmosphere of anticipation; when it came down, there was gloom and despair.

The next morning the word was out—*Coco* was a disaster. Lerner's script was pedestrian, André Previn's score was tuneless, Michael Benthall's direction had no color or drive. Benthall had been Hepburn's choice; he had done well by her in *As You Like It* and *The Millionairess,* but *Coco* was his first musical, and he didn't have the knack for this complicated and demanding form of theater. Before long, he handed over the reins of production to Michael Bennett, a gifted young choreographer who was to emerge during the 1970s as one of the top directors of Broadway musicals. (*A Chorus Line* and *Dreamgirls* are his major achievements to date.)

With Bennett in command, *Coco* began to take on gloss, speed, and excitement. Kate gained confidence, but she remained ill at ease in the musical sections of the show, and often wondered whether she wasn't making a fool of herself. Once she went to pieces during a series of painful, often violent rehearsals, but snapped back and continued to look for new ways to improve the show. The beginning of the second act was a particular problem; there was a lot of exposition about the failure of Coco's fashion show, all of which was deadweight and slowed down the momentum of the show. Kate came up with an alternative opening: as the curtain went up, she strode down a staircase, crossed to the footlights, stared at the audience, and muttered, "Shit!" Then she turned on her heel and walked off the stage.

The first time Kate tried out the new scene there was a gasp, then a gale of laughter and applause. The idea of Katharine Hepburn, Woman of the Year, speaking a naughty word delighted audiences, and this one-liner always brought down the house. It was a clever touch, but as people were quick to point out, a show that gets its biggest laugh from someone saying "shit" is a show that can be summed up with the same word.

Despite bad word-of-mouth publicity during the previews, *Coco* built up a huge advance sale, and opening night—December 18, 1969—at the Mark Hellinger Theatre was a star-studded event, with the Kanins, Irene Selznick, Leland Howard, Laura Harding, and several Hepburns among the audience. (One person was conspicuous by her absence: after promising to attend the premier, Gabrielle Chanel informed Brisson and Lerner that she would see the show at a later date.) The first-nighters worked nearly as hard as the actors on stage; they cheered everything— Cecil Beaton's sets, Andre Previn's songs, Bennett's choreography. And at the end, they rose to their feet and gave Kate one of the longest and noisiest standing ovations in Broadway history.

Hepburn's performance as Coco was one of the seven wonders of the entertainment world. The Gabrielle Chanel who had emerged from Lerner's book was a monster, an opinionated, aggressive, self-centered woman of no great intelligence and little charm, but by sheer personal magnetism Kate gave the character some fascination. She let nothing stand in her way, not even Lerner's dialogue, which she spoke as if it were gold and not a steady stream of clinkers. She couldn't dance, and her singing sounded like a cross between a witch's cackle and a mynah bird's voice, but she shrugged off these limitations, and made the audience ignore them, too. There was no particular joy in her performance; she worked hard and one watched her with feelings of awe rather than enjoyment. Still, it was a spectacular display of showmanship, and Hepburn fully deserved the standing ovation she received after every performance.

The critics all wrote flowery tributes to Kate, but their feelings about *Coco* were largely negative. The poor reviews didn't matter; the show sold out on the strength of Hepburn's name, and went on to recoup its enormous production cost when Kate agreed to extend her contract for an additional three months. *Coco* was a terrible drain on her energy—she was on stage for all but seven minutes of the show's nearly two and a half hours—and yet she enjoyed nearly every minute of the long run. For the first time, she realized that audiences were rooting for her from the moment the curtain went up. *Coco* was, in Walter Kerr's words, "Miss Hepburn's gala benefit performance, for our benefit." People came to the Mark Hellinger Theatre not to see a musical or a great performance, but to pay tribute to Katharine Hepburn, a woman they admired and loved.

During the run, Kate had her usual difficulties with fans who took photographs during the performances or accosted her for autographs after the show. Matinee days presented another problem—the Mark Hellinger was across the street from the construction site for a new skyscraper, and the riveting and sandblasting often drowned out the orchestra and actors for at least half the audience. Sometimes the turntable that moved Beaton's weighty scenery broke down, and Kate and the other actors would have to ad-lib scenes or talk to the audience while the mechanism was restored to working order. The winter of 1969-70 was harsh and snowy in New York, and most of the cast came down with colds—possibly because Hepburn kept the backstage doors ajar during performances. She, of course, stayed healthy, and never missed a day's work until she left the show in July 1970.

Monday through Saturday, Kate kept her version of a light schedule—she took long walks in Central Park, occasionally played tennis, and entertained close friends at after-theater suppers in her Turtle Bay home. Weekends, she visited her family in Hartford or went to Fenwick, where, even in midwinter, she went swimming in the sea. She also found time to record the original cast album of

Coco (technically one of the worst show albums ever produced) and to tape a segment of the show for the Tony Awards TV program. Nearly everyone thought Kate would win the Tony as best actress in a musical, but in an upset, the award went to Lauren Bacall for *Applause*.

Hepburn's last Broadway appearance as Coco was an emotionally-charged event. At the final curtain, the chorus members filed past Kate, each handing her a red rose; by the end of the parade, her arms and eyes were both overflowing. In her farewell speech, she thanked her vocal coaches Roger Edens and Sue Seton, her directors and fellow actors, and finally, the audience. Groping for words, she said, "Well, I love you and you love me, and let's leave it at that." French actress Danielle Darrieux replaced Hepburn as Coco, and though she received excellent reviews, business steadily declined, and the show folded two months later.

During the run of *Coco,* Hepburn had agreed to appear in a film version of Euripides' *The Trojan Women,* to be directed by Michael Cacoyannis and co-starring Vanessa Redgrave, Genevieve Bujold, and Irene Papas. Greek tragedy has rarely been successfully adapted to the screen, and people wondered why Kate would undertake such a dubious project. "My time is running out," she explained. "And one wants to do everything."

The Trojan Women was shot near Atienza, Spain, in the fall of 1970. Making the picture was an unpleasant experience: the weather was dry and hot, tempers were short, and Cacoyannis' views of Greek tragedy did not always match Hepburn's. The director had difficulty in creating an ensemble company out of four actresses with such disparate acting styles as his leading ladies. Nor could he find an appropriate visual look for his material, and when the film opened a year later, critics peremptorily dismissed it as "canned theater." After its first roadshow engagements, the picture received only limited distribution.

This is a pity since *The Trojan Women* is a striking, if not entirely satisfying film. All four actresses are excellent. Vanessa Redgrave and Genevieve Bujold give the kind of daring, larger-than-life performances one rarely sees on the screen, and, though Hepburn is too American to make an ideal Hecuba—when she curses her "old gray head" she suggests Barbara Freitchie rather than a Trojan aristocrat—she has superb moments, particularly in the big bravura scenes, when she seethes with rage and vengefulness. Of all Hepburn's post-*Long Day's Journey* performances, this is the most underrated—and possibly the best.

Returning from Spain, Kate took off on a cross-country tour of *Coco*, which opened in Cleveland on January 11, 1971. For Hepburn, the high point of this record-breaking tour was her appearance in Hartford. It was the first time she had played her hometown since *Without Love* in 1942. Kate stayed with her stepmother in her parents' old house on Bloomfield Avenue, and it was there that a grisly incident occurred. One night, as she returned from the theater, she was attacked by a woman who had hidden herself in a closet. Kate recognized her at once as a maid-chauffeur who had briefly been in her service, but she could find no explanation for this vicious assault. During the struggle, the woman bit the top of Kate's finger until it hung by a shred. Phyllis Wilbourn rushed her to Hartford Hospital, where a specialist grafted the severed finger into one piece. Kate was in physical agony for several days and played many performances of *Coco* with her hand in a splint.

In June 1971, the show closed at the Chandler Pavilion in Los Angeles. Kate moved into Tracy's cottage on the George Cukor estate and took a well-earned vacation. She wasn't idle for very long. Four years had passed since

Spencer's death, twice the amount of time she had given herself before retirement, but Kate showed no signs of slowing down. George Cukor was bubbling with excitement about Graham Greene's *Travels with My Aunt,* and, after reading the novel, Hepburn shared his enthusiasm. They hadn't worked together since 1952, and both agreed that *Travels with My Aunt* provided the perfect opportunity for a reunion.

24

Staying Busy

Travels with My Aunt didn't work out—at least not for Kate. Augusta, the heroine of Greene's novel, is a grand madcap in her early seventies, but the book includes glimpses of her past life, and these flashbacks (one of them taking Augusta back to the greenest of her salad days) were so integral to the narrative that they couldn't be excised from the screenplay. So Kate gracefully bowed out, and the part went to Maggie Smith (who was to win an Academy Award nomination for her performance). Hepburn then thought of traveling to Australia to appear in *Daisy Bates,* a film written by Chester Erskine, but the production was eventually abandoned because of financial problems.

Kate spent the better part of 1972 working on these projects, and when they came to nothing, she was momentarily disenchanted with the motion picture business. Scripts came her way, but most were pedestrian or exploitative, and she refused to appear in anything that offended her professional and personal standards. "The assumption is that the audience is totally uninspired, and that pornog-

raphy and depravity is all they want to see,'' she told
an interviewer. ''I find it offensive and very sad that
producers and actors are so willing to sell out for the
money. . . . It's awfully easy in the entertainment field to
talk yourself into justifying the degrading things you do.''

Ely Landau, producer of *Long Day's Journey* and
Madwoman of Chaillot, shared Kate's distaste for the violence and licentiousness that predominated over all else in
1970s American cinema, and, with more courage than
money, he worked out a method of presenting intelligent
films for the discriminating moviegoer. Landau's project
was called The American Film Theatre, a series of movies
based on famous plays and starring famous players, which
would be presented across the country on a subscription
basis. He asked Kate to star as the mother in Edward Albee's *A Delicate Balance,* which was generally considered
to be the playwright's finest work after *Who's Afraid of
Virginia Woolf?* Kate had reservations about the role, but
as a favor to Landau she agreed to take it on.

And there was much to be apprehensive about. Albee's
well-documented misogyny is felt full-force in the character of Agnes, a suburban matron who flirts with madness as
an escape from an impossible family situation: her husband has left her bed, her sister is alcoholic, her daughter
can't stay married, and her best friends decide to move
into her guest room on a permanent basis. Though Agnes'
anger and superciliousness is well-motivated, she is totally
unlikable, certainly the least sympathetic of all Hepburn's
characters after Mrs. Venable in *Suddenly Last Summer.*
The script also required Hepburn to describe Agnes' dis-
tress over her husband's prediliction for coitus interruptus,
a speech that was at odds with the Hepburn persona and
one that would cause audiences to titter uncomfortably
once the film was released.

Kate, at first, seemed to enjoy the challenges offered by the script. Later, she was to say she accepted the assignment because she wanted to discover what Albee was trying to say in the play. She was also excited by the opportunity of acting with Paul Scofield and her old friend, Joseph Cotten, who headed a first-rate supporting company including Lee Remick, and Kim Stanley as Agnes' alcoholic sister. Stanley would be giving her first screen performance since her award-winning role in *Seance on A Wet Afternoon* in 1964.

Shot in London, with Tony Richardson as director, the production was beset with problems from the start. Shortly after rehearsals began, Kim Stanley suffered a breakdown and was replaced by Kate Reid; the house chosen for location shooting proved to be inadequate for the camera movement Richardson had planned; worst of all, Hepburn became increasingly uncomfortable in her role and was at odds with Richardson over its interpretation. (Richardson couldn't understand why Hepburn despised Agnes because he felt the actress had a great deal in common with the role.) As a result, *A Delicate Balance* is one of the least effective of the generally stagebound American Film Theatre productions.

But the experience wasn't unpleasant enough to keep Kate from immediately accepting another project about which she had serious misgivings. After *A Delicate Balance*, she stayed on in London and started work on David Susskind's production of *The Glass Menagerie* for ABC-TV. Susskind had been after Hepburn to appear as Amanda, the mother in Tennessee Williams' famous play since 1965; at that time she refused on the grounds that the role belonged to Laurette Taylor, who had played it memorably in the original Broadway production. (Hepburn has frequently said that her two favorite actors were Tracy and Taylor.) Two years later, she again rejected Susskind's offer for the same reason, but in 1972, when he pointed out that the part had been played by many actresses since Miss Taylor's death, Kate began to waver. "I'm too thin," she argued. Susskind said she wasn't. "I'm too old to learn the new technique of [TV] taping," she objected. Susskind said the show would be shot like a film. "I want a director I trust." Susskind promised her Anthony Harvey, director of *Lion in Winter*. Unable to come up with any further objections, Kate checked in at a London studio and began rehearsals for her TV debut.

A year or so ago, in a private conversation, Hepburn said, "I've learned that I'm successful only when I'm totally committed to a script; when I'm not, things don't turn out so well." Quite possibly this was a lesson learned from *Delicate Balance* and *Menagerie*. Her doubts about her ability to play Amanda Wingfield were well-founded. She was miscast, seriously so, and the most that could have been expected from her was some indication of how the role should be played. Even from that standpoint, her interpretation was a failure, possibly because she wanted to steer clear of comparisons with Laurette Taylor; possibly because Anthony Harvey's direction was curiously uninflected, taking no advantage of the play's rich vein of comedy, and allowing the cast to drift through drab, dramatically unfocused performances. The entire production had a musty, museum smell to it, and despite surprisingly good reviews, it didn't please the TV public when it was broadcast on December 16, 1973.

When asked why she had finally succumbed to TV, Kate replied, "Curiosity killed the cat." Her curiosity, however, was not killed by *The Glass Menagerie*—during the next few years she was to make several TV appearances, apparently enjoying the challenge of the medium. On the nights of October 2 and 3, 1972, she appeared on the Dick Cavett program to promote the American Film Theatre, and provided a provocative two hours of talk-show entertainment. Cavett's awed-little-boy act was annoying, but Kate was in top form, peppering the conversation with acerbic, outspoken comments, and then turning on the charm and sweetness. Their discussion covered her views on marriage, politics, discipline, privacy, drugs and alcohol ("Cold sober, I find myself absolutely fascinating"), movies, theater, and the people she had worked with. At one point, Cavett asked Kate if she regretted never having played with Laurence Olivier. "Well!" she answered after a startled pause, "Neither Larry nor I are dead yet!"

This exchange proved to be prophetic. A few months later she and Olivier were at work with George Cukor on a TV film called *Love Among the Ruins*, an unorthodox love story of an English barrister and a world-famous Shakespearean actress. (Later a critic remarked, none too kindly, that if the professions of the protagonists had been switched, the two stars would have been more convincingly cast.) Shot in London, and set in the Edwardian period, the production is a testament to Cukor's unfailing good taste and the charismatic presence of Hepburn and Olivier. They almost redeem the foolish plot, but not quite; this is one of those entertainments in which the actors seem to be having more fun than the audience, and their skylarking becomes tedious long before the story reaches its conclusion. When first telecast in March 1975, *Love Among the Ruins* received very mixed reviews, though both Hepburn and Olivier were highly praised. Later both received Emmies for their performances.

After returning to New York, Kate spent a few weeks in her Turtle Bay home before packing up and leaving with Phyllis Wilbourn for California. On arrival they moved into one of the guest houses on George Cukor's estate—from now on, this would be Hepburn's residence whenever she was in Hollywood. She had come to the West Coast to appear in a film that had stirred up a lot of excitement among the columnists, but which Hepburn fans viewed with varying degrees of alarm.

Kate was to star with John Wayne in *Rooster Cogburn,* a sequel to *True Grit,* the film for which Wayne had won an Oscar in 1969. Moreover, the film also looked suspiciously like a rip-off of *The African Queen:* Hepburn was to play a missionary's daughter; Wayne was a one-eyed marshal; and their adventures together included a perilous boat trip over the rapids. Wayne was undeniably a durable superstar, but he wasn't in the same class as Bogart and Tracy, and Kate's admirers didn't look forward to having her cut to size by the Duke. A faint odor of exploitation hung over the entire project.

Hepburn, however, resented the suggestion that there was anything déclassé about taking up with Wayne after just finishing with Laurence Olivier: "Both are national heroes in their respective. countries," she said. "I hadn't acted with either of them before. So I decided to grab them before it was too late." (Wayne was, of course, a national hero only in certain segments of America, his political machismo offending many people.)

Much of the film was shot on location in the pine forests of Oregon's high country, an area that offered few creature comforts, and those few imported by producer Hal Wallis were shunned by Kate. She rarely used her mobile dressing room and did most of her own stuntwork, explaining, "I haven't waited all these years to do a cowboy picture with John Wayne to give up a single minute of it now." Wayne was coughing badly and suffered from an undiagnosed lung ailment—a year later he would undergo cancer surgery—but he insisted on keeping pace with Hepburn; he also did his own stuntwork and riding. He had great respect for Kate. "She wants to do everything, too much really, because she can't ride worth a damn and I gotta keep reining in so she can keep up," he said. "How she must have been at age twenty-five or thirty! How lucky a man would have been to have found her then!"

Wayne went on to say, "I'd hate to think what this picture would be without her." But even with her, *Rooster Cogburn* wasn't much. The critical response was lukewarm at best. Pauline Kael responded to the ambivalent ending when Wayne bids a temporary farewell to Kate by remarking, "These two are hardly at a time of life to postpone romance." Audience reaction was more affirmative, and in box-office terms, *Cogburn* was a modest success.

What is particularly unpleasing about *Rooster Cogburn* is that both stars are presented less as actors than as legends or monuments, and crumbling ones at that. This is an inferior retread of movies both had made to greater advantage in the past, and, as Pauline Kael suggested, there are heavy hints of mortality in every frame in which they appear.

These limitations seem firmly supported by fact. After *Rooster Cogburn,* Wayne was to make only one other film before his death in 1979, and Hepburn was to be professionally inactive for over a year. During that period, there were rumors that Hepburn was in poor health and might be forced to curtail her professional activities. It was fairly well known that she suffered from a palsylike ailment that was incurable, though it could be controlled by medication. And her behavior, which had always been offbeat, now began to seem downright peculiar. One widely reported incident occurred a few months earlier when Kate and Anthony Harvey attended a performance of Harold

Prince's environmental production of Leonard Bernstein's operetta, *Candide*. Like the rest of the audience, she was forced to sit on bleacher seats, which surrounded three sides of the stage, a seating arrangement that provided small comfort for those with weak backs and uncushioned behinds.

At intermission, Hepburn rose from her seat, walked on the stage, and reclined on a canopied bed that was the chief decoration of the set. Near pandemonium erupted in the auditorium—if the culprit of this prank had been anyone other than Hepburn, he or she would have been promptly rousted out of the theater. Some witnesses thought Kate had gone a bit dotty; others applauded, interpreting her action as a protest against the producers' lack of regard for the audience's comfort. That was partly true, but Kate was also suffering sporadic pain from an operation she had undergone at the beginning of 1974. A few years before she had developed osteoarthritis of the hip, and the operation was to alleviate this condition: the surgeons removed some bone and replaced it with a plastic socket. Kate was ordered to take it easy, but she found the command difficult to follow. Before the prescribed recuperative period was over, she was running the rapids in *Rooster Cogburn*.

Though she refused to pamper herself, Kate did become very philosophical about the process of aging, a subject she now frequently discusses in her interviews. "We're very limited by this box we came in," she told one reporter. "The box is me, and it's gradually rotting away. . . . When the vital things go, it dissolves. You'd have to be a fool not to recognize that." Another interviewer, after listening to a variant of this speech, gave Kate a quick appraisal, and said the "box" still seemed to be in pretty good condition. "Not bad," Kate agreed. "Not bad at all."

Hepburn's spell of poor health also seemed to lead her to

examine the direction her career had been taking in the previous five years. After Tracy's death she had said that for the next two years she didn't want to think, just work hard. Those two years had stretched to nearly eight, and too many of her assignments in this period added up to little more than a way of staying busy. She had her reasons for each of the jobs she had taken on, but too many of the reasons sounded like excuses.

One can understand why she wanted to act with Olivier and Scofield, one can forgive her for Wayne, one can even see what drew her to Coco Chanel, but throughout this phase of Hepburn's life, there is a feeling of drifting, a lack of commitment, a sense of distance between actress and the material at hand.

Kate seems to have reached a similar conclusion. After *Rooster Cogburn*, she was to bide her time before committing herself to a new project. Constantly sent scripts by stage and screen producers, she found nothing that intrigued her until she received a new English comedy about a wealthy and terribly eccentric woman in her late seventies. Called *A Matter of Gravity*, it was written by Enid Bagnold, a mildly eccentric woman in her early eighties, the senior member among the corps of practicing English dramatists.

Bagnold's script had something to say about matters that concerned Kate, and she agreed to appear in the play, though she had strong reservations about its popular appeal.

25

Matters
of Gravity

Bagnold was eighty-six when *A Matter of Gravity* went into production in 1975. She had led what she once described as "a zestful life," perhaps something of an understatement for a woman who had been a suffragette, an artist and poet, the platonic confidante of H.G. Wells, and mistress of Frank Harris. As an author, she is best known for her novels, *Serena Blandish* and *National Velvet*, and for her masterpiece, *The Chalk Garden*, the last of the great English comedies of manners.

She and Kate had crossed paths previous to *Gravity*. In the 1930s RKO had bought the film rights to *National Velvet* for Hepburn, but for reasons now forgotten, the project was shelved. (In 1944 MGM filmed it with Elizabeth Taylor in the leading role.) Kate's great friend, Irene Mayer Selznick, had produced *Chalk Garden* in New York and at that time Hepburn and Bagnold had met briefly. But it wasn't until the spring of 1975, when Kate spent a week at Bagnold's home near Brighton in England, that the two really got to know each other.

One of the reasons for Kate's visit was to explore and

possibly sharpen certain sections of the script. According to Broadway scuttlebutt, Mrs. Selznick had browbeaten Bagnold through innumerable revisions of *The Chalk Garden* to strengthen its structure and clarify its point of view. The rumors are probably true since Bagnold's other plays, including *Gravity*, lack focus and craftsmanship. As far as script revisions went, Kate made little headway during her stay with Bagnold in Brighton.

But she did become quite fond of Bagnold, though later she would be exasperated by the Englishwoman's habit of picking up the phone at any hour for a lengthy transatlantic chat. Bagnold's approach to life had grown no less "zestful" over the years. During the Philadelphia tryout of *Gravity*, she caused something of a commotion when she entered the Forrest Theatre one night dressed in a beautiful caftan, but wearing no slippers or stockings.

There is every reason to believe that Bagnold used herself as a model in creating Mrs. Basil, the heroine of *Gravity*, a woman of such enormous individuality that she appears to be senile to small minds, though, of course, she is sharp as a tack. She lives in a large country house, still resplendent despite leakage and a gradual erosion of the foundation. (The house, like the chalk garden of Bagnold's earlier play, begs to be accepted as a symbol of England.) Mrs. Basil intends to leave the estate to her beloved grandson, Nick; as a socialist sympathizer, he wants no part of the estate or of the traditions it entails and urges his grandmother to sell. Nick, however, is in love with a half-caste girl from one of the former British colonies. At first sight, she falls in love with the house, and is willing to take Nick only as an appendage of the estate and the heritage it represents. Mrs. Basil, however, is not prepared to hand over her home as a wedding present; she distrusts the girl and is not quite ready to move on, as she is not pleased by

her vision of the ultimate resting place. She is resigned to
death as oblivion, but she would like to postpone that oblivion for as long as possible.

Several years pass between Acts II and III. Nick's marriage has been a failure, and Mrs. Basil realizes that only
through possession of the house will his wife come to love
her grandson, only through their mutual guardianship will
the house and its traditions be sustained and renewed. She
decides to decamp, taking along as companion her drunken
cook who, at occasional moments, begins to levitate. Witnessing this mystical experience has led Mrs. Basil to
believe that perhaps through uprooting ourselves from
worldly concerns we may all be able to fly upwards. As the
curtain falls, she and the cook leave the house for a lunatic
asylum, though no one now believes she is insane (except,
perhaps, the audience).

As the length of the preceding synopsis may suggest, *A
Matter of Gravity* is not a play that can be easily sum-
marized. The title is an obvious pun on the cook's gift for
aerial acrobatics, but it is also a signal to the audience that
beneath the high-comedy veneer subjects of importance are
being discussed—foremost being the question of death and
legacy. By no means is it a successful play—its multiple
levels and themes never entirely mesh, and the dialogue is
frequently stilted and arch, depending much too heavily on
the seeming non sequitur. The first act is nearly a total
disaster—anyone leaving the theater after the initial inter-
val would have been perfectly justified—and yet, for all its
flaws, it's a peculiarly moving and haunting play. It lin-
gers in the mind.

It was, however, a long shot for production in the 1970s
Broadway market, and certainly the play would never have
stood a chance without a star of Hepburn's proven box-
office draw as Mrs. Basil. And even with Hepburn, *Gravity*

still looked like a risky project. Kate fully realized this, but she was so drawn to the play that she suggested certain financial arrangements to speed along the progress of production. Most stars got 10 percent (or higher) of the box office gross against a guarantee of $5,000 a week. Hepburn took only the minimum salary required by Actors' Equity (plus expenses) until the show had recouped its cost; then, naturally, she was to receive a slightly bigger bite of the profits than usual. (Bagnold and several members of the production team also agreed to similar terms.)

Hepburn never said why she was drawn to the role of Mrs. Basil, but it seems safe to presume that actress and character were both concerned with similar matters of gravity, though their thoughts were by no means identical. Like Mrs. Basil, Kate saw death as "the big sleep," an idea she found "lovely" and not at all frightening as Mrs. Basil does at the start of the play. Hepburn didn't know about God—He was a concept too vast for her mind to consider but she believed in "the lessons of Jesus Christ." She had no religion—like Marx and Shaw she believed religion was "a sop for the masses." She was more in tune with Mrs. Basil on the subject of tradition, the passing of knowledge and standards from one generation to the next, particularly at a time when (in Kate's view) most people were lazy, unprincipled, and concerned only with instant gratification. "It's a me-me-me era," she said. "Right and wrong are mixed up. Integrity is not held in any great esteem. If we behave like mutts and roll around, dissipating, being exhausted, what are we going to be? Mush!"

A Matter of Gravity went into rehearsal early in the fall of 1975 with Noel Willman at the helm. An English actor and director best known (in America) for his stagings of *A Man For All Seasons* and *Lion in Winter*, Willman became close to Kate during the production and was soon to be tapped whenever she needed a partner for tennis. The supporting cast for *Gravity* included Christopher Reeve (later to build up his pectorals and achieve fame as the star of *Superman*), who seemed somewhat out of his depth as Nick, Mrs. Basil's diffident grandson.

The entire cast was, in fact, weak, and the production, even after its Broadway opening (in February 1976) seemed tentative and prosaic, making short shrift of the quirky wit and mysticism suggested by the script. Without a strong company to back her up, Kate fell back on mannerisms, and Mrs. Basil came out more like an aging and offbeat Bryn Mawr socialite than a post-Wildean *grande dame* like Edith Evans (whose presence seems to haunt the play). But, of course, it was Hepburn, not Mrs. Basil, that the public wanted to see.

Despite a general lack of critical enthusiasm, audiences flocked to see *A Matter of Gravity,* both on the road and in New York. The tryout tour opened in Philadelphia for three weeks, then played four weeks in Washington D.C., one in New Haven, four in Boston, and three in Toronto. By the end of the first week in Boston, the production had recouped its cost and opened in New York showing a 100-percent profit on a $160,000 investment. While *Gravity* may not have qualified as an artistic triumph for Kate, it proved beyond any doubt that she was just about the biggest box-office name in the American theater.

During the run of *Gravity*, Kate's every move was covered by the gossip columnists. There was the now-familiar incident in which she furiously upbraided a patron for photographing her during a performance, and as usual her tirade received a warm ovation from the other members of the audience. During the tryout in Boston, she was tailed by a detective while shopping in an expensive department store. Not recognizing Hepburn, who was wearing one of her bag lady outfits, he suspected she might be a thief. Irritated by his doggedness, Kate turned and said imperiously, "Young man, I don't *need* to shoplift!" Placing the voice immediately, he swiftly backed off, murmuring apologies. In Philadelphia, her former husband, Ludlow Ogden Smith, saw the show, visited Kate backstage, and shared breakfast with her the next morning. (Smith was to die two years later.) In Washington she was seen frequently with William Rose, the author of *Guess Who's Coming to Dinner?*, and rumors started that the two were about to embark on a romance. These stories, however, proved to be nothing more than journalistic fantasies.

During the New York run of *Gravity*, Hepburn had a run-in with Stephen Sondheim who lived in one of the brownstones adjacent to Kate's. Sondheim was then finishing the score for *Pacific Overtures*, and his late-night sessions at the piano kept Kate awake. Early one morning she went out in the communal garden that ran behind her house and Sondheim's, and placed her nose against one of the composer's windows. Sondheim and a companion froze when they caught sight of her, standing and staring at them like one of the ancient Furies. She disappeared as swiftly as she had appeared, but Sondheim got her message. From then on, he closed his keyboard cover before Kate returned from the theater each night.

As in the past, Kate found stage acting something of an ordeal. The Broadway performance schedule conflicted with her personal timetable, and experience had done nothing to diminish the stage fright she felt whenever she faced an audience. Her jitters were so severe that she wondered whether she'd find the courage to take another stage project. She limited the New York engagement of *Gravity* to twelve weeks, and though the run was virtually sold out before the opening, she refused to delay the closing date.

She did agree, however, to take the show on the road for a period of several months. Like Katharine Cornell, the Lunts, and Helen Hayes (and unlike most present-day actors), she "*adored* touring," and found it an invigorating experience that staved off the boredom that comes with a lengthy run in New York, where audience reaction is strongly influenced by critical reception.

Before starting the tour, Kate planned to vacation for a couple of months, but then decided to forgo part of her holiday in order to make a picture called *Olly Olly Oxen Free*. She was cast as an elderly woman who helps two children construct and fly a hot-air balloon, a quixotic adventure that teaches the youngsters the values of discipline, fortitude, and individuality. The film ends with the balloon and its passengers coming to ground in the Hollywood Bowl during the middle of a concert, a scene that required Kate to dangle from a rope during the descent. In another sequence she had to put out a fire by throwing herself on it. Asked why she was drawn to films calling for such perilous stunts, Hepburn replied, "Danger *intoxicates* me!" (With age, Kate's tendency to speak in italics has increased dramatically.)

This response led the interviewer to ask Hepburn if she considered herself an eccentric, a question that also related to the type of role Hepburn had played in recent years—she had established a virtual monopoly on dotty characters. Kate's retort was worthy of Mrs. Basil in *Gravity:* "The young always think their elders are eccentric."

The post-production history of *Olly Olly Oxen Free* was nearly as unfortunate as its title. At its first screenings, the picture received such poor audience and critical reaction that it was shelved for many months and has never received more than a very limited distribution. Kate shrugged off the fiasco philosophically. "You take on a play or a picture because there's something about it that fascinates you," she said. "Sometimes it works, sometimes it doesn't." She had had enough failures in her life to realize that one more wouldn't matter, not at this point in her career.

Hepburn returned to New York after completing *Oxen Free,* relaxed briefly, and then went into rehearsals for the tour of *Gravity.* Starting in October 1976, Kate and company went on the road for six months, opening in Denver and then playing Vancouver, San Francisco, Los Angeles, San Diego, and Phoenix. This West Coast trek was even more successful than its previous road engagements a year earlier: the show sold out everywhere, and for Kate, the critical reception was warmer than in New York.

The tour proceeded without incident until *Gravity* opened at the Ahmanson Theatre in Los Angeles. One night after the show, Kate was strolling around the grounds of her home—once again she was staying in a cottage on George Cukor's estate—when she tripped, fell, and fractured an ankle. Two performances were canceled while the future of the tour was debated. The choices were limited: as Hepburn was irreplaceable, *Gravity* must either close or a way must be found to let her continue with the show. Kate said she was ready to go on in a wheelchair, so the staging was hastily reblocked to accommodate its incapacitated leading lady. The results were so effective that Enid Bagnold, in a preface to the acting edition of the play, suggests that the role might always be played in this manner. (Undoubtedly, what pleased her was the sharp contrast between the levitating cook and the chairbound Mrs. Basil.)

Hepburn's fracture healed quickly, and by the end of the tour she was again acting on her own two feet. Once the show closed, Kate went into retreat in Turtle Bay and at

251

Fenwick in Connecticut. Having been in the spotlight for so many months, she now luxuriated in being a private person. Over the years her nervousness about appearing in public had abated somewhat, but there were few public places that held much attraction for her. Her aversion to eating in restaurants had grown even stronger as they began to raise their prices in the late 1970s : informed of what one posh, prix fixe palace was charging for its nouvelle cuisine, she snapped, ''Give me one hundred dollars and I'll cook you the best god-damned dinner you ever ate!''

Her excursions into the everyday world usually took her to museums, movies, or the theater. She had fallen into the habit of seeing practically everything that opened on Broadway, never pulling rank and asking for house seats, but walking to the box office herself and picking up tickets without any fuss. Occasionally there could be a commotion when she was spotted in the auditorium—once during a performance of the Royal Shakespeare Company's production of *Sherlock Holmes*, her appearance created more excitement than what was happening on stage—but for the most part, the public kept their distance. Kate had taught them to respect her privacy.

Hepburn kept up with the current fare, but she disliked practically all the plays and movies she saw. *Jaws,* in her opinion, could have been done much better, and *Last Tango in Paris* was an abomination. (People, she said, were beginning to confuse ''the bedroom with the bathroom.'') What was happening in film and theater depressed her so much that at times she wondered whether she shouldn't toss it all aside and take up another, more public-minded career. And around this time she did become a spokeswoman for Planned Parenthood, allowing this organization to send out leaflets bearing her signature, many of them urging recipients to support pro-abortion legislation. (In taking on this cause, Hepburn was undoubtedly paying tribute to her mother and the work she had done many years before in support of Margaret Sanger and her followers.) She also recorded several voice-over commentaries for TV commercials promoting a Connecticut bank, as (one supposes) a sort of tribute to her native state.

For all her misgivings about the world of show business, Kate kept on entertaining offers from Hollywood and Broadway. Even as she was talking about finding a more fulfilling occupation, she was pondering several projects, one of which looked so promising that it had already been forecast as one of the top pictures of the 1977–8 season.

26

Golden Corn

In March 1977, *Variety* and *The New York Times* announced that Hepburn had agreed to co-star with Bette Davis in *Whitewater*. The picture was the brainchild of producer Hal B. Wallis, who had worked with Hepburn on *Rooster Cogburn* and with Davis on any number of films during her 1940s reign as Queen of the Warners lot. Based on a novel by Paul Horgan, it was (according to a press release) the story of "two spirited women who make a strong impact on a small Texas town during the 1940s." A script had been prepared by Jerome Lawrence and Robert E. Lee (authors of *Inherit the Wind*), and Wallis had already selected Jan Kadar as director, best known for *The Shop on Main Street*, a film made in Kadar's native Czechoslovakia in 1965. Richard Thomas, then at the peak of his fame as John-Boy in the popular TV series, *The Waltons*, had been chosen for the major male role.

The picture raised a lot of anticipatory excitement, but of a decidedly suspect nature. Film fans seemed to expect *Whitewater* to turn out as a camp chef d'oeuvre, a kind of genteel companion piece to *Whatever Happened to Baby*

Jane?, the Grand Guignol travesty that Davis had made with Joan Crawford in 1962, and not without good reason. Two ladies as "spirited" as Davis and Hepburn were perhaps one too many for a single film to manage, and the other talent involved in this project made for a very peculiar mix. Perhaps Hepburn or Davis, perhaps both, had second thoughts; whatever the reason, these initial announcements were just about the last to be heard of *Whitewater*.

After this project collapsed, Kate was to be professionally idle for the better part of a year. Her personality was too dominant to allow her to slip into character parts, as many actresses her age had done, and leading roles for women in their sixties were not easy to come by. As it happened, George Cukor, who had recently directed one of the great international fiascos of movie history, the 1976 Russo-American co-production of Maeterlinck's *The Blue Bird*, was also casting about for a suitable assignment. Movies were out—his age (he was now close to eighty) and *The Blue Bird* made him an untouchable as far as the major studios were concerned—so he came up with the idea for a TV production starring Kate, one which she found terribly exciting. It was to be Cukor and Hepburn together again for the tenth time, joining forces on an adaptation of Emlyn Williams' *The Corn is Green*. (It was also to be their last collaboration—Cukor died in January 1983.)

Williams' semi-autobiographical play had brought Ethel Barrymore her last great stage triumph in 1941, and had subsequently been filmed as a vehicle for Bette Davis (who also starred in a 1974 musical adaptation that never reached Broadway). One of the secrets of the play's enduring appeal is that it provides a showcase for a leading lady of indeterminate age. According to the script, the heroine is in her forties, but the role can easily be adapted to an older actress. Ethel Barrymore was sixty-one when she first played it, and nearly as old as Kate (now almost seventy) before she bid it farewell.

Miss Moffat, Williams' heroine, is an English spinster who comes into a small inheritance, including a cottage in a Welsh mining town. She decides to open a school for the local children and their unlettered elders. One of her pupils is Morgan Evans, a nearly illiterate but innately gifted teenager. Under Moffat's demanding tutelage, Evans begins to blossom, studying zealously though at times unwillingly, as he has already developed a taste for rum and the lasses. Eventually Morgan wins a scholarship to Oxford, only to learn that a village wench is "expecting a little stranger," fathered, of course, by himself. He is about to do right by the girl when Moffat steps in and promises to adopt and raise the child, thereby allowing Morgan to leave the mines and explore the land where the corn is green.

The film was shot on location in Wales and later in a studio in London during the spring of 1978. As when she had followed Laurette Taylor as Amanda in *The Glass Menagerie,* Kate was again in the difficult position of taking on a role identified with an actress she loved and venerated—Ethel Barrymore had been a close friend—but of the two assignments this was the easier: Miss Moffat was closer to Hepburn's own personality than was Amanda, and of the two plays, Kate preferred *The Corn is Green* since its uplifting sentiments echoed many of her own beliefs.

Making the film would have been an entirely pleasurable experience had it not left Hepburn with so little time for the violent physical activity she craved. On one of the few days she was not needed on the set, she decided to unwind for several hours at a women-only swim club in Hampstead

Heath. The pool, fed by spring waters, was icy, but Kate found it "divine."

After swimming several lengths of the pool, she noticed a woman who was trying to coax her ten-year-old daughter to dive off a twelve-foot board. The child would toe the edge, then run backward, clearly terrified. Kate decided to show her how it was done. After making the plunge, she told the girl, "I did that just for you. You can do the same. All you have to do is make up your mind."

The child again reached the edge of the board, only to back off once more. "I'll do it the next time," she said.

"Yes." Hepburn replied. "And I think the next time is right now, don't you?" The girl either had to dive or face Kate's disdain, so she took the easy way out: she dove. Kate ran to congratulate her. "Aren't you thrilled? You see, you can do *anything!*"

Miss Moffat couldn't have handled the situation more deftly or to better results.

When *The Corn is Green* was first telecast in January 1979, it received mainly tepid reviews. Though they had words of praise for Hepburn, the critics dismissed Williams' play as sentimental and old-fashioned, an impression reinforced by the stodginess of James Costigan's adaptation, Cukor's direction, and the playing of the supporting company (headed by Ian Saynor as Morgan Evans). The show attracted only a modest portion of the TV public, and was a real setback for CBS, already losing the battle for supremacy among the three major networks.

Kate had no time to ponder her relative lack of success as a TV actress (none of her excursions into small-screen drama had qualified as a popular hit) as she was soon involved in another project, one that would require a lot of energy and maneuvering if it were ever to reach fruition.

Kate had the vigor and the know-how but still it looked like pretty much of a long shot.

Everything started in September 1978 when the Hudson Guild Theatre, one of the most acclaimed of the many off-Broadway companies, produced *On Golden Pond*, a new play by a virtually unknown dramatist, Ernest Thompson. (A part-time actor, still a few months shy of his thirtieth birthday, Thompson had written other plays, none produced in New York.) The Hudson Guild production was so favorably received that Greer Garson (the former Mrs. Miniver, now making a name for herself as a theater producer) and her partner, Arthur Cantor, decided to move it to Broadway.

Kate hadn't seen *Golden Pond* at the Hudson, but she had been told it was her kind of play, and when it opened a brief out-of-town tune-up in Wilmington, Delaware, she drove down to look it over. Afterward she went backstage and congratulated the cast, headed by Frances Sternhagen and Tom Aldredge, actors well-known to their peers, but without any broad box-office appeal. Later Hepburn let the appropriate people know she would be interested in taking on the leading role if the play were ever filmed.

When *Golden Pond* opened on Broadway in February 1979, it won a hesitant welcome, many critics suggesting it seemed stronger in the intimate surroundings of off-Broadway. Thompson's plot centers on Ethel and Norman Thayer, who at the beginning of the first act, return to spend their fiftieth summer at their house in Maine. It is probably going to be their last holiday since Norman (aged seventy-nine—Ethel is ten years younger) has a bad heart and is fighting off encroaching senility; the last act ends as he suffers what appears to be the penultimate attack. The Thayers' relationship is sensitively drawn, and in itself, could make for a touching one-act play, but Thompson pads the action with a subplot about the Thayers' divorced daughter, her newest suitor, and his precocious thirteen-year-old son. Since these characters are TV sitcom stereotypes, the play goes stale whenever they are on stage, and even at its best, Thompson's script seems a throwback to the middle-class, slice-of-life dramaturgy popular in the 1950s, an anachronism even the most enthusiastic reviewers felt obligated to mention.

These reservations, along with the lack of box-office names and the geriatric subject matter, weren't conducive to sold-out houses. The play limped along for 128 performances and then closed. But the producers had enough faith to move it back to off-Broadway where it lasted for another 253 performances. It still hadn't returned a dime to its investors, and the chances for a film sale would have been slim had it not been for a group of loyal supporters who looked beyond box-office grosses and such considerations as what was or was not old-fashioned.

One of these people was Hepburn. Another was Jane Fonda who was convinced the role of Norman Thayer was perfect for her father. Henry was equally keen, but he had no suggestions for the casting of Ethel. Neither did Jane until she learned that Hepburn was eager to play Ethel, but wasn't sure about her Norman. According to Thompson, it was Jane who was the moving force between the partnership of Hepburn and Fonda.

Surprisingly the two stars had never met, though they had many friends in common (including Tracy and Leland Hayward, who had managed both Fonda and Hepburn in the 1930s), and once before, over forty years before this, they had been set to co-star in *The Mad Miss Manton* before Kate withdrew and left Miss Manton to Barbara Stanwyck. Hepburn has said that one of the reasons she was drawn to *Golden Pond* was its kinship with the pictures she had made with Spencer Tracy. Now that Spencer was gone, Fonda was the next best thing: like Tracy he had a nearly transparent technique, an unstudied, non-neurotic naturalism that owed nothing to Stanislavsky, Stella Adler, or the Actor's Studio. For Kate, he was an ideal choice.

The picture was financed by Jane Fonda's production company (which earlier had produced *Coming Home* and *The China Syndrome)* in conjunction with Sir Lew Grade's Marble Arch Films. There had been some apprehension about the appeal of a movie starring two septuagenarians for younger audiences, and partly for this reason, and partly because she had been nursing an ambition to act with her father, Jane agreed to play the not very gratifying role of Chelsea, the Thayers' alienated daughter. Thompson agreed to build up Jane's role and also alter his one-set script to include some outdoor melodramatics for the camera. And to complete the screen crew, Jane asked Mark Rydell to sign on as director.

Rydell was an unknown quantity to Hepburn, so when his latest picture, *The Rose* (starring Bette Midler), opened during negotiations, she rushed to see it. And what she saw—a predictable study of an overwrought, Janis Joplinesque singer—suggested that Rydell was definitely not the right director for *Pond.* Hepburn started demanding a replacement, but was talked into seeing one of Rydell's earlier films, an adaptation of William Faulkner's *The Reivers.* Few people found much to admire in this poky, oversweet picture, but Kate was one of the exceptions. Maybe she detected Rydell's gift for handling actors, certainly his chief distinction as a film director. For whatever reason, she withdrew her earlier objections and agreed with the Fondas that Rydell was an entirely appropriate choice.

All was set for filming to begin in June of 1980 when two events occurred that threw the future of the entire production into jeopardy. The first happened on a spring day when Kate was playing a few sets of tennis with Noel Willman. Simultaneously with serving the ball, she heard a terrible tear and was then nearly doubled over with pain. Unable to lift her arm, she was taken to a hospital where later she underwent a rotator cuff operation of the kind frequently performed on baseball players. Surgeons usually advise a post-operative convalescence of several months, but Kate was determined to meet the *Golden Pond* starting date, even though she knew she might be in pain for much of the production.

A more serious complication was a threatened strike by the Screen Actors Guild, a possibility that looked more and more like a certainty as *Golden Pond* approached its starting date. If the strike did occur, it could last for months, thereby delaying *Golden Pond* (which had to be shot in summer) for another year. That was out of the question. Jane Fonda had other commitments, and as for the other two stars, who knew whether they'd be able to work then. Despite her hip and shoulder problems, Kate was in generally strong health, but Henry Fonda had a five-year-old pacemaker in his chest, and had recently paid a number of visits to the hospital. He himself realized that *Golden Pond* could well be his final film.

Many producers were getting around the threatened strike by promising to meet retroactively whatever terms were finally worked out by the arbiters. Jane Fonda, however, had to struggle with her political conscience as to whether she should take a step that could be construed as strike-breaking, but she had no option other than abandoning the film entirely. She and her fellow producers reached an agreement with the Screen Actors Guild that allowed

Golden Pond to keep shooting when a strike did occur later that summer. (Throughout the production, Jane was in a very ticklish position, frequently leaving the set to fly to California where she spoke at rallies organized to bolster the morale of the picket-line actors.)

Though *Golden Pond* is set in Maine, the film (for reasons known only to the art director) was shot on Big Squam Lake in New Hampshire. Kate was one of the first to settle in, and a few days later, when Fonda and his wife, Shirlee, had unpacked, she welcomed them with a small dinner party. As a main course, she served bouillabaisse, not a dish she particularly liked, but one she knew Fonda relished. (Naturally she had very definite ideas about the ingredients for an authentic bouillabaisse.) Later that evening, she gave him one of Spencer's old hats, and Fonda was so touched by the gift that he made it part of Norman Thayer's wardrobe. (A gifted amateur painter, Fonda later made a watercolor of this hat and two others he wore in *Golden Pond.* Copies were later distributed to cast and crew as farewell presents.)

On the first day of shooting, Kate was in a hyper-feisty mood. Catching sight of Ernest Thompson, she immediately banished him from the set. ''I wasn't around when you wrote it,'' she snapped, ''so why should you be here when I start to play it?'' She was overflowing with suggestions for Mark Rydell, who listened with a sense of *déjà entendu:* having already passed through the rites of passage with John Wayne (on *The Cowboys)* and Bette Midler, he was now immune to the autocratic ways of Hollywood stars. He had great respect for Kate, and as diplomatically as possible, he let her know that there was only going to be one boss on this production. From then on, Kate was the soul of cooperation, even though she was frequently in extreme physical discomfort.

By the time she reached New Hampshire, Hepburn had practically recovered from her tennis injury, but then she walked into a glass door, her shoulder bearing the brunt of the impact. The vanishing pain now returned with even greater intensity, and Kate discovered she couldn't move her fingers. She was unable to work for the better part of a week, but when she returned, she insisted on making light of the incident, and refused to have the staging reblocked for her convenience. Once again the doctors advised her to take it easy, and though she would have liked to disobey, she grudgingly cut down on the outside physical activity she thrived on.

As a substitute, she took vicarious pleasure in watching Jane Fonda master an athletic feat that provided a dramatic turning point in the film. In the stage version of *Golden Pond*, Norman Thayer has never recovered from the shock of having sired a daughter instead of a son, a disappointment aggravated by his daughter's inability to execute a backflip dive. Such trite motivation is one of the chief weaknesses of Thompson's original script, and in the screenplay he goes even further by having the daughter finally perform the dive, thereby establishing an immediate rapport with her father.

Jane was in peak physical condition—during *Golden Pond*, she held exercise classes, just like the ones outlined in her then to-be-published fitness manual—but her list of athletic accomplishments did not include the backflip. Kate couldn't show her how the dive should be performed, as she had for the girl in Hampstead Heath, but she cheered from the sidelines and applauded when Jane finally arrived at something close to Olympic perfection.

On Golden Pond cost $7,500,000, a modestly priced production for the time, and though Universal (which had taken on the distribution rights) expected it would eventually show a profit, there was fear in some quarters that unless handled with care, the picture might end up by breaking even, nothing more. So *Golden Pond* was presented as an event, rushed out in time to qualify for the Academy Award nominations for 1981, and shown initially only in a handful of theaters across the country so that it could build its own audience through word of mouth.

On its release in November 1981, *On Golden Pond* recieved mixed reviews. Henry Fonda was universally praised—many critics considering Norman Thayer to be the finest portrayal of his career—but the sentimentality of Thompson's script came under sharp criticism. And while Hepburn's interplay with Fonda was widely admired, there were reservations about the emotionalism of her performance. She does, in fact, seem on the verge of tears throughout most of the film and her shaking is frequently out of control. But audiences didn't seem to care: they had learned to accept this tremulousness as an inevitable part of every Hepburn performance, just as opera buffs grow accustomed to the uncertain top notes of their favorite aging prima donnas.

On Golden Pond was a true audience picture. Many people said they saw themselves or their parents in the story of Ethel and Norman Thayer, but probably the source of this emotional response lay elsewhere. Just as the audiences for *Guess Who's Coming to Dinner?* had really responded to Hepburn and Tracy, not the characters they were playing, so now people were caught up by their feelings for Fonda and Hepburn, by an accumulation of connotations and memories stretching back over a span of fifty years. Some of us had grown up with them—and those who hadn't, thanks to the TV late shows, felt as though they had—and to see them, still resiliant, in these twilight years, was both inspirational and genuinely moving. Within a year of its release, *Golden Pond* was to gross close to $100,000,000, making it the most financially successful of all Hepburn's films to date. This unexpected box-office victory led industry prognosticators to foresee a future for movies without special effects, Harrison Ford, and/or other teen-age gimmickry.

At Oscar nomination time, *Golden Pond* collected ten citations, including best picture, best director, best actor and actress, best supporting actress (Jane Fonda), and best adapted screenplay. It was surpassed only by *Reds,* which won twelve nominations.

As to how many of the *Golden Pond* nominees would wind up with a statuette—that was a different story. Henry Fonda looked like a shoo-in and Thompson was the favorite among the screenwriter candidates, partly because the competition was weak, partly as a compensation for *Golden Pond* eventually missing out in the other top categories. It had a dark-horse chance of winning best picture over *Reds,* but Warren Beatty had virtually wiped out Mark Rydell and the other competitors for the best director trophy. Jane Fonda was given no chance against Maureen Stapleton (in *Reds)* for best supporting actress, and Hepburn's prospects looked equally dim. The best actress award, it was predicted, would go either to Meryl Streep (for *The French Lieutenant's Woman)* or Diane Keaton *(Reds)*—it was pretty much of a toss-up since neither actress had any great surge of sentiment or enthusiasm behind her.

On the night of the award ceremony, March 29, 1982, things went pretty much as projected, at least as far as *On Golden Pond* was concerned. Jane Fonda lost to Stapleton, Thompson carried off the screenwriting award, Beatty won over Rydell. Finally it was time for the three top awards. Henry Fonda, everyone's favorite, was voted best actor.

Fonda's health had deteriorated drastically in recent months, and he was too ill to attend the ceremony. Jane accepted for him. She told the audience that she was sure her father had reacted to his victory by saying, "'Ain't I lucky!'—as though luck had anything to do with it."

The next presentation was the award for best actress, and it provided the first real surprise of the evening. The winner was Hepburn. Apparently unable to muster much enthusiasm for either Keaton or Streep, the Academy members had turned against both and chosen to honor Kate instead.

Only moments later came another, even bigger surprise. The best picture award went not to *Reds*, not to *Golden Pond*, but to *Chariots of Fire*, a stunning upset that was to be extensively analyzed in the days ahead. The furor over *Chariots* tended to overshadow Kate's triumph, but her award had an historical importance too impressive to be dismissed lightly. Up to this point, there were three triple winners in the best acting category: Ingrid Bergman, Walter Brennan, and Hepburn, who held a slight edge since she was the only one of the three who had not won at least one of their awards in the supporting actor or actress division. Now, with a fourth Oscar for *Golden Pond*, she was in a class by herself.

27

To Be Continued

Only once in her fifty years as a Hollywood actress has Hepburn ever attended an Oscar presentation, and that was in 1974 to accept an honorary award for her friend, producer Lawrence Weingarten. Cowardice was the reason she gave for not showing up on the twelve occasions when she had been a nominee: "I guess I was afraid I'd lose," she frequently explained. But in 1982, the year of *Golden Pond,* she had another excuse for staying away: she was then appearing on stage in *West Side Waltz,* a new comedy by Ernest Thompson.

Two years earlier, Thompson had received a modest grant from the Ahmanson Theatre in Los Angeles with the understanding that he would use the money to develop a play that would eventually open there. (This company, like the Kennedy Theatre in Washington D.C. and the presently-inactive Vivian Beaumont in New York, presents star-studded productions of uncontroversial plays, both old and new.) Just before he started writing, Thompson met Hepburn and immediately started tailoring his still half-formulated plot to accommodate her personality. *West Side*

Waltz was just as much a star vehicle as *Philadelphia Story,* only not quite so good. Later the Ahamson would be censured for underwriting such a blatantly commercial project but Hepburn thought the play had something important to say. She liked it and agreed to play in it, not only in Los Angeles, but on tour and in New York. She brought in Robert Whitehead and Roger Stevens as co-producers and Noel Willman as director, the same team that had worked with her on *A Matter of Gravity.*

The theme of *West Side Waltz* is a variation on the theme of *On Golden Pond:* the psychological and physical problems of aging. But this time around, the treatment was almost entirely lighthearted, though the heroine is in some ways in a sorrier state than Ethel Thayer. Having already lost her husband, she is alone and proud and outspoken, adjectives that might be used to describe the seventy-two-year-old Kate Hepburn.

Margaret Mary Elderdice is a former pianist who lives in an apartment building seemingly modeled on the Ansonia, a residential hotel in Manhattan's West Seventies once favored by musicians and second-caliber opera singers. She is declining physically, a condition her otherwise alert mind fails to accept. Cara Varnum, a spinster violinist in her fifties wants to move in and take care of her, but Cara is loud and pushy, so Mrs. Elderdice rejects the offer for mutual companionship. Instead, she takes as roomer a young actress who has just been ditched by her homosexual husband. Elderdice swiftly solves the girl's problems and soon finds herself again living alone.

Physical declivity finally overcomes Margaret Mary—in the course of the play she goes from cane to walker to a wheelchair—and she now accepts Cara's earlier proposal. At the end of the third act, the two women are playing a duet for piano and violin. "Now we're cooking," Mrs. Elderdice exclaims jubilantly as the final curtain mercifully descends.

The part of Cara Varnum was nearly as important as Mrs. Elderdice, and Hepburn kept a careful eye on the casting. The choice of Dorothy Loudon came as something of a surprise since she was best known for her work in musical comedy (her performance as Miss Hannigan in *Annie* brought her a Tony), and Loudon admits that initially she was apprehensive about the assignment. But Kate was on her best behavior, and the two women quickly established a good working relationship.

Both actresses had to feign the ability to play musical instruments for their roles, and Kate wanted badly to master the fingering for each piece of music she was supposedly performing. Hepburn had accomplished this feat nearly forty years earlier for *Song of Love*, but she was dubious about carrying it off a second time. The injury she had received while making *On Golden Pond* had left her with limited mobility in her fingers, and she still lacked the flexibility to maneuver her hands along the keyboard with any show of agility. But determination finally triumphed over physical impairment: by practicing several hours each day, she eventually achieved the deportment of a skilled pianist. Inspired by Kate's perseverance, Loudon struggled away with her violin, and by opening night, she looked as though she had been born with a Stradivarius tucked under her chin.

West Side Waltz opened on the West Coast in the spring of 1982, then embarked on an eight-city tour prior to opening on Broadway in November of the same year. All along the way, the reviewers liked Hepburn and Loudon, but turned thumbs down on Thompson's script. Audience reaction ran along similar lines, so Thompson started revising, paying particular attention to the final act, which had been singled out as being especially weak. But neither the poor reviews nor the lukewarm word-of-mouth publicity hurt ticket sales. *West Side Waltz* played to full houses throughout the year.

It was also virtually sold out before it opened its limited three-month engagement in New York. Thompson's alterations had not substantially improved the script, and the notices were generally quite poor. Critics complained that the plot was flimsy, attenuated, and overly dependent on "New York survival jokes of the sub-Neil Simon variety." Kate was regarded as being beyond criticism. Annalyn Swan of *Newsweek* spoke for most of her fellow reviewers when she wrote, "If Hepburn seems to be acting Hepburn instead of crusty old Margaret Mary Elderdice, so what?" Audiences adored her, applauding the wry inflections she brought to even the tawdriest of Thompson's gags. (One example of the play's level of wit: when Cara Varnum reports that she has nearly convinced the neighbors that the tart-tongued Mrs. Elderdice is really "a dove," Hepburn/Margaret Mary snarls, "Tell them not to look up when I fly over.") In *Coco* Hepburn had gotten a big laugh by saying "shit," and now, she was cracking one-liners about bird-dirt. Too bad she didn't fly over Thompson when he wasn't looking.

After the New York engagement, Kate took *Waltz* on the road for another brief tour, and she was playing in Washington on the night she won her fourth Oscar for *Golden Pond.* (Asked by the film's press representatives what they should say if she won, Hepburn replied, "A simple 'thank you' will suffice.")

She was still touring when it was announced that her performance in *Waltz* had brought her another Tony nomination, and it seemed possible that the Broadway community might get on the Hepburn bandwagon and award her

the double crown—an Oscar and a Tony in one year—
something achieved earlier only by Audrey Hepburn and
Ellen Burstyn. But the Tony remains just about the only
major show business award that Kate hasn't as yet captured: the prize went to Zoë Caldwell for her performance
in the Robinson Jeffers' version of *Medea*.

As promotion for both *Golden Pond* and *West Side
Waltz*, Kate granted what was for her an unusual number
of interviews, though she continued to talk about how
much she loathed this side of the business. In an unguarded
moment, she recently admitted that she found the press almost as intimidating as they find her. And as anyone who
has ever interviewed her can testify, she can be *very*
intimidating in the first minutes of a meeting. Setting up
that meeting is in itself a Herculean ordeal: first you have
to brave Phyllis Wilbourn, every bit as prickly as her employer, and if you do pass muster and get Hepburn on the
phone, you have to be prepared to have her mow you down
and tell you that she's said everything she has to say, so
why should she be bothered? If you persist politely, she
may agree to get back to you, and if you're lucky, she does;
but usually at about 8 A.M., waking you up and telling you
to meet her in precisely two hours.

No ground rules are set, but it's well-known that she
never talks about Tracy or about her private life, except in
a highly reflective, abstract way. If you abide by these un-
spoken rules, after a few moments on both sides, Kate will
start to relax and expand. This occurs when she realizes
you won't push her into hidden corners, but are genuinely
interested in what she thinks and feels. Unlike many much-
interviewed stars, who give glib, obviously well-rehearsed
answers to everything they are asked, Kate listens atten-
tively and responds thoughtfully.

The most publicized and provocative of Hepburn's recent interviews was broadcast on American TV in the spring of 1982. The hostess for the evening was Barbara Walters, the celebrated million-dollar network journalist who has interviewed everyone from Burt Reynolds to the late Shah of Iran (who used her as a kind of impartial envoy to the American people in the months preceding his death). In many ways she was an updated version of Tess Harding of *Woman of the Year,* and when Kate's old film was turned into a 1981 stage musical, the heroine was overhauled along Walters' lines.

Therefore there was considerable fascination about the confrontation of these two women, comrades in spirit but separated by an age difference of twenty years. Initially they handled each other with obvious respect, but soon had locked horns over an issue that concerned each deeply : a woman's ability to combine a career with marriage. Kate felt it was an untenable mixture. "If I were a man, I wouldn't marry a woman with a career. I wouldn't be that big a fool. I'd want her to be interested in me, not the career."

She could not see herself as a working mother : "If I had children and they came down with mumps on one of my opening nights, I would want to kill them, I really would." Walters (who *is* a working mother) gasped at this point, and not without reason : practically everything Hepburn had said conflicted with her status as one of the heroines of the feminist movement. In fact she seemed to be repeating lessons learned from Tess Harding and Amanda Bonner in respectively, *Woman of the Year* and *Adam's Rib* (films which, not so incidentally, Hepburn has always defended against the charges of sexism).

Walters next asked Hepburn how she felt about a man marrying an older woman. Kate answered that it might work out provided the man was "a slight sap." (Was she perhaps thinking of Garson Kanin, who was sixteen years younger than Ruth Gordon, and whom she had never forgiven for his best-selling *Tracy and Hepburn,* published in 1974?) Walters was now in a state of near-shock, but Hepburn wouldn't back down. "Look," she said. "You've got to choose. You can't have it all."

Walters then decided to switch to another subject. A few years earlier, Kate had been quoted as saying, "I'm a legend because I've survived over a long period of time. I think people are beginning to think I'm not going to be around much longer, and what do you know, they think they'll miss me like an old monument, like the Flatiron Building." Picking up on this, Walters asked Kate whether she knew she was considered a legend. "Yes," Hepburn replied, but no, of course, she didn't think of herself that way. She did, however, take pride in having endured as a film star for fifty years, an achievement she called "a triumph." (About the only living actresses who equal or surpass Kate in this area are Lillian Gish, Barbara Stanwyck, Claudette Colbert, Myrna Loy, and Bette Davis, some of whom have been only sporadically active during the last two decades.)

The interview ended on a note of whimsy. Barbara asked "If you were a tree, what kind of tree would you be?" "Certainly not an elm," Hepburn answered, "because then I might get Dutch Elm disease." After a moment she decided she'd be an oak, and who would disagree? She is the most durable and enduring of film and stage stars.

Kate has announced no plans for the immediate future, though there have been rumors that she is toying with the idea of playing Rose Kennedy in a biographical TV drama. After the conclusion of the *West Side Waltz* tour, she returned to New York, moving between her homes in Turtle Bay and Connecticut, scrubbing walls, baking brownies, poking around in her garden, catching up on the latest films and plays. Wherever she goes she turns heads, not only because of who she is but also because of what she wears. Now that fashion has caught up with her, Kate can don the most raffish of ensembles and receive praise for her daring individuality. A trend-spotting reporter for *The New York Times* noted recently, "No one on the New York streets looked better than Katharine Hepburn. There she was, striding into the Plaza Theater to see *Diva*, wearing loose trousers, sandals, socks, a white shirt and a glistening black ankle-length raincoat. For last week, at least, that was swagger."

Asked recently whether she had any regrets about her life, Kate answered, "I could have accomplished three times what I've accomplished. I haven't realized my full potential. I could have been a great tennis player, and I'm a pretty good golfer." She would have preferred to have been a painter rather than an actress, though she admits that she has no great skills when it comes to palette and easel. "Acting isn't a very high class way to make a living, is it?" she asked rhetorically. "Nobody ever won a Nobel Prize for acting. You have to remember that Shirley Temple could do it at the age of four. All you have to have is a salable whatever the hell it is that people like to see."

Despite this disparagement of her profession, one also expressed by Spencer Tracy and many other prominent actors, one doubts that Kate would find the routine of daily living—the cooking and planting, the cleaning and Sunday painting, the swaggering along Fifth Avenue—quite so fulfilling if she didn't have the option of returning to the world of stage and screen. Perhaps there is no such thing as a born actor, but Hepburn was definitely born with a highly theatrical personality, one that now and then needs a spotlight to keep it alive and vigorous. As long as she can memorize lines, it seems certain that she will go on acting, even if she needs the support of canes, walkers, or wheelchairs. There are, one imagines, still a few chapters to be written before the book of Kate's life reaches its conclusion.

A Katharine Hepburn Filmography

A BILL OF DIVORCEMENT (1932). RKO. Directed by George Cukor. With John Barrymore, Billie Burke, David Manners.

CHRISTOPHER STRONG (1933). RKO. Directed by Dorothy Arzner. With Colin Clive, Billie Burke, Ralph Forbes, Irene Browne, Helen Chandler.

MORNING GLORY (1933). RKO. Directed by Lowell Sherman. With Douglas Fairbanks, Jr., Adolphe Menjou, Mary Duncan, C. Aubrey Smith.

LITTLE WOMEN (1933). RKO. Directed by George Cukor. With Frances Dee, Jean Parker, Joan Bennett, Spring Byington, Douglass Montgomery, Paul Lukas.

SPITFIRE (1934). RKO. Directed by John Cromwell. With Robert Young, Ralph Bellamy, Martha Sleeper.

THE LITTLE MINISTER (1934). RKO. Directed by Richard Wallace. With John Beal, Alan Hale, Donald Crisp, Dorothy Stickney.

BREAK OF HEARTS (1935). RKO. Directed by Philip Moeller. With Charles Boyer, John Beal, Jean Hersholt.

ALICE ADAMS (1935). RKO. Directed by George Stevens. With

Fred MacMurray, Fred Stone, Evelyn Venable, Frank Albertson, Ann Shoemaker, Hattie MacDaniel.

SYLVIA SCARLETT (1936). RKO. Directed by George Cukor. With Cary Grant, Brian Aherne, Edmund Gwenn, Natalie Paley, Dennie Moore.

MARY OF SCOTLAND (1936). RKO. Directed by John Ford. With Fredric March, Florence Eldridge, Douglas Walton, John Carradine, Gavin Muir.

A WOMAN REBELS (1936). RKO. Directed by Mark Sandrich. With Herbert Marshall, Van Heflin, Elizabeth Allan, Donald Crisp, David Manners.

QUALITY STREET (1937). RKO. Directed by George Stevens. With Franchot Tone, Fay Bainter, Estelle Winwood, Eric Blore, Cora Witherspoon.

STAGE DOOR (1937). RKO. Directed by Gregory La Cava. With Ginger Rogers, Adolphe Menjou, Andrea Leeds, Gail Patrick, Constance Collier, Lucille Ball.

BRINGING UP BABY (1938). RKO. Directed by Howard Hawks. With Cary Grant, Charles Ruggles, May Robson, Barry Fitzgerald.

HOLIDAY (1938). Columbia. Directed by George Cukor. With Cary Grant, Lew Ayres, Doris Nolan, Edward Everett Horton, Jean Dixon.

THE PHILADELPHIA STORY (1940). MGM. Directed by George Cukor. With Cary Grant, James Stewart, Ruth Hussey, John Howard, Roland Young, Virginia Weidler.

WOMAN OF THE YEAR (1942). MGM. Directed by George Stevens. With Spencer Tracy, Fay Bainter, Reginald Owen, William Bendix.

KEEPER OF THE FLAME (1942) MGM. Directed by George Cukor. With Spencer Tracy, Richard Whorf, Margaret Wycherly, Donald Meek, Audrey Christie.

STAGE DOOR CANTEEN (1943). United Artists. Directed by Frank Borzage. With Cheryl Walker, William Terry, Lon Mc-Callister, Selena Royale.

DRAGON SEED (1944). MGM. Directed by Jack Conway and Harold S. Bucquet. With Walter Huston, Aline MacMahon, Akim Tamiroff, Turhan Bey, Hurd Hatfield.

WITHOUT LOVE (1945). MGM. Directed by Harold S. Bucquet. With Spencer Tracy, Lucille Ball, Keenan Wynn, Carl Esmond, Patricia Morison.

UNDERCURRENT (1946). MGM. Directed by Vincente Minnelli. With Robert Taylor, Robert Mitchum, Edmund Gwenn, Marjorie Main, Jayne Meadows.

THE SEA OF GRASS (1947). MGM. Directed by Elia Kazan. With Spencer Tracy, Melvyn Douglas, Phyllis Thaxter, Robert Walker.

SONG OF LOVE (1947). MGM. Directed by Clarence Brown. With Paul Henreid, Robert Walker, Henry Daniell, Leo G. Carroll.

STATE OF THE UNION (1948). MGM. Directed by Frank Capra. With Spencer Tracy, Adolphe Menjou, Van Johnson, Angela Lansbury, Lewis Stone.

ADAM'S RIB (1949). MGM. Directed by George Cukor. With Spencer Tracy, Judy Holliday, David Wayne, Tom Ewell, Jean Hagen.

THE AFRICAN QUEEN (1951). United Artists. Directed by John Huston. With Humphrey Bogart, Robert Morley, Peter Bull, Theodore Bikel.

PAT AND MIKE (1952). MGM. Directed by George Cukor. With Spencer Tracy, Aldo Ray, William Ching, Sammy White.

SUMMERTIME (1955). United Artists. Directed by David Lean. With Rossano Brazzi, Isa Miranda, Darren McGavin, Mari Aldon, Jane Rose. Released in England as *Summer Madness.*

THE RAINMAKER (1956). Paramount. Directed by Joseph Anthony. With Burt Lancaster, Wendell Corey, Lloyd Bridges, Earl Holliman, Cameron Prud'homme.

THE IRON PETTICOAT (1956). MGM. Directed by Ralph Thomas. With Bob Hope, James Robertson Justice, Robert Helpmann.

DESK SET (1957). Twentieth Century-Fox. Directed by Walter Lang. With Spencer Tracy, Joan Blondell, Gig Young, Dina Merrill, Neva Patterson.

SUDDENLY, LAST SUMMER (1959). Columbia. Directed by Joseph L. Mankiewicz. With Elizabeth Taylor, Montgomery Clift, Mercedes McCambridge, Albert Dekker.

LONG DAY'S JOURNEY INTO NIGHT (1962). Embassy. Directed by Sidney Lumet. With Ralph Richardson, Jason Robards, Jr., Dean Stockwell, Jeanne Barr.

GUESS WHO'S COMING TO DINNER? (1967). Columbia. Directed by Stanley Kramer. With Spencer Tracy, Sidney Poitier, Katharine Houghton, Cecil Kellaway.

THE LION IN WINTER (1968). AVCO Embassy. Directed by Anthony Harvey. With Peter O'Toole, Timothy Dalton, Anthony Hopkins, Jane Merrow.

THE MADWOMAN OF CHAILLOT (1969). Warner Bros. - Seven Arts. Directed by Bryan Forbes. With Charles Boyer, Danny Kaye, Yul Brynner, Edith Evans, Margaret Leighton, Giulietta Masina, Richard Chamberlain, John Gavin.

A DELICATE BALANCE (1972). American Film Theatre. Directed by Tony Richardson. With Paul Scofield, Lee Remick, Kate Reid, Joseph Cotten.

THE GLASS MENAGERIE (1973). ABC-TV. Directed by Anthony Harvey. With Michael Moriarty, Sam Waterston, Joanna Miles.

LOVE AMONG THE RUINS (1975). ABC-TV. Directed by George Cukor. With Sir Laurence Olivier.

ROOSTER COGBURN (1975). Universal. Directed by Stuart Miller. With John Wayne, Anthony Zerbe, Richard Jordan, Strother Martin.

OLLY OLLY OXEN FREE (1976). Sanrio. Directed by Richard A. Colla. With Kevin McKenzie, Dennis Dimster. (This film not released until 1978).

THE CORN IS GREEN (1979). CBS-TV. Directed by George Cukor. With Ian Saynor.

ON GOLDEN POND (1981). Universal. Directed by Mark Rydell. With Henry Fonda, Jane Fonda, Dabney Coleman, Doug McKeon.

MEET THE STARS

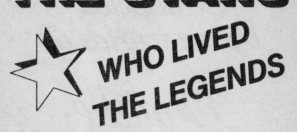

WHO LIVED THE LEGENDS

_____ **BETTE**: The Life of Bette Davis
Charles Higham................................10662-1-25 $3.95

_____ **ELIZABETH TAYLOR**: The Last Star
Kitty Kelley..12410-7-42 3.95

_____ **INGRID BERGMAN**: My Story
Ingrid Bergman & Alan Burgess........14086-2-17 3.95

_____ **KATHARINE HEPBURN**: A Hollywood Yankee
Gary Carey.......................................14412-4-38 3.95

_____ **LANA**: The Public and Private Lives of Miss Turner
Joe Morella & Edward Z. Epstein.......14817-0-13 3.50

_____ **RITA**: The Life of Rita Hayworth
Joe Morella & Edward Z. Epstein.......17483-X-27 3.95

DAVID NIVEN

"David Niven is brilliant!"—*The Boston Globe*

"David Niven was known among his friends as, quite simply, an incomparable companion. Always, when asked why, they were never able to communicate his particular magic. All we have to say is: Read his books."—William F. Buckley, Jr.

☐ **BRING ON THE EMPTY HORSES** 10824-1 $3.95

☐ **THE MOON'S A BALLOON** ...15806-0 $3.95

☐ **GO SLOWLY, COME BACK QUICKLY**................................13113-8 $3.95

DELL BOOKS